George J. Hoc

Ryerson Memorial Volume

George J. Hodgins

Ryerson Memorial Volume

1st Edition | ISBN: 978-3-75234-382-3

Place of Publication: Frankfurt am Main, Germany

Year of Publication: 2020

Outlook Verlag GmbH, Germany.

Reproduction of the original.

RYERSON MEMORIAL VOLUME
BY J. GEORGE HODGINS

1

PREFATORY NOTE.

I have two reasons to give for the part which I have taken in the preparation of the latter part of this Memorial Volume. The first is mentioned in the following paragraph from the brief *resumé* of the historical and personal facts given in the volume, and which I read on the day of the unveiling of the statue, as follows:—

> "It devolves upon me, as Chairman of the (Ryerson Memorial Statue) Committee, and at the kind request of my colleagues—no less than as the life-long friend and fellow-labourer of him whose deeds and memory we honour to-day—to trace back to their source the origin and underlying principles of our system of education, and to show that these underlying principles and other vital forces were so combined by a master-hand as to form the groundwork, as they have, in their combination, become the charter of our educational system of to-day."

The second reason is contained in the following paragraphs—containing a brief record of Dr. Ryerson's thirty-two years in the Public Service, taken from *The Story of My Life*, page 351.

> "During my connection with the Education Department—from 1844 to 1876—I made five educational tours of inspection and enquiry to educating countries in Europe and the United States. I made an official tour through each county in Upper Canada, once in every five years, to hold a County Convention of municipal councillors, clergy, school trustees, teachers and local superintendents, and thus developed the School system as the result of repeated inquiries in foreign countries, and the freest consultation with my fellow-citizens of all classes, in the several County Conventions, as well as on many other occasions.

> "During the nearly thirty-two years of my administration of the Education Department, I met with strong opposition at first from individuals—some on personal, others on religious and political grounds; but that opposition was, for most part, partial and evanescent. During these years I had the support of each successive administration of Government, whether of one party or the other, and, at length, the co-operation of all religious persuasions; so that in 1876 I was allowed to retire, with the good-will of all political parties and religious denominations, and without diminution of my public means of subsistence.

> "I leave to Dr. J. George Hodgins, my devoted friend of over forty years, and my able colleague for over thirty of these years, the duty of filling up the details of our united labours in founding a system of education for my native Province which is spoken of in terms of strong commendation, not only within, but by people outside of the Dominion."[1]

My own estimate of Dr. Ryerson's educational life and labours is contained in the following paragraphs, which were written by me in 1883:—

Dr. Ryerson's fame in the future will mainly rest upon the fact that he was a distinguished Canadian Educationist, and the Founder of a great system of Public Education for Upper Canada. What makes this distinguishing excellence in his case the more marked, was the fact that the soil on which he had to labour was unprepared, and the social condition of the country was unpropitious. English ideas of schools for the poor, supported by subscriptions and voluntary offerings, prevailed in Upper Canada; free schools were unknown; the very principle on which they rest—that is, that the ratable property of the country is responsible for the education of the youth of the land—was denounced as communistic and an invasion of the rights of property; while "compulsory education"—the proper and necessary complement of free schools—was equally denounced as of the essence of "Prussian despotism," and an impertinent and unjustifiable interference with "the rights of British subjects."

It was a reasonable boast at the time that only systems of popular education, based upon the principle of free schools, were possible in the republican American States, where the wide diffusion of education was regarded as a prime necessity for the stability and success of republican institutions, and, therefore, was fostered with unceasing care. It was the theme on which the popular orator loved to dilate to a people on whose sympathies with the subject he could always confidently reckon. The practical mind of Dr. Ryerson, however, at once saw that the American idea of free schools was the true one. He moreover perceived that by giving his countrymen facilities for freely discussing the question among the ratepayers once a year, they would educate themselves into the idea, without any interference from the State. These facilities were provided in 1850; and for twenty-one years the question of free schools *versus* rate-bill schools (fees, etc.) was discussed every January in from 3,000 to 5,000 school sections, until free schools became voluntarily the rule, and rate-bill schools the exception. In 1871, by common consent, the free school principle was incorporated into our school system by the Legislature, and has ever since been the universal practice. In the adoption of this principle, and in the successful administration of the Education Department, Dr. Ryerson at length demonstrated that a popular (or, as it had been held in the United States, the democratic) system of public schools was admirably adapted to our monarchical institutions. In point of fact, leading American educationists have often pointed out that the Canadian system of public education was more efficient in all of its details, most practically successful in its results, than was the ordinary American school system in any one of the States of the Union. Thus it is that the fame of Dr. Ryerson as a successful founder of our educational system, rests upon a solid basis. What has been done by him will not be undone; and the ground gone over by him will not require to be traversed again. But I forbear, as I hope to devote a volume to the private and personal history of our educational system.

———————

The first part of this volume contains an interesting account from the leading daily papers of Toronto of the ceremony of unveiling the great statue to a distinguished native of Ontario and a truly representative man— representative of her enterprize, energy and progress. As such, many of the leading men of the Province assembled on the Queen's Birthday to do honour to his memory. It also contains the addresses in full of those gentlemen who were appointed by their respective institutions, etc., to that duty, and who kindly consented to take part in the ceremonies and proceedings of the day.

The second part of the volume contains a statement of the origin, with illustrations, of the underlying principles of our system of education— primary, secondary and university.

There has also been added at the end some historical and personal sketches —some of them of a humorous cast—but all illustrative of the early days of education in this Province, and its vicissitudes of light and shade. They admirably serve to bring out in strong relief the present state of efficiency of our system of public instruction, as well as the substantial progress which has been made by it in its various departments since the early educational pioneers of Upper Canada first attempted to give it form and substance, over fifty years ago.

The photograph from which the frontispiece is printed was by Mr. J. Bruce, of 118 King street west, Toronto.

J. G. H.

TORONTO, 24th May, 1889.

PERSONAL NOTE.

A few days after the ceremony of unveiling the Statue, I received the following very kind note from Rev. Dr. Ryerson's only son:—

27 CECIL ST., TORONTO,
May 28th, 1889.

MY DEAR DR. HODGINS,—The 24th of May was indeed a red-letter day to me and to my family; and one I shall never forget.

The Statue and Pedestal are beyond anything I expected; and the likeness is excellent.

Allow me to thank you very heartily for your eloquent Historical Paper, and the touching references to my dear Father.

I know that all you did was a labour of love. But I cannot allow this event to pass without expressing to you our deep gratitude for the time and pains you have taken in successfully carrying out this splendid memorial to my revered Father. Mrs. Ryerson joins me in very kind regards.

4

Believe me,
Yours very faithfully,
C. EGERTON RYERSON.

J. George Hodgins, Esq., LL.D.,
Toronto.

THE RYERSON MEMORIAL VOLUME.

PRELIMINARY.

The Rev. Dr. Ryerson's death occurred on the 19th of February, 1882. Early in the next month the following circular was issued:—

A preliminary meeting of trustees, inspectors and teachers connected with Public, Separate and High Schools—past and present—will be held in the theatre, or public hall, of the Education Department, on Tuesday afternoon, the 14th instant, at 4.30, to consider the proposal to erect a monument or other tribute of love and esteem to the memory of the late revered founder of the educational system of Ontario.

J. GEORGE HODGINS,
Convener.

Toronto, March, 1882.

The following account of the meeting appeared in *The Mail* newspaper of the 15th March:—

A meeting of those connected with educational matters was held in the theatre of the Normal School yesterday afternoon, to consider the proposal to erect a monument or other token of esteem to the memory of the late Dr. Ryerson.

There were present, Drs. Hodgins, Davies, Carlyle, Tassie; Inspectors Hughes, McKinnon, McBrien, Little, Fotheringham; Messrs. James Bain, G. McMurrich, and Crombie, Public School trustees, Toronto; Thomas Kirkland, M.A., Normal School; Mrs. Riches, Misses E. A. Scarlett, M. L. Williams, Boulton and Tomlinson; Messrs. McAllister, Doan, Lewis, Spence, McCausland, Martin, Clarke, Coyne, Parker, Cassidy, Campbell, teachers of Toronto city schools. Dr. Hodgins was appointed chairman, and Mr. James L. Hughes secretary.

Letters expressing regret at inability to attend were read from Mr. G. W. Ross, M.P., Inspectors Scarlett, Bigg and Platt, and Mr. W. J. Gage. Also a letter from the Minister of Education, to the effect that every inspector and teacher was at full liberty to take such action as he might think proper in connection with so laudable an object as the erection of a memorial to the late superintendent.

Dr. Hodgins related the circumstances which had led to the calling of a meeting, and said that the object was to unite all persons in any way connected with schools in a tribute of affection to the late chief, even the children might contribute a mite. There was some difference of opinion as to whether the tribute should take the form of a monument in the cemetery, or a statue in the Normal School grounds. He mentioned Dr. Ormiston as having taken a very strong interest in the matter.

On motion of Mr. McAllister, seconded by Mr. McMurchy, a resolution expressing the approval, by the meeting, of the proposal to erect a memorial was unanimously adopted.

Mr. Hughes suggested that a central committee of organization be appointed, and that local associations be formed in every county.

Messrs. Fotheringham, McMurchy, George McMurrich, McAllister and Brother Odo, were appointed to nominate the central committee. Their report was presented to the meeting, and adopted with some amendments.

In the discussion which took place, the general opinion was that the memorial should take the form of a statue of the late Chief Superintendent, to be erected in the Normal School grounds, Mr. Bain being one of those who strongly urged this view.

Mr. Inspector Fotheringham thought that the amount of the contribution should be limited so as to make it general, and suggested one dollar for each teacher and trustee, and ten cents for each child, corporate bodies being left to their own discretion.

The chairman having called for suggestions as to the formation of local committees, Mr. Little, Inspector for Halton, thought that the inspector for each county should appoint the teachers and trustees of each school to open a subscription list.

Mr. McBrien, Inspector for Ontario County, suggested that the inspectors should send a postcard to every teacher in the county, requesting him to convene a meeting in his section.

Mr. McKinnon, Inspector for Peel, was in favor of Mr. Little's plan.

There was also considerable discussion as to whether others besides those directly connected with the schools should be asked to contribute. It was urged on the one hand that the tribute would come more fittingly from those more peculiarly interested in education, and on the other that it should be made national in its character, especially as a large majority of the people had been educated, and their characters formed under the school system of which Dr. Ryerson was the founder.

These questions were left for future consideration, and, after a vote of thanks to the chairman, the meeting adjourned.

As the result of that meeting the following circular was issued by the secretary on the 15th March:—

At a preliminary meeting of trustees, inspectors and teachers connected with Public, Separate and High Schools, held in the public hall of the Education Department on the 14th instant, the following gentlemen were appointed members of a central committee to carry out the resolution unanimously agreed to by the meeting, viz.: to collect funds with which to erect a monument or other tribute of love and esteem to the memory of the late revered founder of the educational system of Ontario, viz.:—

Dr. *Hodgins*, chairman; Rev. Principal *Davies*; Principal McCabe; Rev. Dr. Ormiston, of New York; President Wilson and Prof. G. P. Young, Toronto University; Archbishop Lynch; Rev. Provost Body, Trinity College; Rev. Principal *Caven*, Knox College; Rev. President Castle, Toronto Baptist College; Rev. Father Vincent, Superior, St. Michael's College; Rev. President Nelles, Victoria University; Very Rev. Principal Grant, Queen's University; *A. McMurchy*, M.A., President of Ontario Teachers' Association; Very Rev. Dean Grassett, Chairman of Collegiate Institute Board; Edward Galley, Esq., Chairman, Public School Board; Vicar-General Rooney, Chairman, Separate School Board; Dr. McLellan, Inspector, High Schools; Mr. White, Inspector, Separate Schools for Ontario; Rev. Brother Tobias, city Inspector of Separate Schools; J. S. Carson, Esq., Chairman of inspectors' section Ontario Teachers' Association; R. Lewis, Esq., chairman of Public School section; D. C. McHenry, M.A., chairman of High School section; also the Public School Inspectors throughout the Province as *ex officio* members, (Messrs. *D. Fotheringham* and *J. R. Miller*). Mr. *James L. Hughes* was appointed secretary of the committee, and Mr. *Walter S. Lee*, treasurer.[2]

APPEAL FOR FUNDS FOR ERECTION OF THE STATUE.

At a subsequent meeting of the committee, Rev. Dr. Ormiston and Dr. Hodgins were requested to draw up an appeal soliciting aid for the proposed memorial. Dr. Ormiston did so as follows:—

Appeal to Trustees, Inspectors, Teachers and Pupils—past and present—connected with Public, Separate[3] and High Schools, and to the other friends of Education in the Province of Ontario; from the General Committee appointed at Toronto on the 14th

8

March, 1882, for the collection of funds with which to erect a Monument, or other Tribute of Esteem and Admiration to the memory of the late Rev. Dr. Ryerson, founder of the Educational System of Ontario:

"Although still young our Province has already been called to mourn the removal of not a few of her gifted sons, who have severally adorned the different walks of public life. In weight of character, wealth of manhood, and width of human sympathy, the late Chief Superintendent of Education, stood amongst the foremost and mightiest of them all.

Egerton Ryerson was a man of rare diversity of gifts, of remarkable energy, and of abundant mental resources. It would have been easy for him to have excelled in any one sphere of human greatness, but it was his to stand high in several. He was a many-sided man; richly endowed in various ways. He was a laborious farmer—a zealous student—a successful teacher—an eminent preacher—a prominent ecclesiastic—an influential editor—a forcible writer —a sagacious counsellor—a most efficient principal and professor—but he was chiefly noted as a great public educationist.

For a third of a century he was the head and inspiring genius of our school system, establishing, moulding, adapting, controlling it; and this, the main work of his life, will endure and command in the future, as it has in the past, the admiration of all, both at home and abroad. During all these years he was the teacher's true friend, and the ardent well-wisher of the young. His sympathies—tender and true—as helpful as they were healthy, went out to every earnest worker, whether in acquiring or imparting knowledge. The enquiring left his presence directed; the downcast, cheered; the doubtful, confirmed.

Unselfish, generous, disinterested, he devoted himself wholly to his work. How often did his lip quiver and his eye fill when he addressed the gatherings of teachers and pupils, upon whom he looked not only with the eye of a patriot, but of a parent,—"Ye are my children all."

We can never forget him; we profoundly mourn our loss; we fondly cherish his memory. Affection, gratitude, a sense of what is due to so eminent a man, impel us to perpetuate that memory in some suitable way, which will render such a noble life an inspiring example to young men now and in the coming days.

In obedience then, to one of the purest and loftiest instincts of our nature, let us unite in paying a common tribute of admiration and regard to the memory of him to whom we all sustained a common relationship, and to whom we also, without distinction as to nationality, political preferences, or religious belief, can pay sincere homage, as the founder of our present excellent and comprehensive system of education.

In honoring him we do honor to our common country, and recognize our obligation to pay fitting homage to the great men of our Dominion, whose names, with his, are inscribed high upon the roll of Canada's famous sons."

At intervals, during the years 1882-1886, circulars were issued by the committee to inspectors, trustees and masters of High, Public and Separate Schools, urging the collection of the necessary funds to erect the proposed memorial. In order to aid in this work, 7,500 copies of a biographical sketch of Dr. Ryerson and his educational work, prepared by the chairman, was sent to the inspectors for distribution. The chairman also made the following suggestions to inspectors (with a view to facilitate the collections from pupils), which was generally acted upon, viz.:—

"Permit me to suggest a simple way of securing a response from each school: You might request the teacher to give notice that, on the following week, he would devote *five minutes* at noon of each day to taking down a list of contributions (from a cent upwards) to the fund.

"In this way the pupils—and everyone in the locality, through the children—would have an opportunity of contributing his or her mite to the erection of a statue to one of Canada's most honored sons."

The final circular issued by the committee was as follows:—

The appeal on behalf of the Ryerson Memorial Fund has been responded to by about two-thirds of the public, and less than one-third of the High-Schools in Ontario. The sum thus received amounts to $4,425.00, including accrued interest on the moneys received and invested.

The 7,520 masters and teachers now employed in the Public and High Schools of Ontario, have not yet been appealed to, as a body, to contribute to this most desirable and patriotic object, although many of them have sent in their subscriptions. The General Committee have, therefore, decided to make this appeal to them through the various teachers' associations. The committee trust, therefore, that the individual masters and teachers concerned (if they have not already done so) will heartily and promptly respond to this appeal.

The words with which Dr. Ormiston closes his appeal on behalf of this fund we would heartily commend to your sympathy and kind consideration. We do so with the earnest hope that you will give them a substantial and practical application. Dr. Ormiston says:—

"In obedience then, to one of the purest and loftiest instincts of our nature, let us unite in paying a common tribute of admiration and regard to the memory of him to whom we all sustained a common relationship, and to whom we also, without distinction as to nationality, political preferences, or religious belief, can pay sincere homage, as the founder of our present excellent and comprehensive system of education.

"In honouring him we do honour our common country, and recognize our obligation to pay fitting homage to the great men of our Dominion, whose names, with his, are inscribed high upon the roll of Canada's famous sons."

The Rev. T. Bowman Stephenson, L.L.D., delegate from the British to the General Conference of the Methodist Church in Canada, in his recent address to that Conference, said, referring to the late Rev. Dr. Ryerson:—

That gentleman "visited us in England twice. Old man as he then was, he seemed younger than most of us. I take him to have been one of those rare men who are never young and never old—old in wisdom whilst young in years—young in heart and feeling when already the snow is on the head. Eloquent, logical, far sighted, generous, independent, courageous, with an unhesitating faith in duty, and a boundless love of freedom and justice, he 'served his generation.'—O how well the inspired words describe him—by the will of God, 'he fell on sleep.'"

THE FINANCIAL RESULTS OF THE APPEALS MADE—PARTICULARS OF THE STATUE.

The following is the financial result of the labours of the committee up to the date of its final meeting on the 1st of June, 1889, viz.:—

Subscriptions received	$4,647 95	
Legislative grant	2,000 00	
City of Toronto grant	500 00	
Interest on deposits	1,119 14	
		$8,267 09
Cost of bronze statue	$5,100 00	
Coat of granite pedestal	2,600 00	
Fees and incidentals	381 09	
		$8,081 09
		$186 00
To be expended on the Memorial Volume		186 00
Height of bronze figure		9 feet 6 inches.
Height of granite pedestal		10 feet 6 inches.

The granite of the pedestal is from a quarry at St. George, in New Brunswick—a Province which was the first early home of Dr. Ryerson's father and mother, after the close of the American Revolutionary War. Dr. Ryerson's mother was a native of New Brunswick as were his elder brothers and sisters.

PROGRAMME OF ARRANGEMENTS FOR UNVEILING THE STATUE.

The following was the programme of arrangements agreed to by the Committee to be observed on the Queen's Birthday, 1889, at the ceremony of unveiling of the statue of the Rev. Egerton Ryerson, D.D., LL.D., founder of the school system of Ontario, 1844-1876, ceremony to commence at two o'clock p.m.:—

Chairman for the Day.—The Hon. George W. Ross, LL.D., Minister of Education for Ontario. *Dedicatory Hymn.*—("All People that on Earth do Dwell," Old Hundred) to be announced by the Rev. John Burton, B.D. *Selection of Scripture.*—To be read by the Rev. John Potts, D.D., Secretary of Education of the Methodist General Conference. *Dedicatory Prayer.*—By the Rev. G. M. Milligan, B.A., Minister of Old St. Andrew's Church, Toronto. *Opening Address.*—By the Hon. George W. Ross, LL.D., Chairman of the Day. *Unveiling of the Statue.*—By the Hon. Sir Alexander Campbell, K.C.M.G., Lieutenant-Governor of Ontario. *Patriotic School Song by the City School Children.*—"Hurrah, Hurrah, for Canada!" to be led by Mr. Perrin, Music Teacher, City Schools. *Historical Paper on Education in Ontario.*— The abstract only was read by J. George Hodgins, M.A., LL.D., Deputy

Minister of Education for Ontario. *Address on behalf of the Ontario Teachers' Association.*—By Mr. McQueen, President of the Association, 1889. *Address on behalf of the Citizens of Toronto.*—By His Worship the Mayor, E. F. Clarke, Esq., M.P.P. (Mr. Clarke having gone to England, the address was read by Alderman McMillan, President of the City Council, and Acting Mayor *pro tem*). *Patriotic Song by the City School Children.*—"The Maple Leaf for Ever!" *Address on behalf of the University of Toronto.*—By the Hon. John Macdonald, Senator. *Address on behalf of Victoria University.*—By the Rev. N. Burwash, S.T.D., Chancellor of Victoria University. *Address on behalf of Queen's University.*—By Sandford Fleming, Esq., LL.D., C.M.G., Chancellor of Queen's University. *Address on behalf of Trinity University.*— By the Rev. Professor William Clark, M.A. *Address on behalf of McMaster University.*—By T. H. Rand, Esq., D.C.L. *The National Anthem. Benediction.* —Pronounced by the Right Rev. Arthur Sweatman, D.D., D.C.L., Bishop of Toronto.

Representatives present.—The Mayor and Corporation of the City of Toronto, Chairman and members of the High School and Collegiate Institute Board of Toronto, Chairman and members of the Public School Board of Toronto. Upper Canada College, Hon. John Beverley Robinson; Knox College, Rev. William McLaren, D.D.; Wycliffe College, Colonel Gzowski, A.D.C.; McMaster Divinity Hall, Rev. Chancellor McVicar, D.D. LL. D.; Brantford Ladies' College, T. M. Macintyre, Esq., Ph. D.; Alma Ladies' College, Colin Macdougall, Esq., Q.C.[4]; Oshawa Ladies' College, Rev. A. B. Demill.

The following replies from other Colleges were received by the Secretaries, viz.:—

"ASSUMPTION COLLEGE, SANDWICH, March 12, 1889.

"DEAR SIR,—I beg to return thanks for your invitation to the unveiling of the Statue to the late Doctor Ryerson.

"I do not think it will be possible for any representative of this College to be present on that occasion.

"I remain, dear Sir, yours respectfully,
"(Sgd) DENNIS O'CONNOR.

"J. CARLYLE, Esq., Secretary."

"ST. MICHAEL'S COLLEGE, TORONTO, 15th March, 1889.

"DEAR SIR,—I received in due time your letter inviting me to the unveiling of the Statue to the late Dr. Ryerson on the 24th of May next. Your invitation I must respectfully decline, and thanking you for it.

"I remain yours very sincerely,
"(Sgd) P. VINCENT.

"JAMES CARLYLE, Esq., Secretary."

"DEAR SIR,—I am in receipt at your circular, dated March 12th, with which you kindly favored me. Please accept my best thanks for your cordial invitation to send a representative of our College to the unveiling of the Statue of the late Dr. Ryerson. I am greatly sorry to state that it will be hardly possible to anybody of us to go on the 24th of May. Please excuse us and believe me.

"Yours sincerely,
"(Sgd.) J. M. FEAYARD, O.M.J.

"Mr. J. CARLYLE, Secretary."

No replies were received from the other Colleges in Ontario to which invitations had been sent by the Secretaries. The following representatives were also present:

Ontario Teachers' Association, Public School Section, Mr. Robert Alexander; Inspectors' Section, Mr. David Fotheringham; High School Section, Mr. Archibald McMurchy, M.A.

Inscription on the pedestal of the bronze statue of Rev. Dr. Ryerson, as approved by the General Committee, November, 1887, to be placed on the front of the pedestal, facing Bond Street:—

EGERTON RYERSON,
FOUNDER
of the
SCHOOL SYSTEM OF ONTARIO.

To be placed on the rear of the pedestal:—

BORN
IN CHARLOTTEVILLE, COUNTY OF NORFOLK, ONTARIO,
MARCH 24, 1803.
DIED
AT TORONTO, FEBRUARY 19, 1882.

Record of Rev. Dr. Ryerson's services, as approved by the General Committee, November, 1887, and intended to have been engraved on the Pedestal. It was afterwards decided not to do so, but to insert the name only, as founder of the Ontario School System.[5]

THIS STATUE
IS
ERECTED
AS A MEMORIAL
OF THE GREAT PUBLIC SERVICES OF THE

REV. EGERTON RYERSON, D.D., LL.D,

SON OF COLONEL JOSEPH RYERSON,
A BRITISH OFFICER WHO SERVED DURING THE AMERICAN REVOLUTION,
AND WHO WAS ONE OF
THE UNITED EMPIRE LOYALISTS
WHO SETTLED IN THIS PROVINCE.

A DISTINGUISHED MINISTER OF THE METHODIST CHURCH,
1825-1852.
HE OBTAINED FOR THAT CHURCH A ROYAL CHARTER IN ENGLAND
FOR THE ESTABLISHMENT OF
UPPER CANADA ACADEMY AT COBOURG,
1828-1841.
AFTERWARDS
THE UNIVERSITY OF VICTORIA COLLEGE,
OF WHICH HE WAS THE FIRST PRESIDENT.

IN FOUNDING
THE SCHOOL SYSTEM OF HIS NATIVE PROVINCE,
AND IN PROMOTING THE
ESTABLISHMENT OF FREE SCHOOLS,
HE DISPLAYED THE RARE GIFTS OF A
FAR-SEEING AND ENLIGHTENED STATESMAN,
AND FOR THIRTY-TWO YEARS WAS
THE ABLE ADMINISTRATOR OF THAT SYSTEM,
1844-1876.

ERECTED BY CONTRIBUTIONS FROM SCHOOL TRUSTEES INSPECTORS, TEACHERS,
PUPILS AND OTHERS;

AIDED BY A GRANT FROM THE CITY OF TORONTO AND
THE LEGISLATURE OF ONTARIO.

CHAPTER II.

CEREMONY OF UNVEILING THE STATUE, 24TH MAY, 1889.

The ceremony of unveiling of the Statue is thus described by *The Globe* of May the 25th (abridged):—

The number of truly great men is not large in any country.

Ontario is not old yet in its physical and intellectual development, and yet it is with pride her people recall the memory of a few great men who are now with the overwhelming majority. Among the greatest of Canadian public men was Rev. Dr. Egerton Ryerson, the founder of the Ontario Public School system of education. Posterity recognizes this, and posterity seeks to perpetuate his memory in that loving manner which bespeaks gratitude, thankfulness and patriotism. The generation that now is speaks affectionately and reverently of him, who, by sheer force of character, founded a system of education which places the child of the poor man on an equal equality with that of the rich, and who so admirably developed his system that every office in the State is open through a complete system of elementary and secondary education to all classes in the Province. But this generation has done more. It erected a monument to the great man, so that generations yet unborn may not be unmindful of the heritage which shall be theirs, as the result of the untiring zeal and ability displayed by the Chief Superintendent of Education in Ontario for the moral and intellectual advancement of his country.

The unveiling of this monument, fittingly erected in a commanding position of the Normal School grounds, which were the scene of the labors of the grand teacher, took place yesterday afternoon before a large concourse of people. There were there statesmen and politicians, presidents of universities and eminent divines, men learned in the law and merchant princes, manufacturers and agriculturists, teachers and pupils—all being assembled to do honor to the name of him whose monument was unveiled and whose virtues were extolled. The gathering was truly historical and unique in its character—there being seen representatives of the old class of teachers who presided over the school, houses of the country when there was no system of education in Ontario, and who, therefore, could the more appreciate the revolution wrought by the master mind of Dr. Ryerson, when he undertook to mould into shape the heterogeneous elements of public instruction over forty years ago. Then, again, it is seldom in the history of a nation that all classes, creeds and colors could be got together to do honor to the memory of one man, and seldom could there be seen such an array of intellectual leaders in all the walks of life as held seats on the platform when Her Majesty's representative unveiled the form of him whose memory is sought by it to be perpetuated. The sky itself seemed to favor the auspicious occasion. The weather could not have been finer if it had been designed to gladden and rejoice the hearts of those who were present, and thereby to assist in making the proceedings pass off as pleasantly as possible.

A temporary platform was erected nearly in front of the monument commanding an admirable view of it, while seats were placed on both sides of the centre of attraction.

(Among those present not mentioned in the programme were: Ex-Governor Aikens, of Manitoba, Sir Daniel Wilson, Hon. Oliver Mowat, Rev. Dr. Scadding, Rev. Dr. Rose, Judge McDougall, Rev. Leroy Hooker, Thomas Hodgins, Q.C., Mr. F. E. Hodgins, Rev. Dr. Parker, Rev. Dr. D. G. Sutherland, Mr. Wm. Houston, Lt.-Col. Allan, Rev. John Hunt, Mr. D. Rose, Dr. H. H. Wright, Professor Ashley, Mr. J. J. Withrow, O. A. Howland, Mr. A. Marling, James Beatty, Q.C., Rev. Dr. Thomas, Mr. J. E. Bryant, Mr. F. B. Hodgins, and Members of the City Corporation, etc. A very large number of ladies were also present, and many unenumerated old friends of the venerable ex-Chief.)

The proceedings were opened by Rev. John Burton giving out Psalm 100, which was sung by the audience. Rev. John Potts, D.D., read a portion of Scripture, and the dedicatory prayer was offered by Rev. G. M. Milligan.

THE HON. G. W. ROSS' ADDRESS.

Hon. G. W. Ross, Minister of Education, spoke as follows:—

We are assembled to-day to do honor to the founder of the school system of the Province of Ontario. On the 18th of October, 1844, the Rev. Egerton Ryerson received a commission from Sir Charles Metcalfe as Superintendent of what was then called the Common Schools of Upper Canada. At the time he entered upon his duties there were in existence 2,885 Common Schools, with a registered attendance of 96,756 children of school age. The entire revenue from all sources for school purposes amounted to $340,000. When he retired in 1876 there were 5,092 schools, with a registered attendance of 489,664 pupils, and a revenue of $3,373,035. Besides the Common Schools in existence there were 25 Grammar Schools attended by 958 pupils, and maintained at an expense of $16,320 annually. At the close of his long career there were 104 High Schools attended by 8,541 pupils, and maintained at an annual expense of $304,948. The accommodation for the pupils attending the

Common Schools was supplied by 2,887 school houses, of which 213 were brick or stone, 1,008 frame and 1,666 log. The teachers numbered 3,086, and were possessed of such varied qualifications as might be expected when I tell you that they obtained their certificates in most cases from the Boards of Trustees which employed them. When he surrendered his commission there were 4,926 school-houses, of which 1,931 were brick or stone, 2,253 frame, and only 742 log, all in charge of a staff of highly educated and accomplished teachers, numbering 6,185.

The school law in existence at the time of Dr. Ryerson's appointment to office consisted of 71 sections, and was as crude in many respects as the education which was obtained under it. There were practically no authorized text-books, no Boards of Examiners, no Inspectors, no Department of Education. It was an era of primitive simplicity, but an era, nevertheless, the possibilities of which no man could estimate, the development of which no man could foresee. "The deep surge of nations yet to be" had struck our shores. Thousands of sturdy pioneers were at work hewing down our forests and wrestling with such social and political problems as are incident to a primitive order of things. The materials out of which to organize society on a higher plane were abundant though undeveloped. It was a great opportunity for a man possessed of a genius for organization. In the appointment of Dr. Ryerson the opportunity and the man met face to face, and the splendid system of education which we to-day enjoy is the best proof that the man was as great, if not greater, than the opportunity. But, while the opportunity was a great one, it must not be forgotten that the difficulties to be overcome, to a less vigorous and courageous man, would have been overwhelming.

The executive machinery for administering the affairs of several thousand distinct corporations, with all the complex details necessarily connected with electing trustees, collecting rates, appointing teachers, framing a curriculum of studies, regulating the discipline of pupils and supplying text-books, had all to be re-cast, if not invented, and put into operation. Cabinet Ministers, Members of Parliament and Municipal Councils had to be indoctrinated with the new education. The press had to be directed, and the whole people educated to receive with favor a school system which ignored well established theories and deeply founded prejudices. Even popular indignation had to be set at defiance, and amid misrepresentation and calumny the master builder had often to do his work and to await the verdict of posterity for the vindication of his wisdom and foresight.

It is well known, when Dr. Ryerson first proposed to make all the Common Schools of Upper Canada free alike to rich and poor, to citizen and alien, that he was charged with encroaching upon the rights of the subject, that he was charged with appropriating the money of the taxpayer who perhaps had no children to be educated for the benefit of the thriftless and pauperised classes of the community. What was his answer? It was this:—"The education of the people irrespective of rank or race or creed is a better investment even for the taxpayer than houses or lands, because it guarantees the safe possession of all his goods—it does even more—it guarantees his personal liberty and therefore the taxpayer must be made to pay for the common safety of the people."

When he asked authority for trustees to erect school houses wherever, in their opinion, the public interests required them, he was told such a law would be arbitrary and harsh, that it would place too much power in the hands of a few men. His answer was: "School houses are cheaper than gaols, teachers are cheaper than police officers, the taxpayer must be made to pay for the common morality of the people." When he said: "Teachers must be educated and trained for their work, the success of thousands of children depend upon skilful handling and discipline in the school room, we must have Grammar Schools and Normal School and Township libraries and Boards of Examiners," he was told that the country could not afford such luxuries, that he must wait till the people were richer. His answer was: "Efficiency is the highest economy. If the springtime of life is wasted, life's greatest opportunities are wasted. The taxpayer must be made to pay for the common intelligence of the people." As a result of all this courage—may I not call it heroism—in the defence of sound principles of education he placed his native Province in the van of all the States of America and all the Colonies of the British Empire. Well may we to-day assemble to do honor to his memory. Not only Ontario, but Canada, owes much to his breadth of mind, his sagacity and his tremendous force of character.

For thirty-two years his active brain and busy pen were devoted to the work of propagating sounder views on popular education. For thirty-two years he labored to establish the democracy of mind—the common citizenship of every child attending a Public School. With a patriotism which no man ever questioned, with talents which no man could fail to appreciate, with a tenacity of purpose which no difficulty could daunt, he devoted his life to one purpose, the establishment of a school system which would fully meet the wants of a free, strong and progressive people. (Applause). It is said of Augustus that he found Rome brick and left it marble. It may be said of Dr. Ryerson that he found our school system without any definite organisation, he left it highly organized. He found it weak in influence and poor in circumstances, he left it endowed with houses and lands and millions of treasure. He found it tolerated as traditionally respectable, he left it enthroned in the affections of a free people.

Well may we honor his greatness, for we share in all it has produced. Well may we search our quarries for a fit emblem of the durability of his work, on which to carve his name, that generations yet unborn may recall the record of his life and be stirred to emulate his example. And yet when we have done all this, when we have committed his memory to the keeping of the bronze and granite now before us, I believe the judgment of those who know his work will be that all the monuments which mortal hands can erect, and all the eulogies which affection or admiration can prompt his contemporaries to utter, will be ephemeral and perishable compared with the educational edifice which his own hands builded or the intellectual life which of his own genius he imparted to his fellow countrymen.

THE STATUE UNVEILED BY SIR ALEXANDER CAMPBELL.

At the close of his address Mr. Ross invited the Governor to unveil the statue. Before doing so the Governor, turning to the audience, said in feeling terms:—

"Dr. Ryerson was known throughout the length and breadth of this Province. No Representative of Her Majesty has had ever as pleading a duty given to him to discharge as that which falls to my lot in unveiling the monument of that great man."

Sir Alexander, accompanied by the Minister and Deputy Minister of Education, proceeded then to the statue, and the work of unveiling was only the question of a few moments. As soon as the British Canadian flag, which covered the massive form of the statue, was raised, the audience raised a cheer which is rarely heard within the Normal School grounds, It was the reflex of the inner gratitude of the sharers in a great heritage.

The sculptor, Mr. McCarthy, who did his work well, was then introduced to the Lieutenant-Governor by the Minister of Education.

The statue having been exposed to full view the song "Hurrah for Canada" was sung by city school children, led by Mr. Perrin, music teacher, city schools. The children acquitted themselves admirably.

EDUCATIONAL RETROSPECT BY THE DEPUTY MINISTER OF EDUCATION.

It was fitting that the next speaker should be a gentleman so long and so closely connected with Dr. Ryerson in moulding the educational institutions of the Province. The Chairman therefore introduced Dr. Hodgins, Deputy Minister of Education, who read a masterly and comprehensive historical paper on Education in Ontario. Dr. Hodgins traced the growth of education in the Province from 1841, dealing minutely and with a thorough knowledge of details with the difficulties encountered by Dr. Ryerson in gaining public endorsation for his scheme of popular education, and the phases through which the system passed until at the Centennial Exhibition, held in Philadelphia in 1876, the Chief Superintendent of Education was gratified by the Commissioners making the following award:—

For a quite complete and admirably arranged exhibition, illustrating the Ontario system of education and its excellent results. Also for the efficiency of an administration, which has gained for the Ontario department a most honorable distinction among Government educational agencies.

Dr. Hodgins concluded as follows:—Having been intimately concerned in all of the events and educational matters to which I have referred, it may not be out of place for me to add a few words of a personal character in conclusion. At the end of this year I shall have completed my more than 45 years' service, as chief of the staff of the Education Department of Ontario. For over 40 years I enjoyed the personal friendship of the distinguished man whose memory we honor here to-day—32 years of which were passed in active and pleasant service under him. How can I, therefore, regard without emotion the events of to-day? They bring vividly to my recollection many memorable incidents and interesting events of our educational past known only to myself. They also deeply impress me with the fleeting and transitory nature of all things human. The chief and sixteen councillors, appointed and elected to assist him, have all passed away. His great work remains, however, and his invaluable services to the country we all gratefully recall to-day, while his native land lovingly acknowledges those services in erecting this noble monument to his memory. Truly indeed and faithfully did Egerton Ryerson make good his promise to the people of this Province, when he solemnly pledged himself, on accepting office in 1844—

To provide for my native country a system of education, and facilities for intellectual improvement, not second to those of any country in the world.

God grant that the seed sown and the foundations thus laid, with such anxious toil and care—and yet in faith—may prove to be one of our richest heritages, so that in the future, wisdom and knowledge, in the highest and truest sense, may be the stability of our times!

THE TEACHERS' REPRESENTATIVE.

The audience was then introduced to Mr. R. McQueen, President of the Ontario Teachers' Association, who eulogised Dr. Ryerson for his marked individuality, tenacity of purpose, and the grand results he achieved through his influence for popular education in his native country. He deserved a monument from a thankful posterity because his whole aim in life was to ameliorate the condition of his fellow-countrymen. He was there in behalf of the teachers of Ontario to express their joy at the tribute paid to the memory of a great teacher and founder of a system of education.

THE ACTING-MAYOR RESPONDS.

In the absence of Mayor Clarke, Ald. McMillan was called on to reply in behalf of the citizens of Toronto. The Acting-Mayor said that Canada owes Dr. Ryerson a deep debt of gratitude. His life was grand and versatile; he was a teacher and a Christian; a combination of the scholar and gentleman; a leader of men. He impressed his genius on the educational institutions of the Province, he was loyal to the country of his birth, and he abhorred falsehood and oppression. Therefore it was eminently fitting that his greatness and worth should be commemorated by a public tribute.

The school children at this stage sang the well-known Canadian song: "The Maple Leaf for Ever."

THE UNIVERSITIES OF ONTARIO.

The Universities of Ontario owe much to the painstaking care of the late Dr. Ryerson over the development of Public and High School education. The efficiency of the University and its possible influence depend on a sound and thorough system of elementary education. The High School depends on the Public School and the University on the High School. Our Universities have made tremendous strides during the last ten years, and without a doubt the cause of this has been due to the fact of the elementary schools putting forth the fruit of the good seed sowed thirty years ago. The Universities therefore were not unmindful of what they owe to the genius of Dr. Ryerson at yesterday's re-union. These five institutions were well and ably represented on the platform. The addresses of these representatives were one series of eulogies on the life and labors of him, whose memory they met to do honor to.

Senator Macdonald, after praising the Ontario system of education, turned to the young people of the audience and said: "You are forcibly reminded to-day that Canada will cherish the memory of all those of her sons who will work patriotically and nobly for the good of their country."

Rev. Dr. Burwash spoke of Dr. Ryerson as a public educator, but he would be great, the speaker said, in any other profession. Ontario, however, remembers him as an educator, statesman, philanthropist and Christian teacher in the highest sense of the word.

Chancellor Fleming honored the name of Dr. Ryerson for having laid such a broad and national system of education as enables Ontario to rank among the first of enlightened nations.

Rev. Professor Clark thought that the spirit of Dr. Ryerson was to provide such a system of education as would make men of earnestness, character and patriotic ardor. The University with which he was identified honored the name of Dr. Ryerson, and he was there to add his tribute to the worth of so great a Canadian.

Professor Rand, eulogised also the elementary and secondary system of education in Ontario, declaring that its founder richly deserved to be commemorated by a public monument.[6]

The audience then sang the national anthem. Bishop Sweatman pronounced the benediction, and the statue of the great educationist was left to posterity to admire and to preserve intact and inviolate.

The report of *The Empire* necessarily traversed the same ground. I can therefore only give the salient points in addition to those referred to by the *Globe*, it said:—

The great educational lights of the Province were present in front of the Education Department building yesterday afternoon, when the statue of the Rev. Dr. Ryerson was unveiled. The day was appropriate for doing honor to the memory of a man who had so ably served his Queen and country. A large crowd of citizens witnessed the unveiling and listened to the addresses that were delivered.

The following relatives of Dr. Ryerson were present: Mr. Charles Egerton Ryerson, (his only son), Mrs. C. E. Ryerson and their two sons, (Egerton and Stanley), Mrs. Edward Harris, (his only daughter), Dr. G. S. Ryerson (his nephew) was absent with the Grenadiers at Berlin, Mrs. G. S. Ryerson and son were present; also, Mrs. Hardy (his niece) and her daughter, Miss Ethel Hardy, Dr. John Beatty, of Cobourg, and Mr. James R. Armstrong, (brothers-in-law), Mrs. J. R. Armstrong, Mrs. George Duggan, (sister-in-law), His Honor Judge McDougall, (a connection by marriage)."

The main points of *The Mail* report were as follows:—

It would perhaps be too much to say that, while the gay and thoughtless were seeking amusements in other parts of the city, it was only the wise who repaired to the grounds of the Education Department to take part in the unveiling of the Statue of the late Egerton Ryerson; yet it cannot but be admitted that those who assembled to witness and assist in this ceremony were men and women worthy to have the privilege of publicly honoring the memory of Canada's greatest educationist. Among those present were men who have attained to eminence in every department of public life, and it was but right that they should pay the tribute they did to the memory of him who was the founder and for many years the head of the greatest of all departments. There were men present who for years were associated with Dr. Ryerson in his great work; men whose characters were to a great extent moulded by his example, and men whose ambitions have been wakened and whose purposes have been inspired by the contemplation of his achievements.

Early in the afternoon the crowd begin to gather around the statue, the front part of which was veiled by a large British flag, the folds of which hung almost to the foot of the pedestal. In front of the statue, under the shade of a couple of the maples that help to make the grounds of the Education Department and Normal School so attractive, a platform had been erected for the use of those who were to take part in the ceremony, and around it were placed a number of seats.

At the close of his address (given on pages 9-11), Hon. Mr. Ross invited Sir Alexander Campbell to unveil the statue. Before proceeding with the ceremony Sir Alexander advanced to the front of the platform and briefly expressed himself as feeling highly honored by being called upon to perform such a task as the one that on this occasion had devolved upon him. He thought no pleasanter duty could fall to the lot of a Lieutenant-Governor of any province than that of assisting in honoring one of the province's noblest men. He then stepped down, and taking hold of the cords that kept the flag in place, drew them aside and the drapery fell to the ground. As the sunlight flashed on the exquisitely chiselled features, and the form so well known to many of those present stood out for the first time as it will stand, it is hoped, for many years to come, a prolonged cheer burst from those who had up to this moment watched Sir Alexander's movements with almost breathless interest. After a pause of a few moments, during which the naturalness and finish of the statue was freely commented on, Hon. Mr. Ross called forward Mr. Hamilton McCarthy, the sculptor, and amid great applause introduced him to Sir Alexander, who spoke in flattering terms of the pleasure he felt in meeting a man who had shown himself capable of producing so excellent a work of art.

The bronze statue, nine feet six inches in height, represents the late Dr. Ryerson in the attitude of addressing an audience in the cause of education. The head is turned a little to the right, with the lips slightly parted, and with the massive brow and flowing locks, give a correct and forcible expression, in harmony with the action of the advanced arm and firm position of the right leg. The proportions of the figure are well kept through the ample folds of the Doctor's gown, which in their various lines, lend richness and interest to the work, and take away the stiffness of the modern costume. The left hand is raised nearly to the breast, and in it is grasped a book. A little to the left and rear of the figure stands a short pedestal bearing three books, carelessly laid one upon another; and on one of the panels of the pedestal is the arms of the Department of Education under Dr. Ryerson's *regime*. Dignity of bearing, repose and action, and distinct force of character, eminent qualities in the personality of the late doctor, mark the expression of the figure; and it is evident that no pains have been spared by the artist in the modelling of the details.[7] Mr. Hamilton McCarthy has also been very successful in the design of the pedestal, which has excited general admiration. It is 10 ft. 6 in. in height, and is of New Brunswick granite. The conception is unique in character. Pilasters at the four angles terminate in buttresses to the ground, and support above beautifully designed capitols with dentils on the face. The pyramidal form of the whole work gives it an effect of rising out of the ground. The finely polished panels of the die, in each of which a classic shield is outlined, contain the inscriptions.

Mr. McCarthy can be congratulated upon the success of his work, and the province can be congratulated upon the possession of so noble an addition to the few works of art now in the country. Mr. Gullett, the contractor for the erection of the pedestal also performed his duties carefully and faithfully, as not the slightest hitch occurred, and no damage was sustained by the granite.

COMMENTS OF THE PRESS ON THE UNVEILING OF THE STATUE.

The *Evangelical Churchman* of May the 9th, anticipating the unveiling of Dr. Ryerson's statue, said:—

> "On the 24th of this month, the Queen's Birthday, Ontario will do honor to one of her most distinguished sons. On that day will be unveiled the statue to the memory of Egerton Ryerson, the founder of the school system of his native province. The ceremony will be unique in many ways, not the least interesting fact in connection therewith being that the statue of Dr. Ryerson will be the first one erected by the Province of Ontario to one of its own sons. Dr Ryerson was a thorough Canadian and was born in Ontario. Thus this signal honor to his memory acquires additional lustre, and does much to redeem Ontario from the reproach an often uttered that a prophet is not without honor save in his own country. It reveals, indeed, another fact which, in a new country, is not without a peculiar significance. It is this, that national life is commencing in earnest, and that national characteristics are developing themselves. A country which can step aside, as it were, in the rush and hurry of existence to do honor to one of its sons, is not without aspirations after a national existence, is not wholly given up to considerations of material interest, and possesses within it something that is full of promise of permanence and true greatness."

The Hamilton *Times* of the 25th of May, under the beading of "The

Memory of a Great Canadian," said:—

"The unveiling of the Ryerson statue in the Normal School grounds, at Toronto, yesterday, was the occasion of recalling the achievements of the late Dr. Ryerson in connection with Ontario's educational system. From 1844 until 1876 Rev. Egerton Ryerson was Chief Superintendent of Education in this Province.... But Dr. Ryerson's services to Canada did not begin in 1844. He was a great man before he touched the educational System. He was born in the County of Norfolk in 1803, and when he was about 20 years of age he was studying in Hamilton in a little house on Jackson Street, not far from the place where the new Y.M.C.A. building is in the course of construction.... In 1826 Archdeacon Strachan preached a sermon on the death of Bishop Mountain. The Methodists at that time were the most numerous religious body in upper Canada but Dr. Strachan set forth the claim of the Church of England to the Clergy Reserves.... Mr. Ryerson was junior preacher under the late Rev. James Richardson, who had his arm shot off while in naval service near Sackett's Harbour during the war.... When Dr. Strachan's sermon was published, it was agreed that Mr. Richardson and Mr. Ryerson should each write a reply to it. They separated, each going to a different part of their large circuit, and when they met a few weeks later young Ryerson had prepared his paper, but Mr. Richardson had nothing ready. It was read before the other preachers and published. The battle had now begun, and it did not end until the Clergy Reserves were secularised in 1854. During nearly all that time Mr. Ryerson was a leading character in Canadian public life. He wrote, he spoke, he worked, appearing before Parliamentary committees, interviewing the statesmen of Great Britain and occasionally taking his stand upon the hustings.... Dr. Ryerson was born in 1803 and became Superintendent of Education in 1844. He was only 42 years of age at the time of his appointment, yet he had performed a greater share of work, and had attained a greater degree of prominence in those forty-two years than most public men can boast of as the achievements of a lifetime. How many men in this latter end of the century get into the thick of the fight and make their influence felt while under 40 years of age? The point we wish to impress is this: Had Egerton Ryerson died in 1844, instead of becoming Superintendent of Education and living until 1882, his history would still have been worth writing, and he would have deserved a monument For the services he performed for his native Province. His long connection with educational affairs to a great extent blotted out the memory of his earlier work and struggles in another connection. He had much to do with founding Victoria College and getting that institution fairly established.... The impression remains with us to this day that if Dr. Ryerson had been a lawyer he would have made all other Canadian lawyers look small; if he had gone into politics he would have been perpetual Premier: in short, he was the ablest native Canadian who has so far helped to make history.

The *Christian Guardian* of the 29th May, said:—

The unveiling of the statue of the late D. Egerton Ryerson, last Friday, in the Normal School grounds in this city, recalls the memory of a worthy and honored Canadian, widely known as a successful journalist, a gifted and learned divine, and an eminent educationist. It will hardly be questioned that the principle of perpetuating the memory of benefactors of a country is a laudable one, or that the individual in this case was worthy of this honor. No one who has travelled in Britain or other European countries, has failed to have his attention arrested by statues, or other memorials, of eminent men whom the county delighted to honor. It is well adapted to inspire the young with high purpose to note that however partisan strife may obscure the patriotic services of public men during active life, when the work of life is over, as a general rule, men of all parties cheerfully recognize the value of the service rendered by those who have faithfully labored for the public good. Owing to the intensity of political feeling in Canada, there is a strong tendency to underestimate the work of our statesmen and politicians, until they have gone where human praise or blame cannot affect them.

Though Dr. Ryerson passed through many fierce controversies, and at times came into conflict with hostile opponents, to-day men of all creeds and parties are ready to give him his

26

due meed of praise as one of the greatest of Canada's sons, who achieved a work in organizing and building up a system of public education that shall tell powerfully for good through all coming time. He founded no cities; he led no armies to victory; he had no special influence on the material prosperity of the land; but in organizing a system of public schools, which placed the elements of a sound education within the reach of every boy and girl in this Province, he has exercised an undying influence over the future intellectual life of the country, that shall largely determine its place in the scale of civilization.

It is not only since his death that the strife of tongues has ceased, and the value of his work has been generally acknowledged. For several years before his death the echoes of old battles had become silent; old strifes were healed; and he lived in a peaceful Beulah land awaiting the Master's call to cross the dark river. In the beginning of 1879 at the request of the editor of the *Guardian*, he wrote an article for the Jubilee number of this paper, of which he was the first editor. After giving an interesting account of the origin and growth of the paper, he concluded by saying; "May the success of the past be as a dim dawn to the success of the future! Such is the prayer and hope of the first editor of the *Guardian*—now retired from all office in Church and State, near the fifty-fifth year of his ministry and the seventy-seventh year of his age—*looking* for a better country and *waiting* for a heavenly home."

The *Presbyterian Review* of the 30th May, said:—

The various speakers dwelt upon the immense service which the late Dr. Ryerson rendered to the country in laying broad and deep the foundations of our educational system, and testified their satisfaction that gratitude and veneration had found expression in the noble work of art before them, which would perpetuate his name to many generations of students and scholars.... Dr. Hodgins and the other gentlemen associated with him on the Ryerson Statue Committee are to be heartily congratulated on the result of their well-directed efforts and well-sustained efforts to assist in perpetuating the memory of a native-born Canadian who, notwithstanding some errors of judgment, proved himself worthy to be held in grateful remembrance by his countrymen.

The *Week* of the 31st May, said:—

That was a grand purpose to which Rev. Egerton Ryerson pledged himself on accepting office as the first Superintendent of Education for Ontario in 1844, "To provide for my native country a system of education, and facilities for intellectual improvement, not second to those of any country in the world." The form and loftiness of the promise marked the courage, individuality and conscious strength of the man who made it. The statue in the Toronto Normal School grounds, which was unveiled with appropriate ceremonies on the 24th inst., will henceforth stand as the testimony of the people of Ontario, especially of its teachers and others interested in educational work, to the faithfulness and ability with which the pledge was redeemed through thirty-two years of indefatigable toil and struggle. The artistically wrought monument in bronze will also serve as a fitting reminder to all who visit the Educational Department that the people of Ontario do not mean to let those who faithfully served their country in its earlier days be forgotten. A monument "more enduring than bronze" stands out to view wherever a free public school is efficiently doing its work in training the young of both sexes and of all classes to become intelligent and patriotic citizens of this growing commonwealth. Whether it be literally true or not that Dr. Ryerson "placed his native Province in the van of all the States of America and all the colonies of the British Empire," as the Minister of Education avouches, his plan was certainly comprehensive and statesmanlike, and was followed out with a courage, perseverance and success, for which the Province must ever remain his debtor.

The Toronto correspondent of the *Montreal Witness*, under date of 31st of May, says:—

One of the noblest public tributes ever paid to the memory of any man in Canada was paid the other day to the memory of the late Rev. Egerton Ryerson. From the time of his death, early in 1882, till now, the work of collecting subscriptions for the erection of a statue has gone steadily on. The amounts contributed were individually small, but the contributors were numerous, and now in front of the Departmental Buildings, in St. James' Square, stands a memorial of him which will fairly convey to future generations some idea of what the man himself was in personal appearance. The massiveness and rugged strength are there, and there were, after all, the most marked traits of Dr. Ryerson's personality, though he was by no means lacking in sympathy and intellectual ability.... The addresses were admirable alike for brevity and good taste, and nothing occurred to mar the success of the ceremony.

The *Educational Journal* of June 1st, said:—

The statue of the late Dr. Ryerson, which has been so long in course of preparation, has been set up on the Normal School grounds, and was unveiled, with appropriate ceremonies, on the 24th ult.

The ceremony of unveiling was performed by Sir Alexander Campbell, the Lieutenant-Governor, who said that he thought no pleasanter duty could fall to the lot of any Lieutenant-Governor than that of assisting in honoring one of the Province's noblest men.

The status is of bronze, nine feet six inches in height, and stands upon a pedestal of New Brunswick granite, ten feet six inches high. It represents Dr. Ryerson in the attitude of addressing an audience in the cause of education. The head is turned a little to the right, with the lips slightly parted, and with the massive brow and flowing locks, gives a correct and forcible expression, in harmony with the action of the advanced arm and firm position of the right leg. The proportions of the figure are very well kept through the ample folds of the doctor's gown, which in their various lines, lend richness and interest to the work, and take away the stiffness of the modern costume. The left hand is raised nearly to the breast, and in it is grasped a book. A little to the left and rear of the figure stands a short pedestal bearing three books, carelessly laid one upon another; and on one of the panels of the pedestal is the arms of the Department of Education. Dignity of bearing, repose and action, and distinct force of character, eminent qualities in the personality of the late doctor, mark the expression of the figure; and it is evident that no pains have been spared by the artist, Mr. Hamilton McCarthy, in the modelling of the details of both statue and pedestal. The statue stands in a commanding position in the Normal School grounds. It will add a new object of interest to the many attractions which these grounds present to teachers and others visiting the Department.

The *Irish Canadian* of the 6th of June, under the heading of "A Graceful Tribute," said:—

On the 24th of May (the Queen's Birthday), was unveiled the statue erected in the Normal School grounds to the memory of the Rev. Egerton Ryerson, the founder of the common school system of education in Ontario, and its Superintendent from its inception in 1844 till 1876, when he retired in the fullness of years, and after his labors had been crowned with signal success. The Catholics of this Province, in the matter of education, have nothing for which they should be thankful to the distinguished divine.... For all that, Dr. Ryerson was a man of great and good parts; and, from a Common School point of view, he has left a noble heritage in a system of education that will bear favorable comparison with the best of any land.

It was the occasion of the unveiling of his statue that his co-laborer in the Education Department—Dr. J. George Hodgins—paid the memory of Dr. Ryerson a graceful tribute. Who so capable for so delicate a task as he who had been Dr. Ryerson's right-hand man, his able support, during his long and varied career in the Education office? And happily has the story of the ups and downs of the Common School system been told by the learned Deputy Minister, to whose ripe judgment, in no small degree, was due the system's unmeasured success. The part that Dr. Hodgins played, however, is kept in the background; and we see only what Dr. Ryerson done during his lengthened incumbency, and the difficulties with which he had to contend in maturing his plans and bringing them as nearly as possible to his own ideal of perfection.

Dr. Hodgins' retrospect goes back to the period of the U. E. Loyalists, and thence downward to 1876. It leads us by degrees from the primitive system in vogue prior to the grammar schools (in one of which the late venerable Bishop Strachan taught as master), through a series of changes aiming at higher education, till we arrive at the year in which the foundations of the present system were laid. The corner-stone having been placed, the superstructure rose in fair proportions; and the edifice having been completed, to furnish it with all the adjuncts necessary to the best educational training was the Superintendent's constant care. How Dr. Ryerson finally overcame every obstacle to his darling object is told with tender affection by Dr. Hodgins, who, in laying a chaplet on the grave of his dead chief, does honor not only to the memory of a good man, but also to his own generous instincts.

The *Canada Educational Monthly* for June-July, said:—

The Rev. Dr. Ryerson has long been widely known as a gifted and learned divine, as well as a successful journalist, who took a prominent part in the religious and moral development of our country in its early days, ... but the fitting memorial which was unveiled on Her Majesty's seventieth birthday, is erected to him chiefly as a worthy Canadian and an eminent educationist....

The life work of this able man has now passed into other hands; in itself it forms a whole superstructure, and if the enlightened principles which he laid down and acted upon are carried out in their integrity, they must exercise an undying influence for good upon the intellectual life of the country, upon its gradual advance in the scale of civilization and refinement, and upon its moral and religious life.

The ceremony of unveiling the statue brought together many true, patriotic and representative men. Some of his personal friends and fellow-workers were there, and others who remembered him with affection and gratitude. The Government, the city, the public and secondary schools, the colleges and universities were all represented, and all united in honoring the memory of the founder of the Ontario school system.

CHAPTER III.

THE ADDRESSES DELIVERED AT THE UNVEILING.[8]

THE TEACHERS' ASSOCIATION OF ONTARIO.

Mr. Robert McQueen, President of the Ontario Teachers' association, spoke as follows:—

Your Honor, Mr. Chairman, Ladies and Gentlemen:

We are gathered here to-day to do honor to the memory of one to whom this country owes a debt of deep and lasting gratitude; and should I fail entirely to give expression to any thought worthy of the man or the occasion, I feel certain that all will be overlooked, when I simply utter the two words "Egerton Ryerson." He was a man of marked individuality of character, of energetic action, of great power of will, and tenacity of purpose. His life-work bears the marks of his individuality and energy, the results he achieved are evidences of his power of will and his tenacity of purpose. And, in view of the results which he achieved, it is a meet and a becoming thing, that, as a people, we should meet and do honor to his memory, as we have gathered here this day to do.

Men, even great men, only act permanently, as they act upon the institutions of their country. The greatness that centres in the individual is dependent upon and contingent on the existence of the individual, and the influence exercised by him as it centres in him, dies with him, passes away when he leaves the scene. But the man who leaves his impress on the institutions of his country, exercises an influence that is permanent in its action, pervasive in its power, and, within the range of these institutions, is universal in its beneficence. Every amelioration of these institutions is an abiding good, shared in by all who come within their sphere of operation. It becomes the common heritage of all.

Such was the impress made, such still is the influence exercised by the individual to whose memory and life-work we have met this day to do honor. His connection with, his charge over, and his influence upon the educational institutions of this country, reaching backward nearly half a century from the present time, and lasting over a period of nearly thirty years, was that of a formative and meliorating kind. From the time of his acceptance of office in 1844, down to the period when he resigned his trust, his energies were directed, his powers brought to bear on organizing, modelling and consolidating the school system of this province.

Let us for a few moments trace briefly the history of that system for the last fifty years. The Education Bill of 1837 may be said to have been the first legislative attempt at organization. This bill provided for the annual expenditure of fifteen thousand pounds for common school purposes, and that as soon as the permanently available Public School Fund of this Province amounted to ten thousand pounds per annum, a superintendent of common schools should be appointed by the Governor under the Seal of the Province, whose duty it should be to report annually to the Legislature on all matters pertaining to the administration of the public schools. The union of the Provinces brought the Act of 1841, introduced by the Hon. Mr. Day. This Act was simplified and improved by the Bill of 1843, introduced by the Hon. F. Hincks. By the provisions of that Act the Secretary of the Province was *ex-officio* Chief Superintendent of Schools. In 1844 that office was tendered to the late Dr. Ryerson, and in the autumn of that year it was accepted by him on two conditions: (1st), that the administration of the school system should constitute a separate and distinct non-political department; (2nd), that he should be permitted to act by a deputy for one year and have leave of absence for that period, in order to enable him to visit and examine the educational systems of other countries, in Europe and America, before attempting to lay the foundations of a system in Upper Canada. The whole of 1845 was spent in these inquiries and investigations. The results were embodied in a report to the Legislature in 1846. Along with this report was a Draft School Bill, which was introduced and carried through by the Hon. W. Draper, and became law in June, 1846. In a few mouths a draft bill for cities and incorporated towns was submitted and carried through by the Hon. J. H. Cameron, and became law in June, 1847; these two Acts, with modifications and improvements, suggested by time and experience, were incorporated in the School Bill of 1850, which was introduced by the Hon. F. Hincks, and was the first Act to which the Earl of Elgin gave the Royal Assent after the removal of the Seat of Government to Upper Canada.

The provision of this bill embodied the basis of our present system. It introduced the principle of free schools, leaving the adoption of that principle to the option of each school section. Subsequent changes and modifications were embodied in the Act of 1870, which abolished the office of township superintendent, introduced the county inspectorate, and made free schools compulsory. This Act may be said to be the last touch of the "Master Hand." In order to apprehend the true nature and extent of that impress which he made, of that influence which he exercised and exerted, we have only to look around, to look on that noble structure, whose foundations he was permitted and honored to lay, and whose superstructure he was so largely enabled to rear. Our school system is his true memorial.

I have already said that it is a meet and a becoming thing for a nation to honor the memory of its public benefactors. The nation that ceases to cherish and manifest a grateful remembrance of those who have devoted their energies to the promotion of its welfare and spent their lives in its service, gives evidence of deterioration and decay, gives evidence that it is on the down grade of national existence. To-day we have gathered here to give expression to our gratitude in tangible form, by the erection in this public place, of this costly and enduring memorial of the individual and his life-work, that by its very presence it may speak to all who behold of the grateful sense of benefits received, cherished by the people of this Province. Yet there is another way in which we may manifest our gratitude, viz., by seeking to conserve, to consolidate, to ameliorate, our school system, which has thus come down to us from the moulding hand of the departed; and not only seeking to preserve what has thus been handed down to us, so far as the school system itself is concerned, but to seek to make it practically effective in its operation, so that all who live under its shadow, may share to the full of the blessings and privileges which it is fitted to confer and intended to bestow. Our sense of gratitude will thus assume a practical and beneficent form. That the management of our school system has fallen into, and now is in good and wise hands, we all feel confident. That its success depends largely on the energy, the zeal and the faithfulness of those who are entrusted with the education of the youth of this Province, our high and public school teachers, together with the co-operation of the people at large, of all classes and of all creeds, all will be prepared to admit. In one word: It is only by the united and concerted action of all three, the executive skill, the zeal and energy of the teachers, and the popular sympathy and support that we can hope to secure the full benefit of our school system on the one hand; and on the other, show ourselves worthy of the heritage that has been handed down to us by those who have gone before us.

ADDRESS OF THE ACTING MAYOR.

Alderman McMillan, President of the City Council and Acting Mayor of Toronto, in the absence of Mayor E. F. Clarke, M.P.P., in England, spoke as follows:—

I regret very much that His Worship the Mayor is not with us to-day to represent the citizens of Toronto on this interesting occasion.

It is his loss, however, and I fear it will be your loss also, that it has fallen to my lot to act as his substitute and to speak on his behalf and on behalf of the citizens of Toronto.

Knowing my own unfitness for the task, I have hesitated; feeling my own inability, I have shrunk from the duty imposed on me. Deeply conscious as I am of the fact that it requires more eloquence than I possess to do justice to the occasion, or to speak in fitting terms of the great work of the eminent divine and educationist to whose memory this statue has been erected.

No more appropriate place could have been selected for its erection than here on the grounds of the department which is the creation of his genius, and in front of a building which stands a monument to the energy of its founder.

He will be but a poor student of the history of his country who has not yet learned from its pages the deep debt of gratitude which every Canadian owes to the man whose memory is held in most affectionate rememberance by all classes of the community.

He will be a poor judge of mental power or moral worth who has not yet learned to prize the grandeur of his life-work or the versatility of the attainments of the man who was not only a deep thinker and a notable teacher but an earnest and a humble Christian—a happy combination of the scholar and the gentleman.

During a long and eventful career, and at a crucial period in our country's history the active part he played in public affairs has left on the institutions of our province the impress of his vigorous intellect. Prompted by pure motives, and guided by sound judgment, he gave evidences of an uncommon genius, which he devoted to the service of his country and the best interests of the people, and thus he became a leader among men.

In the school system of this province he built for himself a more lasting monument than the granite and bronze we now raise to his memory.

With fluent speech and ready pen he has oft been the defender of our most sacred rights and cherished privileges. A lover of truth, he abhorred falsehood. A lover of freedom, he hated oppression; and the cause of truth and of freedom found in him an able and willing champion. A staunch defender of British connection, he yet manfully battled for equal rights and privileges to all classes of the people.

He loved the land of his birth with no ordinary affection and, during a long and busy life, he helped to mould her destiny and shape her course—guiding her feeble and often erratic steps, leading her into the paths of truth and righteousness which, we are assured, most surely exalteth the nation.

In the pages of Canadian history the "Story of his Life" and labors will ever be instructive reading.

In the chronicles of the Methodist Church of Canada (the church of his choice) his name will always stand pre-eminently conspicuous as one of her ablest scholars and one of her most eminent divines—an earnest preacher and a devoted missionary. Filled with a fervent love for his Lord and Master, he labored earnestly in His vineyard seeking souls for His hire.

I am proud of the privilege I enjoy of being here on behalf of the citizens of this great city—pleased to be able to bear testimony to the high appreciation we have of his services and the strong affection we bear to the memory of the Rev. Egerton Ryerson. I am also pleased to have this opportunity of being allowed to tender my own humble tribute of respect to the memory of him who was both a statesman and a scholar, a patriot and a Christian.

REPRESENTATIVE OF THE UNIVERSITY OF TORONTO.

The Honourable Senator John Macdonald, speaking on behalf of the University of Toronto, said:—

I wish first to express my regret—a regret I have no doubt in which you share—that some one better fitted than myself had not been selected to represent the University of Toronto upon this important occassion. My embarrassment is lessened however, and possibly your disappointment, in view of the handsome tribute paid to the memory of the great man by the Minister of Education in his admirable address, by the presentation of the historic paper by the Deputy Minister, and last, though not least, by the speech of Alderman McMillan on behalf of the city of Toronto.

Patriotism is that passion which aims to serve one's country, either in defending it from invasion or protecting its rights and maintaining its laws and institutions in vigour and purity. If then we accord, as we ought to do, a place among the patriots of our country to those who readily respond to its call in the hour of danger, to those who bring their wisdom and judgment to bear in the making of laws for its good and healthful government, to those, also, who as diplomats in the carrying on of delicate and subtle international negotiations do so in such a way as not only to maintain their country's honor but to make their country respected, what place shall we assign to him who devoted his life to the best interests of the young of his own province in order that they might be fitted rightly to take their part in life, to do this all the better by reason of that educational system of which he was the moving spirit and which it was his to found? What place I ask, if it be not the very first place in the front rank of that distinguished class. Egerton Ryerson may fairly be regarded as the founder of the school system of his own province and as a consequence must, throughout all time, occupy a foremost place in the history of his country.

His was a life spent not in the promotion of his personal ends. Indeed it may be affirmed that his devotion to his life-work so absorbed his time, his thoughts and his energies as to have disqualified him for making that suitable provision for the close of life for which his great abilities so eminently fitted him.

It would scarcely be fair to claim for him all the honour of perfecting the school system of Ontario, scarcely fair to say that to him exclusively belongs the results seen to-day which give to the school system of Ontario so prominent a place among the school systems of other countries. A measure of the praise is doubtless due to the able staff of workers by which he was supported. His was the directing mind; 'twas theirs to carry out his plans.

It would not be fair to ascribe to the architect all the credit for the grace, symmetry and safety of the most magnificent public buildings. True, he it was who planned the foundations, made them deep and broad, as that they might be safe and enduring. True, he it was who gave grace and beauty to the elevation, as that it might not only answer its purpose, but that it might be at the same time "a thing of beauty;" but how easily might not only the safety of the building be imperilled but its beauty marred by careless and by ignorant treatment; but skilful treatment has produced the needed strength, and has secured the grace of outline, and the building is perfect and harmonious in all its parts.

What the architect is to the building that was Egerton Ryerson to our school system. His it was to lay the foundation upon which a structure which might be at once the pride and the glory of our Province could be erected; his it was to lay these deep and broad and enduring. How wisely and how well he did his work. How well his efforts have been supplemented by the able band of workers who were associated with him the splendid school system of our Province to-day abundantly testifies.

It is fitting, therefore, that his statue should be placed on these grounds, so that the coming generations may be made familiar with the general appearance of the man who has done so much for the educational interests of his country.

But it is not here, faithful as the bronze may speak of the man, that his most fitting and most enduring monument must be found. The group of happy faced children which throng our sidewalks wending their way each morning to our schools, the pupils of our Model Schools, our High Schools, the under-graduates of our Universities, and these seen not only in their school period, but in their subsequent career taking their place in our country as its legislators, its professional men, its merchants, mechanics, farmers, its matrons, taking their places in life, and taking them all the better for their own good and that of their country for the training, sound, thorough and scholarly, which they have received in the schools, colleges and universities of their own country, helping them to make their homes homes of comfort, elegance and refinement.

Here must be found the true and abiding monument of the man; here the enduring fruit of his life-work, more imperishable also than either brass or marble.

Statistics have been freely given, and these need not be repeated.

Not often does it fall to the lot of one man to leave behind him such a record as that left by Dr. Ryerson in his life-work of thirty-three years.

To see the old-log school house, with its imperfect appliances, supplanted by the palatial school buildings with their perfect equipment of our own day.

To see the work done by our High Schools, our Colleges and Universities, which challenges not the attention only, but the admiration of other countries, that is an honour, even with the capabilities which exist in a young country like ours, reserved but for few, and yet among that number he stands out promptly whose statue has this day been unveiled by His Honour the Lieutenant-Governor.

Any words of mine are poor and weak indeed in dealing with a matter so full of interest, not to the people of Ontario only but to the people of Canada, but full of interest to my own mind, as it must be to the mind of others, is the estimate placed upon Dr. Ryerson's work by many eminent men, all well qualified to judge from an educationalist standpoint. Dr. Hodgins has spoken of the late Dr. Fraser, Bishop of Manchester.

Few men were so well able to form an opinion upon any educational system. Himself a great scholar, an Oriel man, an enthusiast on all matters connected with the educational system of his own country, appointed by the Royal Commission as an assistant commissioner to visit and report upon the educational system of the United States and Canada, thus speaks of our school system and of Dr. Ryerson. After referring to the system says: "It shows what can be accomplished by the energy, determination and devotion of a single earnest man. Through evil report and good report, he has found others to support him in the resolution that free education shall be placed within the reach of every Canadian parent for every Canadian child."

Egerton Ryerson has deserved well of his country. His best days and his best energies were given to the upbuilding of its grandest institution. Well should his country guard and cherish his memory, so that the young who are here assembled to-day may learn this lesson, that he who devotes his life for his country's good, his country will hold his memory not in fragrant only, but in perpetual remembrance.

REPRESENTATIVE OF VICTORIA UNIVERSITY, COBOURG.

The Rev. N. Burwash, S.T.D., President and Chancellor of Victoria University, spoke as follows:

Ladies and Gentlemen:

It is particularly appropriate that on this occasion Victoria University should speak. We meet to do honor to one of the greatest of Canada's sons. Dr. Ryerson has written his name indelibly upon the pages of his country's history. He has done so not merely by superior gifts of intellect, although to few men have more noble talents been entrusted. Nor has he done so merely as the successful leader of a great party in Church or State, although he was a leader, one of the first three in one of Canada's greatest movements towards a perfect political constitution. The success of this movement, after a struggle stretching through the lifetime of a full generation, and its results of which all good men now approve, might well ennoble the name of any man. But that for which we honor Dr. Ryerson's name and memory to-day is his work as an educator; and from Victoria University he first received the call to consecrate his life to his work. He was the first President of Victoria College. He, a Canadian of the Canadians, was the first Canadian to occupy that position in our Province; and Victoria has maintained the Canadian succession unbroken from his day to the present. Victoria was the first institution in this Province in active operation as a teaching institution with University powers. And it fell to Dr. Ryerson to shape its character and curriculum, and to give it a form, many features of which it has retained to this present hour.

It was from this duty of laying the foundations of our University in this young Province that Dr. Ryerson was called to the wider field of fashioning the primary and intermediate education of the whole people.

It would be presumption on my part to attempt to speak to-day of the difficulties which beset him in his task, and of the skill and judgment with which those difficulties were met and overcome. That has already been the more appropriate duty of one who has just spoken, and who was for long years his most valued and honored associate in his life-work.

But, as a Canadian of the fourth generation, and as a Canadian school boy who has enjoyed the advantages of the great work which to-day we commit to the perpetual memory of our country, I may venture to refer to the peculiarly Canadian character of the system founded by Dr. Ryerson. The early schools of this country were very varied in their type. Prepossession and usage rule imperiously in education. Each little colony or settlement, as it was called, had its national prepossessions. Here was an attempt to reproduce a miniature English Eton or Rugby. There was a genuine Scottish parish school with its Bible and Catechism. Here was an Irish school with its predilection for difficult problems in arithmetic and algebra. There was a Yankee school with its spelling-matches and dialogues on examination day. These were the heterogeneous elements of forty-five and fifty years ago. To-day, we have everywhere the Canadian school as unique in its character as any of these, and as well-known in its results all over this continent. The skilful mind that took possession of these materials, that carefully separated the good from the bad, that patiently and wisely removed or overcame prejudices, that calmly waited till the public mind was ready for each progressive movement, and then with vigor pushed it forward to speedy completion—this was the ——le gift which Dr. Ryerson devoted to his country's service. Gathering his materials for building up a perfect educational system from all lands, and from the wisdom and experience of all ages, this great man wrought out his life-task in the face of political prejudices, of national prejudices and of sectarian prejudices. I know of no man of his day who rose more fully than did he above the narrowness of all these. From the elevation of a broad catholicity, he grasped the great outlines of a comprehensive and national system of education for the Upper Canadian people, and patiently did he work toward that as his ideal. It would be too much to say that he completed the ideal. Such is not often given to mortal man. There are problems in this work still unsolved. There is still something for us to do. But in the solution of these problems we may well thank God for the broad, strong foundations, and structures planned, and so nearly completed by this master workman.

In the inaugural address with which Dr. Ryerson opened his work in Victoria College, I find this passage "The education imparted in this college is to be British and Canadian. Youth should be educated for their country as well as for themselves." This motto, never forgotten, has given character to his great life-work, and has given us a system of public schools and intermediate schools which more enduring than any monument will perpetuate to our children for generations to come, the name of Egerton Ryerson.[9]

REPRESENTATIVE OF QUEEN'S UNIVERSITY, KINGSTON.

Sandford Fleming, C.E., LL.D, C.M.G., Chancellor of Queen's University, spoke as follows:—

Your Honor, Mr. Chairman, Ladies and Gentlemen:

In the name of Queen's University, and at the special request of the Senate of that institution, I come here to-day to take part in these interesting proceedings. On behalf of higher education in Eastern Ontario I have the honor to bear tribute to the memory of Dr. Egerton Ryerson.

However unworthy the individual whom Queen's has sent on this occasion, I am warranted in stating that no institution in this country is more thoroughly alive to the importance of sound education for all classes of the community than the University I come here to represent. Moreover, I venture to say that there is no one here present who more fully appreciates the incalculable value of the school system of Ontario and the work accomplished in its establishment, by him to whose memory we are this day assembled to do honor.

It is not simply an agreeable duty I am called upon to perform, I feel it to be a high privilege to be allowed to take part by my presence on this auspicious occasion. I have but to look back over a period of forty years to recall the living form of the sculptured figure before us, and to remember the time when in the zenith of his strength and intellectual power, he brought to bear on the great work of his life that wisdom and foresight, that indomitable perseverance and patriotism, that zeal and devotion with which he was gifted. I have but to recollect his persistent efforts to initiate and put in successful operation a comprehensive system of common school education in this province, to express my unalloyed satisfaction that those efforts—those great and sustained efforts were not in vain. I rejoiced then, as I rejoice now, that the noble work in which he took so conspicuous a part has been crowned with signal success. I thought then, and I think now, that the people of this province, I may indeed say the people of the whole of Canada, of all ages, of all classes, of all colors and of all creeds, owe a deep debt of gratitude to Dr. Ryerson, and I cannot be wrong in the firm opinion that we all do well to revere and perpetuate his memory.

While Dr. Egerton Ryerson attached most importance to the establishment of the common schools of the country on a sound and efficient basis, he also warmly sympathized with every effort to promote higher education. He took an active part in founding Victoria University, of which he was chosen the first president. He was a strenuous supporter of that institution up to the day of his death, firmly believing that the resources of the country could support, and that the people of Ontario should possess, well endowed, independent seats of learning of different types.

As a member of the community I have always had the highest esteem and veneration for this great pioneer of education in Canada. I feel now and have always felt with unnumbered thousands that his life has indeed been that of a foremost public benefactor. I am, therefore, greatly gratified that it has fallen to my lot, on behalf of Queen's University and higher education in Eastern Ontario to bear tribute to the memory of the founder and first administrator of our system of public instruction, a far-seeing Canadian, an enlightened statesman, a man who in his distinguished career rendered the most important services to the country of his birth.

I am glad to have an opportunity of taking part in the formal inauguration of the work of art which we see before us. At the same time I cannot forget that Dr. Egerton Ryerson has left behind him an inheritance to unborn generations of Canadians in the schools which we behold everywhere throughout the land and the free public instruction which they represent. These are now and must always be recognized as his best and most enduring monument.[10]

REPRESENTATIVE OF TRINITY UNIVERSITY, TORONTO.

The Representative of Trinity University, Rev. Professor Clark, remarked that he had the honor of representing the smallest of the universities of Ontario, but one in which they strove to do their work in a spirit of loyalty to their country as well as to their own convictions. He had naturally prepared to make some remarks on the distinguished and illustrious man in whose honor they were then assembled; but, as he supposed, nearly everything which had occurred to him as being suitable to be said had been anticipated by previous speakers.

As he looked upon those Normal Schools by which they were imprinted, he could not help being reminded of the words inscribed on the interior of St. Paul's in memory of its founder, Sir Christopher Wren, "*Si monumentum requiris circumspice.*" "If you ask for his memorial look around you." With equal propriety we might point to those schools as a monument and memorial of Dr. Ryerson, the founder of the educational system of this Province, no less fitting than the statue which had just been uncovered. But more enduring than the building or the effigy was the intellectual and moral work which he had accomplished in our educational institutions, for that work was eternal. Its effects and influences would never pass away, but would go on leavening generations yet unborn. Whatever changes or revolutions might occur, his work and its consequences would still live on.

In one respect, perhaps, it was fortunate that others should have borne testimony to Dr. Ryerson's work and ability, and to the greatness of the work which he had done. His own knowledge of the man and of the work was only second-hand, and he could not speak with the freshness and vividness of those who had personal knowledge of them. "*Segnius irritant animos demissa per aurem.*" But although he had not direct and immediate knowledge of Dr. Ryerson, he had the opportunity of studying several of the publications which gave an account of his history, and especially of his educational work—more particularly some of those written by Dr. Hodgins. From these he had learnt something of the spirit in which the work had been accomplished, and the principles which were embodied in it; and these would account for the eulogiums which had already been bestowed upon the work and its principal doer.

They might learn from such investigations something that would help to guard them from dangers which attended their educational work. It seemed to him that Dr. Ryerson's conception of the work of education was singularly simple, earnest, deep and comprehensive, free from affectation and one-sidedness. They were in danger of forgetting some of these elements, of making education showy instead of solid,—of forgetting that it was the education and discipline of the man and of the mind that we had to accomplish, and not the outward adornment of him, or the mere imparting of knowledge. Some of our dangers have been forcibly pointed out by the President of University College, Sir Daniel Wilson, in the March number of the *Canada Educational Monthly*. It would not be proper to go into details on such an occasion, but he would recommend those who were interested in these questions to study that article.

There was great danger of their being one-sided in education, of their taking up cries on one side or another. We have often heard of a foolish Anglomania by which some people were possessed. But there are other manias which are quite as silly. There was an Americano-mania and a Canada mania (*mania Canadensis*, said the Minister), and they were all equally foolish. It was egregious folly merely to imitate an Englishman or an American. But it was equally foolish to imagine that we had everything and could do everything by ourselves. Our business was not to make Englishmen or Americans or Canadians, but to make men, furnished with sufficient knowledge, with cultivated, disciplined minds, with vigorous wills. This is our work, and we must do it with our might, remembering the limitations of our position and realizing what we could and could not accomplish. We must not at present expect the results of the education given at the great German universities or at Oxford and Cambridge, but we might make the best with the materials at our disposal. We might foster in the rising generations a love of truth and goodness, and instil into them a deep sense of duty, and thus help to qualify them for the position they would have to occupy, and the work which they had to perform.

REPRESENTATIVE OF MCMASTER UNIVERSITY.[11]

Professor Theodore H. Rand, M.A., D.C.L., representative of McMaster University spoke as follows:—

Twice before it has been my privilege to unite in doing honor by a public memorial to the name of distinguished educationalists,—that of Horace Mann, of Massachusetts, and Alexander Forrester, of Nova Scotia; but in view of the breadth of the area over which Egerton Ryerson wrought, and the really national character of his work, this has been an occasion of surpassing interest to me, and one, I am sure, which marks an epoch in the educational history of Ontario. In speaking as a representative of McMaster University, which is just now being organized as one of the instruments of the higher education of this country, I may be permitted to say that the Christian denomination which controls the destiny of that University has in all parts of the world been in active sympathy with popular education, and in two of our Canadian provinces has been foremost in efforts to secure the efficient organization of systems of free education under government control.

When a country has risen to the position of making adequate public provision against the blighting and destructive influences of ignorance, it has undertaken the discharge of one of those contingent and great obligations which, perhaps, will always await any people who are pressing forward to the attainment of the possibilities of Christian civilization. With all its imperfections our system of public education in an eminent degree commands the affectionate regard of our people and the admiration of strangers. While Ontario was not the first of our Canadian provinces to organize a free system of public schools, and while she has not maintained intact the principle which lies at the basis of the common schools, the grandeur of the outline of our system and the general completeness of its details are, I believe, unsurpassed by those of any other system on this continent or throughout the empire. This is especially true of the completeness of the provision made for passing from the elementary schools into the work of the higher education. Ontario occupies this advanced position to-day, with all its immeasurable advantages, largely because of Egerton Ryerson. He was possessed of a profound conviction that mind is the great creative power by which all resources of nature are to be turned to account. He had no idea that material good is a good at all only as it is a means for the development of the moral and social possibilities of the individual and of the nation. He did not argue, as many others in the country did, that since the area of the Province is vast, its population widely scattered, its forests waiting to be felled, its lands to be cleared and drained, therefore the organization of an efficient school system was a thing of the far future. On the contrary, having before him such examples as Prussia, Scotland, Ireland, the New England, Middle and Western States, and believing that our civic institutions should afford social conditions inferior to those of no country in the world, he poured all the energy of his great heart and mind into the effort to make available even to the remotest hamlets of the Province the blessings of knowledge. Intelligence, industry and morality were felt to be inseparably bound up with the progress of education. A system good enough for the rich and poor alike, and supported at the public expense, was his aim and his final achievement. The Christian communism underlying our systems of public education on this continent is proving one of the great safeguards of society against the forms of a false communism; and there is yet room, in my judgment, for a still wider application of kindred principles in our social system.

The work of Egerton Ryerson furnishes an additional illustration of the truth that systems of popular education are, so to speak, the gift to the people of the Colleges and Universities. His relations to the higher education enabled him to grasp all the elements involved in the great problem he undertook to solve for Ontario, and to bring all parts of the educational system into helpful and sympathetic relations. Our Universities must always be sources of stimulus and enrichment to the schools of the Province at large, if they discharge in any original and adequate measure their functions to society.

In attributing so important a share to Egerton Ryerson in the establishment of our school system, I am not, of course, unmindful of the public men who seconded his efforts, and above all, of the teachers and inspectors by whose self-sacrificing toils educational advance was rendered possible, and has been sustained. Were he whom we honor in our midst to-day he would be the first to speak thus, and especially of his friend, Dr. Hodgins, who for so many years was his able assistant and valued confidant. This bronze memorial is well—may it long testify to the patriotic virtues of a noble man—but it is as nothing, I trust, in comparison with the living and imperishable memorials of enriched and ennobled human lives. As time witnesses the increasing development of the material and spiritual forces of the present and coming generations of our people, as our social and national institutions are more fully perfected and widely recognized, we shall have hereby and herein perennial memorials of the founder of the school system of Ontario throughout all coming time.

CHAPTER IV.

EDUCATION IN ONTARIO—PAST AND PRESENT.

An Historical Retrospect by J. George Hodgins, M.A., LL.D., Barrister-at-Law, and Deputy Minister of Education for Ontario.

To-day will long be memorable in the educational history of Ontario—for to-day has been unveiled the first statue ever erected in this province to one of its own sons.

It will be still more memorable from the fact that that special subject of public interest and national concern which has been signally honoured to-day, is the pre-eminently important one of popular education. These two facts combined give to the celebration and pleasant incidents of the day a peculiar significance and a special interest.

Significance of the Event of To-day.

One of the first indications of a growing national life and a patriotic national spirit is the erection of statues to noble sons who have rendered such valuable services to the state as are recognized and honoured here to-day.

It is a most hopeful sign, as well as an assuring and happy augury for the future of a country, when its patriotism takes the grateful and graceful form of doing honour to those who have aided in laying the foundation of its future greatness and prosperity. This, we all rejoice has been done by Ontario to-day in the unveiling of the statue of the distinguished founder of her educational system. She has reared to-day to one of the sons of her soil a noble monument, expressive of grateful acknowledgment for services of the greatest importance and value to her and to the thousands of her sons and daughters yet unborn.

The erection of this statue emphasizes in a striking manner a notable fact, chronicled by John Milton, which the mature judgment of the nineteenth century has everywhere endorsed, that—

"Peace hath her victories no less renowned than war."

That is, that it is not heroic deeds of valor alone which call forth a nation's gratitude. It further shows us that unswerving devotion to duty in any of the departments of the public service, or professional or private life, which have to do with matters which concern a nation's progress and welfare, is equally recognized, if not more signally honoured, than were deeds of prowess in the days gone by. We have, at all events on this continent, many notable examples of distinguished honour being done to literary men, to men of science and to noted educationists. Any one who has visited the chief city of Massachusetts cannot fail to have seen, on the broad terrace in front of the capitol, a massive bronze statue to Horace Mann, the well-known Founder of the Public School system, not only of Massachusetts, but practically of the New England States.

THE ONTARIO SYSTEM OF EDUCATION—ITS INFLUENCE ABROAD.

So, in like manner we unveil to-day the statue, not only of the Founder of the School System of Ontario, but of one, the impress of whose hand, and the practical suggestions of whose mature experience, may be recognized in the systems of education of some of the Maritime Provinces, and in those of Manitoba and British Columbia. The first Superintendent of British Columbia, and the second of Manitoba were trained in the schools of Ontario, and were thus experienced pioneers in the new Provinces of their educational systems. Also in the West Indies the educational example of Ontario was felt to be of some value by Sir Francis Hincks, when Governor of the Windward Islands.[12]

Even the grand old Mother Country has not failed to acknowledge her indebtedness to him whom we honour to-day, for practical suggestions in the solution of the educational problems which confronted her public men, notably the Duke of Newcastle and the Right Hon. W. E. Forster,[13] during the years reaching from 1860 to 1870.

In 1860, at the request of the Duke of Newcastle, who accompanied the Prince of Wales to Canada, Dr. Ryerson prepared an elaborate sketch of the system of education in Upper Canada, and contrasted it with the English and other European systems of education. This report was embodied in a letter to the Duke, dated 12th October, 1860.

As to the appropriateness of our erecting a Statue to Egerton Ryerson in Ontario, as was done to Horace Mann, in Massachusetts, I may here quote a reference to the equal value of the labors of those two noted men which was made twenty-five years ago by that acute observer and experienced educational commissioner, the late well-known and distinguished Bishop Fraser, of Manchester. He said:

"What Education in New England owes to Horace Mann, Education in Canada owes to Egerton Ryerson."

To-day we honour ourselves by seeking to discharge that obligation, at least in part.

46

There is one circumstance connected with the erection of this statue which, to my mind, gives it a peculiar value and significance. The erection of statues by popular vote, or by the Legislature, gives a *quasi*, if not a real national character to such erection, but, a statue erected from the proceeds of thousands of small contributions, as in this case, shows that deep down in the hearts of the people of this country there must have been genuine regard for the man whom they thus seek to honour. When a memorial takes such a form as that we may well regard it as more enduring and precious than either the bronze or marble which constitute the material of its structure.

COMPREHENSIVE CHARACTER OF THE ONTARIO EDUCATIONAL SYSTEM.

It devolves upon me, as Chairman of the Committee having charge of this work, and at the kind request of my colleagues,—no less than as the life-long friend and fellow-laborer of him whose deeds and memory we honor to-day—to trace back to their source the origin and underlying principles of our system of education, and to show that these underlying principles and other vital forces were so combined by a master-hand an to form the groundwork, as they have, in their combination, become the charter of our educational system of to-day.

And here, in this connection, a thought or two strikes me; and each thought contains for us a moral and a lesson.

The first is that educational systems are essentially progressive in their character and purposes, and truly they "never continue in one stay."

The second is that the earliest sources of what might be called our educational inspiration are now uncertain guides, and, as such, are to-day of doubtful authority.

No one will venture to affirm that even—as it was then considered—the broad and comprehensive scheme of public education sketched by Dr. Ryerson in 1846, should be considered as the acme of our educational achievements of to-day. Nor would any one at all conversant with the condition and progress of education on this continent alone be content to draw his inspiration from, or limit his range of observation to, the New England States as formerly. The examples to be seen, and the experience to be consulted, and the systems to be studied, must to-day, so far as the United States is concerned—be sought for in the far-off Western States.

In this matter I speak of what I know; and I speak, therefore, with the more emphasis on this point, because of the primary importance of keeping this Province and the Dominion educationally abreast of the most advanced States of the American Union—our near neighbors, and our energetic and actively progressive educational rivals.

As an illustration of these notable facts, I may state that having been selected by the United States Bureau of Education to act as one of the seven international educational jurors, at the New Orleans Exhibition in 1885, it was, during six weeks, my duty with others, to examine into and report upon the condition and results of the various state systems of education in the Union, and in other countries.

CHARACTER OF SYSTEMS OF EDUCATION ABROAD, AND LESSONS THEREFROM.

I need not more than state, what you likely anticipate, that France, by her enlightened educational legislation of 1881—providing for manual, or industrial, training in all of her schools—and Germany, by her earlier and more systematized educational legislation, stand at the head of European States, as does Japan at the head of the whole Eastern World. But, in this connection, the interest to us should be to note the fact that the educational centre in the United States has within the last few years been gradually shifted from the east to the west. As an illustration, I may say that the highest award for the extent, variety and completeness of its educational system in all its details, was unanimously made by the jurors to Minnesota, while Massachusetts and other New England States, with New York, Pennsylvania, etc., were entitled to only second and third class honors. France and Japan justly received first-class honors, while England and other countries (omitting Germany) had to be placed in the second and third class ranks as educating countries.

A revelation of these and other suggestive facts in regard to the progress of education in countries outside of our own, more than ever convinced me of the wisdom of Dr. Ryerson's policy of observation while head of the Education Department. He laid it down, not so much an educational axiom, as a wise dictum—the result of his educational experience, that—

"There is no department of civil government in which careful preparation, varied study and observation, and independent and uniform action, are so important to success and efficiency, as in founding, maturing and developing a system of public instruction."

He, therefore, wisely devoted a large portion of his time to this "careful preparation," as well as to "varied study and observation" of systems of education in Europe and America. And this fact largely accounts for the "success and efficiency" of his efforts in "founding, maturing and developing" our system of public instruction.

In a reply to a resolution from the Council of the County of Norfolk, in 1851, Dr. Ryerson thus referred to this subject:—

"There is no poetry in the establishment and development of a public school system; it is a matter-of-fact-work from beginning to end; and its progress, like the growth of body and mind in an individual, is gradual, and is the joint result of time and labour. I am happy, however, to know that our school system has already become so far developed in its principles, objects and character as to command the attention and almost unanimous approbation of the country. I have laid it down as a first principle to educate the people through the people themselves, by their own voluntary co-operation and exertion, through the usual elective municipalities and other acknowledged and responsible organs of a free people."

EDUCATIONAL LESSONS TO BE LEARNED OUTSIDE OF ONTARIO.

When we reflect upon the fact of the immense growth, and the comprehensive character of the educational machinery in operation on this continent alone, and the vast sums expended to keep it in motion, we cannot fail to be profoundly impressed with the serious and grave responsibility which is constantly imposed upon our educational leaders, of being forever on the watch-tower of observation, to note the changes, improvements and advances which are continually taking place in the educational world outside. We are too apt to be content with our own progress, and to measure ourselves by ourselves. In this connection the words recently addressed to the Kingston Board of School Trustees by the Very Rev. Principal Grant, are of special value as an apt illustration of my meaning:—

"During my absence I have studied the school systems of many countries, and have learned lessons that ought to assist me in coming to right conclusions. The world is wider than Canada, or than America. The British Empire itself is wider than this continent, and within its boundaries there are so many educational systems and methods that a man who travels with eyes and ears open cannot help learning many things that confirm opinions previously held, and suggest improvements on what he may have thought perfect, or the necessity of revising his former judgments. He gets new points of view, and that of itself is a great matter."

Our American neighbors became fully alive years ago to the evils of the fluctuating and uncertain character of the prevailing system of educational administration in vogue amongst them. They saw that new and officially untrained men, of merely local experience and knowledge, were constantly being elected to take charge of the administrative department of the schools of a state. Such men were often able educators, but by no means experienced educationists, or masters of systems of education. The American people, shrewd and practical as they are, felt the absolute necessity, therefore, of furnishing such men, and the vast army of their educationists and educators, with full and accurate information on systems and plans of education all over the world. With this object in view, they established a central observatory, or Bureau of Education at Washington. I need hardly say how ably the work of this Bureau was systematized and most efficiently performed under the direction of the Hon. John Eaton, Commissioner of Education. His successive reports and periodical circulars of information are mines of educational wealth. Their fullness and comprehensiveness have been a marvel. They have aroused and stimulated educational workers everywhere. They are largely welcomed, and are highly prized in these Provinces and elsewhere, as suggestive, and as invaluable storehouses of information, and of the practical details of education all over the world. They have, therefore, largely supplied the place of personal inquiry and research, and yet have greatly stimulated both.

It was Dr. Ryerson's ideal that sooner or later a similar Bureau would be established by the Central Government at Ottawa, the object of which would be, not only the supplying of abundant and reliable information to each province on the subject of systems and plans of education, but also, by intercommunication, to secure a general harmony of aim and purpose. And that further, without attempting any interference in local administration, the Bureau would be the means of keeping up an active yet friendly intercolonial rivalry; and thus, on Dominion and national lines, to build up the confederacy, and to stimulate and encourage the efforts made in each province for the promotion of substantial educational progress, combined with efficiency and economy.

THREE EDUCATIONAL PERIODS IN THE HISTORY OF ONTARIO.

The educational history of Ontario naturally divides itself in three periods, viz.:—

1. The early settlement, or United Empire Loyalist period.

2. The period preceding the union of Upper and Lower Canada in 1840.

3. The period since that union, and including the administration of the Education Department by the Rev. Dr. Ryerson, down to 1876.

The United Empire Loyalists period takes us back to a period antecedent to that of their historical prominence as a factor in the events of the war of the American Revolution. In order, therefore, to estimate the value of the educational influence of those times on the future of the provinces in which the U. E. Loyalists settle, we must take a glance at the Colonial chapter in the History of American Education.

COLONIAL CHAPTER IN THE HISTORY OF AMERICAN EDUCATION.

It is, therefore, interesting in taking note of our educational progress to give a brief glance at what was done by our fellow colonists at a corresponding early period in the history of the "old thirteen colonies," which formed the nucleus of the present American Confederation.

It has been the custom, probably unwittingly, but chiefly on the part of certain American writers, to exalt every good in their political and social condition, as of revolutionary origin, and reluctantly to admit that anything which was really excellent in both, in the early colonial times, was of British origin. One unacquainted with the processes and progress of civilization in America would, on consulting such writers, suppose that, Minerva-like, the young Republic had sprung from the head of Revolutionary Jove, fully equipped, if not fully armed for the battle of life, into the arena of the new world, and that this phenomenon happened just at the extinction of British power in the old colonies, and as the result of it. The policy of these writers has been either to ignore the facts of history, or to keep entirely out of view the forces which had been operating in the British colonial mind, before and at the time of the Revolution. They have never stopped to enquire as to the source whence they derived their idea of political freedom, but have attributed it to their own sagacity, or regard it as the outgrowth of their own enlightened speculations and thinkings when emancipated from British control. There never was a greater mistake as to fact, or a greater wrong done to the memory and example of such noble English patriots as Hampden and his compeers, who laid down their lives for political principles which, considering the times in which they lived, were even more exalted and ennobling than those which were professed by the American revolutionists of 1776. In fact, no proper parallel can be instituted between them. John Hampden, in our humble judgment, was as far superior to John Hancock, "President of the Continental Congress," in the purity of his political motives and aspirations, as Cromwell was above Jack Cade.[14] However, it is not our purpose to discuss this question, but rather to vindicate the sagacity of the old colonists, who (at a time when loyalty was the rule, and not the exception), laid the foundation of those educational institutions, which to this day are the glory of the American Republic.

Nor were the British colonists into those early times peculiar in their zeal for the promotion of Education. The Dutch, Swedish, and Irish colonists who settled in Pennsylvania, New York, and Maryland did their part in his great work, and on the whole did it well, according to the spirit of the times.

In 1633, the first schoolmaster opened his school in the Dutch Colony of

New Amsterdam; and in 1638, the "articles for the colonization and trade of New Netherlands," provided that, "each householder and inhabitant shall bear such tax and public charge as shall hereafter be considered proper for the maintenance of schoolmasters." General Eaton, the United States Commissioner of Education, in his valuable report for 1875, says:

"We find, in numerous instances, the civil authorities of these Dutch colonies acknowledging, (1) The duty of educating the young, (2) The care of the qualification of the teacher, (3) Provision for the payment of his services, and (4) The provision of the school-house. When, in 1653, municipal privileges were granted to the New Amsterdam [New York], the support of schools was included."

In 1642, the instruction sent to the Governor of New Sweden [Pennsylvania], was "to urge instruction and virtuous education of youth and children." In 1693-6, large numbers of primers, tracts and cathechisms were received from Sweden, for these schools on the Delaware. This was the educational state of the Swedish settlement in what was afterwards known as Pennsylvania, on the arrival of its noble English founder, William Penn. His views on education were well expressed in the following declaration:

"That which makes a good Constitution must keep it, viz.: men of wisdom and virtue; qualities which, because they descend not with worldly inheritance must be carefully propagated by virtuous education of youth, for which spare no cost; for by such parsimony, all that is loved is lost."

The first real systematic efforts to promote popular education began in New England, from thence it has spread in all directions. In 1635 the first school was opened at Boston, Massachusetts, and brother Philemon Purmount was appointed schoolmaster by the Town Committee. Thirty acres of land were given for his support. In 1642 the General Court, (or Legislature) passed a resolution enjoining on the local authorities:

"To keep a watchful eye on their brothers and neighbors, and above all things to see that there be no family in so barbarous a state, that the head thereof do not himself, or by the help of others, impart instruction to his children and servants, to enable them to read fluently the English language, and to acquire a knowledge of the penal laws, under a penalty of twenty shillings for such neglect."

Speaking on this subject, in his inaugural address in 1853, President Walker of Harvard University said:

What most distinguishes the early settlers of Massachusetts, is the interest and care they took in education, and especially in the institution of a system of common schools, to be sustained at the public charge.

Here they were first. In other things they thought wisely and acted nobly; but in this, and perhaps in this alone, they were original. Honor, immortal honor to the men, who, while still struggling for a scanty and bare subsistence, could yet find the means and the heart to do what had never been done or attempted before: placing the advantages of a competent instruction within the reach of all. By taking this course, what a noble confidence they manifested in the truth of their principles and in the justice of their measures.... But the founders and early settlers of Massachusetts did not limit their views of education to common schools. Many of their leading men had studied at the English Universities and were imbued with, or at least, could appreciate the highest scholarship of that day. They also knew, on general grounds and as practical men, that the public good requires the advancement, as well as the diffusion, of knowledge; in short, that both must go together; that the streams will soon cease, if the fountains fail.—Pages 33,34.

To be brief on this point I may state that in 1847, the first legislative enactment in favor of schools was made in Massachusetts; and in 1670, the Governor of Connecticut declared that "one-fourth of her revenue was devoted to schools."

General Eaton in his comprehensive report of 1875 says:

"History, with hardly a dissenting voice, accords to the English Colonists of New England, the credit of having developed those forms of action, in reference to the education of children, which contained more than any other the distinct features of the systems adopted in this cuntry."

In the early colonial times, before the revolution, there were nine colleges established in seven out of the thirteen colonies.

These colleges, with the date of their foundation, are as follow:—

1. Harvard—Massachusetts, in   1638
2. William and Mary—Virginia, in   1693
3. Yale—Connecticut, in   1700
4. Nassau Hall (now Princeton)—New Jersey, in 1748
5. Kings (now Columbia)—New York, in   1754
6. Brown—Rhode Island, in   1765
7. Dartmouth—New Hampshire, in   1770
8. Queen's (now Rutgers)—New Jersey, in   1771
9. Hampden—Sydney, Virginia, in   1775

The Legislature of Massachusetts, aided by the Rev. John Harvard, founded Harvard Congregational College, in 1638, and the colonists of Connecticut, established the Yale Congregation College in 1700.[15]

The New Hampshire colonists endowed the Congregational College at Dartmouth with 44,000 acres of land in 1770. The Episcopalians of the English colony of New York, aided by the Legislature, founded King's now Columbia College, in 1753. Indeed, so true were the English colonists to the educational instincts of the mother land, that when the Dutch Province of New Netherlands fell into their hands in 1644, the King's Commissioners were instructed "to make due enquiry as to what progress hath been made towards ye foundaçon and maintenance of any College Schools for the educaçon of youth."—(Colonial History of N. Y., Vol. III. p. 53.)

The English Province, *par excellence*, of Virginia made various praiseworthy efforts to promote education. In 1619, soon after the settlement of Jamestown, Sir Edwin Sandys, President of the Virginia Company, had 10,000 acres of land set apart for the establishment of a University at Henrico for the colonists and Indians. The churches in England gave £1,500 sterling in the same year to aid in the education of the Indians. In 1621, 1,000 acres of land as an endowment, and £150 were granted to establish a school at Charles city. Other efforts were made in the same direction in 1660 and 1688. The colony also nobly determined to establish a University; and in 1692-3, the project was practically realized by the founding by the King and Queen, under royal charter, of the Church of England College at Williamsburgh, of William and Mary. To this College the King gave nearly £2,000, besides 20,000 acres of land, and one penny per pound on all the tobacco exported from Maryland. The Legislature also gave it in 1693, the duty on skins and furs exported, and on liquors imported.[16] The plans of the College were prepared by Sir Christopher Wren. Among the first donors to the College was the celebrated Robert Boyle.[17] Of all the colonial Colleges few exercised a greater educational influence among the leading men than did this royal college. Jefferson, Munroe, Marshall (afterwards Chief Justice of the United States), the two Randolphs, and Governor Tyler, of Virginia, received their education here.

The Irish Roman Catholic Province of Maryland was not, at least in purpose, much behind her English sister. In 1671 an Act was passed by one of the Houses of the Legislature for the establishment of a School or College, but owing to religious differences the other House did not concur. In 1692, the Legislature passed an Act for the encouragement of learning; and in 1696, King William's Free School, Annapolis (afterwards St. John's College), was established.

New Jersey was one of the colonies which early promoted higher education by founding the Presbyterian College at Princeton, under the name of Nassau Hall, in 1746, and the Dutch Reformed College at New Brunswick (N.J.), under the name of Queen's, now Rutger's College, in 1770.

The little colony of Rhode Island did not fail in its duty to higher education, for in 1764 it founded the Rhode Island College, now Brown University.

The Quaker colony of William Penn, following the example of the Anglicized Dutch colony of New York, established the University of Pennsylvania at Philadelphia—the metropolis of the colonies in 1755.

Of these nine ante-revolution Colleges, Harvard, Yale, Columbia and Princeton maintain an equally high reputation, while Brown University, the University of Pennsylvania, Rutgers, William and Mary and Dartmouth Colleges are more or less about the average standard of American Colleges.

Governor Oglethorpe, the founder of Georgia, was a graduate of Oxford. He, with other English University colonists, conceived the idea of a College for this, the then youngest of the English colonies. The project of his friend, the Irish Bishop Berkeley, of Cloyne, of founding a College in the Bermudas having failed, he secured £10,000 of the Bishop's funds to aid him in his settlement of the colony. The seed sown by Oglethorpe bore fruit; and while Georgia was still a colony, provision was made for a generous system of education.

D. C. Gilman, Esq. (President of the John Hopkins' University, Baltimore), in his admirable sketch of the growth of education in the United States during the last century, pays a high tribute to the nine Colonial Colleges to which we have referred. He says:—

> "These nine Colleges were nurseries of virtue, intelligence, liberality and patriotism, as well as learning; so that when the revolution began, scores of the most enlightened leaders, both in council and upon the field (on both sides) were found among their graduates. The influence of academic culture may be distinctly traced in the formation of the Constitution of the United States, and in the political writings of Adams, Hamilton, Jefferson, Madison, Munroe and many other leading statesmen of the period. A careful student of American politics has remarked that nothing more strikingly indicates the education given at Cambridge than the masterly manner in which different problems of law and government were handled by those who had received their instruction only from that source."[18]

Prof. Charles Sprague Smith, A.M., (of Columbia College) in his essay on *The American University*, read June, 1887, thus refers to the character of these colonial colleges:—

> "In New England the higher system at general education, brought over from Old England, was divided here, as there, into the two studies of the College and the Grammar School; the latter being superceded in quite recent times by the so-called Academy. The curriculum of the American (or Colonial) College was, in the main, modelled upon that of the parent country, special consideration being given to theological science, etc."—Page 13.

A recent American publication on revolutionary topics, thus deals with the question of the superior education of the British colonists who formed the first American Congress:—

"An examination of the Continental Congress, composed as it was of leading men of all the colonies, affords some light upon the topic of popular education at that period. The Congress, whose sessions extended through some ten years, comprised in all some three hundred and fifty members, of whom one-third were graduates of colleges. A recent writer in one of the most intelligent and accurate of American journals has[10] taken pains to collect and array a paragraph of important statistics upon this subject, which we have taken leave to insert here, though without verification, that, however, being hardly necessary for our present purpose.

"There were in the Continental Congress during its existence, 350 members, of these 118, or about one-third of the whole, were graduates from Colleges. Of these, 28 were graduates from the College of New Jersey in Princeton, 23 from Harvard, 23 from Yale, 11 from William and Mary, 8 from the University of Pennsylvania, 4 from Columbia College, 1 from Brown University and 1 from Rutger's College, and 21 were educated in foreign Universities. These 118 graduates were distributed in the Colonies as follows:—New Hampshire had 4 College graduates among her delegates; Massachusetts had 17; Rhode Island had 4 graduates; Connecticut had 18 graduates; New York out of her large delegation had but 8 graduates; New Jersey had 11 graduates; Pennsylvania had 13 graduates; Delaware had 2 graduates; Maryland had 7 graduates; Virginia had 19 graduates; North Carolina had 4 graduates; South Carolina had 7 graduates; Georgia had 5 graduates. We find that Princeton had representatives from 10 of the colonies; Yale from 6; Harvard from 5; the University of Pennsylvania from 3; William and Mary from 2; and Columbia, Brown and Rutger's from 1 each. Fifty-six delegates signed the Declaration of Independence. Of these, 28, or just one-half, were College graduates."

Incidentally, and as illustrative of the influence of college-bred men in the Legislature, Mr. Adams, speaking of the great liberality of South Carolina in founding a college in that State, says:—

"But no State ever made a better investment. During the first part of this century the general accomplishments and political ability of the statesmen of South Carolina were the just pride of the State, and would have been the pride of any State. In forming this high standard of intellectual and political power the influence of the College was immeasurable."—*North American Review*, January, 1876, pages 215, 216.

It is gratifying to us, British Colonists, and to the descendants of the U. E. Loyalists, thus to have from so important a source, an acknowledgment so candid and so honorable to men, many of whom were the founders of Ontario and the Maritime Provinces of the Dominion. It is an historical fact of equal significance, and an element of social and political strength to us in these British provinces, to know that it was to the thoroughness and breadth of culture which the American "Revolutionary heroes" received in early days in British colonial institutions which fitted them afterwards to take so prominent and effective an intellectual part in the great struggle which took place when they were in the prime of manhood. Another gratifying reflection arises out of the fact that the high place which the United States has taken in later years as a great educating nation is due to her following out the traditional policy of the Colonists of ante-revolution times.

This fact is clearly brought out by Mr. Gilman in the *North American*

Review for January, 1876. We only quote the following remarks on this point, he says:—

> "When the new constitution of Massachusetts was adopted in 1780 public education received full recognition. An article (the spirit of which was fully in accordance with the legislation of 1647 [more than 200 years before]) was adopted, and *still remains the fundamental law of the State....* The constitution of New Hampshire, as amended in 1784, transcribes very nearly the same words of that section of the constitution of Massachusetts already quoted," etc.—Pages 198, 199.

Thus Andrew Ten-Brook, Esq., in his *American State Universities*, says:—

> "The introduction of an educational system into the New England Colonies may be deemed substantially contemporaneous with their settlement. It was of such a character, too, and so energetically prosecuted, that education suffered little if any deterioration in passing from Old to New England. It was even more on this side than the other side of the ocean.... Thus Common School instruction at least was provided for all. Higher schools, too, had an early beginning. What afterwards was Harvard College was established but six years after the settlement of Boston.... Every town [township] of fifty families was obliged to support a school, and the same general state of facts existed throughout New England. Classical schools followed in regular succession. These were modelled after the Grammar Schools of England, in which the founders of the Colleges had themselves received their first classical training.... As early as 1701, the law of Connecticut required every parent to see that he had no child or apprentice in his household who could not read the Word of God, and 'the good laws of the colony.' The system embraced a High School in every town [township] of seventy families, a Grammar School in the four chief county towns to fit pupils for college, and a College to which the general court [Legislature] made an annual appropriation of £120."—Pages 1-3.

Mr. Ten-Brook, speaking of these New England schools, which were afterwards transplanted to each of Western States, says:—

> "They were the elements of that noble system out of which has grown the present one, by the natural laws of development," etc.—Page 18.

Mr. C. K. Adams, in his interesting paper on State Universities in the *North American Review* for October, 1875, in speaking of the educational policy of the colonies, "pursued up to the time of the Revolution, says:—

> "In general terms it may be stated that, through all the dark periods of our Colonial history, the encouragement of higher education was regarded as one of the great interests of the State. It was no doctrine of the Fathers that higher education was less entitled to the fostering care of the commonwealth than was the education offered by the Common Schools."—Page 374.

The "Free School" idea, of which we hear so much as the outgrowth of "modern American civilization and enlightenment," was due to Colonial thought and foresight. It was first broached by Jefferson, three or four years before the treaty with Great Britain was signed by which the United States became a nation. His plan was so comprehensive that we reproduce it here. In a letter to the veteran philosopher, Dr. Priestley, he thus unfolds it:—

> "I drew a bill for our [Virginia] Legislature, which proposed to lay off every county into hundreds, or townships, of five or six miles square. In the centre of each of them was to be a free English School [to be supported, as his bill provided, "by taxation according to

property."]

The whole Commonwealth was further laid off into ten districts, in each of which was to be a college for teaching the languages, geography, surveying, and other useful things of that grade, and then a single University for the sciences. It was received with enthusiasm (he goes on to say), but as he had proposed to make the Episcopal College of William and Mary the University, "the dissenters after a while began to apprehend some secret design," etc.— *Ten-Brook's American State Universities*, pages 9, 10.

A writer in the *North American Review* for October, 1875, in referring to Jefferson's scheme, says:—

> "The view entertained by Jefferson was by no means exceptional. Indeed, a similar spirit had pervaded the whole history of our Colonial life."—Page 379.

Thus this comprehensive scheme of public instruction for Virginia unfortunately failed; and that noble "Old Dominion" is in consequence to-day immeasurably behind even the youngest of her then New England contemporaries in the matter of public education.

As to the abiding influence of the old Colonial ideas in regard to higher education, we quote the following additional remarks from Mr. Gilman, in the *North American Review*, he says:—

> "In reviewing the history of the century, it is easy to see how the colonial notions of college organization have affected ... the higher education of the country, even down to our own times. The graduates of the older colleges have migrated to the Western States, and have transplanted with them the college germs ... and every Western State can bear witness to the zeal for learning which has been manifested within its borders by enthusiastic teachers from the East."—Page 217.

Mr. Ten-Brook, in his *American State Universities*, also says:—

> "The New England colonists left the mother country in quest of greater religious freedom. Their religious system was put first, and carried with it a school system as perfect in organization, and administered with equal vigor. This formed an active leaven, which, at a later day, was to spread to other parts.... Everywhere there was a considerable infusion of men who had received in the European universities a liberal culture, which they desired to reproduce on those shores. Early action was full of promise. Probably, at a period from just before the Revolution to the end of it, the average position of the colonies in regard to lighter education relatively as to age, and to the population and wealth, was quite as good as it is at the present time."—Pages 16, 17.

This opinion of the writer is a virtual admission that in reality higher education in the United States has not advanced in quality, though it has in quantity. To be in 1876 merely where education was "relatively" in 1776, is no advance at all, but rather retrogression. The cause of this declension, the writer thus incidentally admits:—

> "Most of the colonies established, or aided, the (ante-revolution colleges named). The

principle of the State support to higher learning was not merely accepted, but was the prevalent one."—Page 17.

Mr. Gilman, President of the Johns Hopkins' University, touching on the same point, says:—

"There was a civil as well as an ecclesiastical element in most of these foundations. Harvard and Yale were chartered, and, to some extent, controlled by colonial government of Massachusetts and Connecticut, and were for a long time nurtured by appropriations from the public chest....—Page 215.

"These institutions were colleges of an English parentage and model, not Scotch nor continental universities.... They were disciplinary in their aim, and had more regard for the general culture of large numbers, than for the advanced and special instruction of the chosen few. They were also, to a considerable extent, ecclesiastical foundations—finding the churches and ministers their constant, and sometimes their only efficient supporters. Harvard, Yale and Dartmouth were controlled by the Congregationalists; Princeton was founded by the Presbyterians; and New Brunswick, N.J. (Queen's, now Rutgers) by the Dutch Reformed; William and Mary was emphatically a child of the Church of England; and King's College (now Brown University) was under the patronage of the Baptists....

"The declaration of the original supporters of these colleges indicate a desire to train up young men for service of the State, not less distinctly and emphatically than to desire to provide an educated ministry. Individual aid was also expected and invited, and the names of Harvard and Yale perpetuate the remembrance of such generous gifts."

Then follows a eulogy upon these colonial colleges, and a tribute to the intellectual vitality of their teaching, as shown in the mental equipment and breadth of culture exhibited by men who took part in the perilous and stormy times of the American revolution. To this we have already referred. Mr. Gilman, in following up his remarks in the extract which we have just given, says:—

"Hence these nine colleges were nurseries of virtue, intelligence, liberality and patriotism, as well as of learning; so that when the revolution began, scores of enlightened leaders, both in council and in the field (and on both sides), were found among their graduates. The influence of academic culture may be distinctly traced in the formation of the Constitution of the United States, and in the political writings of Adams, Jefferson, Madison, Munroe, and many other leading statesman of the period. A careful student of American politics has remarked that nothing more strikingly indicates the influence of the education given at Harvard, 'than the masterly manner in which difficult problems of law and government were handled by those who had received their instruction only from that source.'"—Pages 215, 216.

THE UNITED EMPIRE LOYALIST PERIOD IN UPPER CANADA.

We might pursue this branch of our subject further, were it desirable. But that is not necessary. Our object was to show that to British Colonial foresight, zeal, and self-sacrifice, was due, not only the foundation of the best colleges and universities on the continent, but the introduction and diffusion of the principle of "free and universal education for the masses of the people." This we have done on the authority of American writers themselves. We might multiply examples on the subject; but the fact is already sufficiently established. We should rather seek to draw lessons of instruction from the noble example of the devotion to education on the part of our British colonial progenitors, whose descendants have shed such a lustre of heroic self-sacrifice and patriotism on the history and exploits of the United Empire Loyalists of the thirteen colonies. To the Americans they have left a rich legacy from the colonial times in such universities as Harvard, Yale, Columbia and Princeton—of which the descendants of the expatriated Loyalists, no less than those of the victorious revolutionists, are so justly proud. Let us, as worthy representatives of these clear-headed and far-seeing Loyalists, bequeath to our children as noble a heritage as the fathers of the founders of this Province did to New England, and indeed to the whole Republic.

Trained in such an educational school, and animated with the educational zeal of these old colonial times, the "United Empire Loyalists" brought with them into Canada their love for education and their devotion to the sovereign.

In order to keep up the historical sequence of this Retrospect, I shall now refer to the early beginning of Educational life in Upper Canada, and then take up the thread of the narrative at the point where the educational forces— afterwards directed by the Rev. Dr. Strachan and the Rev. Dr. Ryerson—took practical form and shape. (See page 59.)

GOVERNOR SIMCOE'S EDUCATIONAL VIEWS IN 1795.

Lieutenant-General J. Graves Simcoe, the first Governor of Upper Canada, arrived here in 1792. He was a man of comprehensive views and noble impulses in regard to university education. He was educated at Eton College and partly at Merton College, Oxford, but entered the army before taking his degree. He served with distinction under Wolfe at Quebec, and during the American revolutionary war.

In April, 1795, Governor Simcoe addressed a letter to the Protestant Episcopal Bishop of Quebec.[20] In that letter Governor Simcoe uses the following striking language in describing the social condition of the people in the rural parts of Upper Canada, and the utter absence of schools and churches, as contrasted with their existence on the United States side of the lines. He said:—

> "There was nothing, in my late progress, that has given my equal uneasiness with the general application of all ranks of the most loyal inhabitants of the Province, that I would obtain for them churches and ministers. They say that the rising generation (of the U. E. Loyalist settlers) is rapidly returning into barbarism. They state that the Sabbath, so wisely set apart for devotion, is literally unknown to their children, who are busily employed in

searching for amusements in which they may consume the day. And it is of serious consideration that on the approach of the settlements of the United States, particularly on the St. Lawrence frontier, these people, who, by experience, have found that schools and churches are essential to their rapid establishment (as a nation), may probably allure many of our most respectable settlers to emigrate to them, while in this respect we suffer a disgraceful deficiency."

The remedy which Governor Simcoe suggested for the state of things which he so graphically described is thus set forth in the same letter to the Bishop of Quebec. It was, as will be seen, entirely general in its character:—

"Nothing has happened since I left England, in the least, to invalidate, to my own conception, the policy of the measure I then proposed. And as far as may be now in the power of His Majesty's ministers, I most earnestly hope that what remains to be effected—that is by giving the means of proper education in this Province, both in its rudiments and in its completion, that from ourselves we may raise up a loyal, and, in due progress, a learned clergy."

EARLY BEGINNINGS OF EDUCATION IN UPPER CANADA, 1785-1805.

A few particulars as to the kind of schools which existed in Upper Canada before and after the date of this letter may be interesting. For instance, the first school opened (so far as I have been able to learn) was by the Rev. Dr. John Stuart, a Protestant Episcopal clergyman, and a United Empire Loyalist, who had been chaplain to the provincial volunteers, and came into Upper Canada with them as a refugee.[21]

In the year 1785 Dr. Stuart opened a select classical school at Cataraqui, (Kingston); and a Mr. Donovan taught the Garrison school there. In 1786, Mr. J. Clarke taught a school in Frederickburg, and Mr. Smith one in Ernestown. In 1789, Mr Lyons kept school in Adolphustown. In the same year, Deacon Trayes, a Baptist, opened one at Port Rowan. In 1792, Rev. Mr. Addison, an Episcopalian, opened a school at Newark (Niagara), then the seat of government. In 1794, the Rev. Mr. Burns, a Presbyterian, (father of the late Judge Burns) opened a school at the same place; and in 1796, Mr. Richard Cockrel opened an evening school in Newark; Mr. Cockrel shortly afterwards transferred his school to the Rev. Mr. Arthur and removed to Ancaster, where he opened another school. A notice in the *York Gazette* in 1796 stated that "as schools were now opened, ignorance would be no longer tolerated." In 1797, Mr. James Blayney opened a school at Niagara. In 1798, Mr. Wm. Cooper opened a school in George St., little York, (Toronto). In 1800, the late Bishop Strachan opened a private school at Kingston, and in 1804, one at Cornwall. In 1802, Mr. and Mrs. Tyler opened a school near Niagara; and in the same year, Dr. Baldwin, (father of the late Hon. Robert Baldwin) opened a classical school at York, and in 1803, the first school in Prince Edward district was opened at "High Shore," Sophiasburgh; another at "Grassy Point," was taught by John James. Rev. Wm. Wright, (Presbyterian) kept the first school at Meyer's Creek, (Belleville) in 1805. He was followed by Mr. Leslie. In that year, Rev. Mr. Strachan held the first public examination of his school at Cornwall.

STATE OF EDUCATION IN UPPER CANADA, 1795-1799.

As to the actual state of education in Upper Canada at this time, we get a brief glimpse from the travels of the Duc de la Rochefoucauld, who visited Kingston in July, 1795. He says:—

> "In this district there are some schools, but they are few in number. The children are instructed in reading and writing, and pay each a dollar a month. One of the masters taught Latin, but he has left, without being succeeded by another instructor in the same language."

As to the character of the private schools thus established, and the facilities of education which they afforded, we learn incidentally from letters and early books of travel, what they were. In a *"Tour through Upper Canada, by a Citizen of the United States,"* published in 1799, we learn that the policy of the government of that day, was to exclude "schoolmasters from the States, lest they should instil Republicanism into the tender minds of the youth of the province."

FIRST OFFICIAL EDUCATIONAL MOVEMENTS IN UPPER CANADA, 1797, 1798.

As the result of the correspondence between the Governor and Bishop Mountain, the question of a University and free grammar schools was discussed. The Governor referred the matter to the Upper Canada Legislature, which, in 1797 memorialized King George III, soliciting a grant of land for the endowment of a grammar school in each district, and a University for the whole Province. To this request the King gave his assent, and, in 1798, the "chief civil officers" in Upper Canada recommended that "500,000 acres of land be set apart for the establishment of a grammar school in each district and a central University for the whole Province." They also recommended a grant for the erection of a "plain but solid and substantial building for a grammar school in each district, containing a school room capable of holding 100 boys without danger to their health from too many being crowded together, and also a set of apartments for the master, large enough for his family and from ten to twenty boarders."

The salaries proposed to be given were: £100 for the head master, £50 for the assistant master; and £30 for repairs, etc., Kingston and Newark (Niagara) were recommended as eligible sites for schools; after which, when the funds were sufficient, schools were to be established at Cornwall and Sandwich. York (Toronto) was recommended as entitled to the University, and for the establishment and support of which a sum at least equal to that granted to the four schools was named.

In 1799, an act was passed by the Upper Canada Legislature "to provide for the education and support of orphan children." It authorized the township wardens, with the consent of two magistrates, to bind and apprentice, until they became of age, children deserted by their parents. In the same year an orphan school was opened near St. Catherines.

EDUCATIONAL PIONEERS IN UPPER CANADA.

Governor Simcoe authorized the Hon. Messrs. Cartwright and Hamilton, to select a person to take charge of the proposed college. The celebrated Rev. Dr. Chalmers having declined the appointment, it was accepted by Mr. (late the Right Reverend Doctor) Strachan (Bishop of Toronto) then a schoolmaster at Kettle, Scotland; but his arrival at Kingston, on the 31st of December, 1799, he found that the project of a college had been abandoned, Governor Simcoe, in the meantime, having left for England.

It was soon discovered that half a million of acres of land would endow but few grammar schools, land being then only worth a shilling per acre: the schema had, therefore, to be abandoned. Meanwhile the Hon. Mr. Cartwright made an arrangement with Mr. Strachan to instruct his sons, and a select number of pupils for three years. In 1804, Mr. Strachan, having been ordained, removed to the mission of Cornwall, where, at the request of the parents of his former pupils, he opened a private school.

For several years this school was the only one of any note in Upper Canada; and in it and in Mr. Strachan's school at York, were educated many of those gentlemen who have filled some of the most important positions in the province. Subsequently Mr. Strachan's school was constituted the grammar school of the Eastern district. In 1806, a temporary act was passed by the Legislature and made permanent in 1808, establishing a classical and mathematical school in each of the eight districts into which Upper Canada was then divided. In the same year(1806) at the suggestion of Dr. Strachan an Act was passed, granting £400 for the purchase of apparatus for illustrating the principles of Natural Philosophy, which were to be deposited in the hands of a person employed in the instruction of youth. In 1807 an appropriation of £800 a year for four years was made to provide for the salaries of masters in the Grammar Schools to be maintained in each of the districts into which Upper Canada was divided. These masters were to be engaged by trustees appointed by the governor, and the governor's sanction was also necessary for the teacher's appointment. There is still in existence the letter, dated, April 16th, 1807, signed by Governor Gore, appointing the Rev. George Okill Stewart, D.D., Archdeacon of Kingston, first Head Master of the Home District Grammar School at York (Toronto).

North of what is now Adelaide Street (formerly Newgate Street), bounded westward by Church Street, and eastward by Jarvis Street, was a large field, almost square, containing about six acres—for many years the playground of the District Grammar School.

In the south-west corner of it, some hundred feet or more from the street boundaries, was elected the plain wooden building, about fifty-five feet long by forty wide in which, on the first Monday of June, 1807, when the population of the town was only about five hundred, the Grammar School was opened. It was attended by the sons and daughters of the well-to-do citizens of York, and on the few existing records may be found many a well known name.

In 1812, the Rev. John Strachan. D.D., was appointed Rector of York, and succeeded the Rev. Mr. Stewart as Head Master of this school.[22] Mr. Barnabas Bidwell (father of the late Hon. M. S. Bidwell) kept a good Latin School at Bath, on the Bay of Quinté, in 1811. In 1813, he removed to Kingston, where he taught for twenty years until he died in 1833.

In 1820, the "Central School at York" was opened under the mastership of Mr. Joseph Spragge, father of the late Chief Justice Spragge. Lieutenant-Governor and Lady Sarah Maitland took a special interest in the success of this school.

In a *View of Upper Canada*, published at Baltimore in 1814, by Mr. M. Smith, (who resided in the Province from 1808 until the breaking out of the War in 1812) he said:—

"The greater part of the inhabitants are not well educated, for, as they were poor when they came to the Province and the country being but thinly settled for a number of years, they had but little chance for the benefit of schools. But since the country has become settled, or the inhabitants rich, or in a good way of living, which is almost universally the case, they pay considerable attention to learning. Ten dollars a year is the common price given for the tuition of each scholar by good teachers."—Page 52.

In 1813, Rev. John Langhorn (a Church of England missionary at Earnestown and Bath from 1787 to 1812, and teacher of a school) made a present of his library to the inhabitants of the Bay of Quinte district. In 1814 Rev. Robert Baldwin was appointed Grammar schoolmaster at Cornwall, vice Rev. John (afterwards Dean) Bethune resigned. In 1815 the Midland District School, so-called, was incorporated.

Dr. Strachan resigned the head mastership of the District School on July 1st, 1823. He was succeeded by Mr. Samuel Armour, M.A., a graduate of Glasgow University, who afterwards became a clergyman of the English Church, and officiated many years in the township of Cavan.

The Rev. Thomas Phillips, D.D., an accomplished scholar, came out from England in 1825 to take charge of the school, and remained in the position of headmaster, much honored and beloved by his pupils, until, in 1830, chiefly by the exertions of the Governor, Sir John Colborne, Upper Canada College was established and the work of the college began in the old District Grammar School building. Classes were opened in the new buildings erected in another part of the city for the college in 1831, and the Grammar School was closed, the building being removed from its original site to the line of

Nelson street (now Jarvis street), and fenced into a plot about 70 × 120 feet. The remaining portion of the six acres was handed over to Upper Canada College.

On the active remonstrance of the citizens living in the eastern part of Toronto, the school was re-opened and secured to the city, Mr. Charles N. B. Cosens being appointed headmaster in 1836, and succeeded by Mr. Marcus C. Crombie in 1838.[23]

EARLY EFFORTS TO ESTABLISH COMMON SCHOOLS 1816-1820.

In 1816, seven years after the establishment of District Grammar Schools, a praiseworthy effort was made to provide for the establishment and maintenance of common schools."[24] A liberal grant of $24,000 a year, for four years, was made as an experiment. Whether the experiment was a success, or not, does not appear, but in 1820, the grant was reduced to $10,000 a year.

STATE OF EDUCATION IN UPPER CANADA, 1784-1819.

In regard to the state of education of Upper Canada in 1817, and the fluctuating character of its progress since the settlement of the Province, in 1784, up to that time, Mr. Gourlay, a well-known Canadian politician and author, writes as follows:—

> "There is no college in Upper Canada, but there are said to be several townships of land set apart for the purpose of endowing such institution, when the population and circumstances of the Province shall require it.
>
> "No provision is made by law for free schools. The inhabitants of the severel townships are left to a voluntary support of schools, according to their own discretion.
>
> "An Act of the Provincial Legislature, in 1807, granted a hundred pounds a year to the teacher of one school, in each of the eight districts under the direction of trustees. In some districts the school thus provided for is made a free school; but in other districts the salary is considered as a public encouragement to a teacher of literary eminence, in addition to the compensation received for the tuition of each scholar."—*Statistical Account of Upper Canada, etc., by Robert Gourlay, 2 vols., London, 1822.*

The Rev. Dr. Strachan became a master of one of these schools, and Rev. George Ryerson and his brother, Egerton, master and usher of another.

As to the state of feeling in the rural parts of the oldest settled portions of Upper Canada, we make the following extracts from a letter written to Mr. Gourlay from the township of Grimsby, in 1818, by a highly respected resident there, William Crooks, Esq. Mr. Crooks remarks:—

> "The state of education is at a very low ebb, not only in the township, but generally

throughout the [Niagara] district; although the liberality of the legislature has been great in support of the district (Grammar) schools, (giving to the teachers of each £100 per annum), yet they have been productive of little or no good hitherto, for this obvious cause, they are looked upon as seminaries exclusively instituted for the education of the children of the more wealthy classes of society, and to which the poor man's child is considered as unfit to be admitted. From such causes, instead of their being a benefit to the Province, they are sunk into obscurity, and the heads of most of them are at this moment enjoying their situations as comfortable sinecures. Another class of schools has, within a short time, been likewise founded upon the liberality of the legislative purse, denominated common, or parish, schools, but like the preceding, the anxiety of the teacher employed, seems more alive to his stipend than the advancement of the education of those placed under his care: from the pecuniary advantages thus held out, we have been inundated with the worthless scum, under the character of school masters, not only of this, but of every other country where the knowledge has been promulgated, of the easy means our laws afford of getting a living here, by obtaining a parish school, which is done upon the recommendation of some few freeholders, getting his salary from the public, and making his employers contribute handsomely beside.

"It is true, rules are laid down for their government, and the proper books prescribed for their use; but scarcely in one case in ten are they adhered to, for in the same class you will frequently see one child with Noah Webster's spelling book in this hand, and the next with Lindley Murray's. However prone the teachers are to variety in their schools, much blame is to be attributed to the trustees, who are in many instances too careless and I might almost add too ignorant to discriminate right from wrong, in the trust they have undertaken for the public benefit. It is, therefore, not to be wondered at why the parish school system should meet with almost universal reprobation from most discerning men.

"Of these parish schools, we are burdened with a liberal share, having no less than three of them. If the establishment of this system was meant by the legislature to abbreviate the present enormous price of education, they have been miserably deceived; for I can see no alteration or reduction from the charge made before the passing of the act. The price then was 12s. 6d. [i.e. $2.50,] and is now the same, per quarter."

In July, 1819, provisions was made for an additional district grammar school; for holding annual public examinations; for reporting the condition of the schools to the governor, and for educating ten common school pupils, free of charge, at each of the nine public grammar schools already established; but the provincial allowance to teachers of grammar schools was reduced to £50 in all cases where the numbers of pupils did not exceed ten.

FITFUL EDUCATIONAL PROGRESS FROM 1822 TO 1829.

In 1822, Sir Peregrine Maitland, the Lieutenant-Governor, submitted to the Imperial Government a plan for organizing a general system of education, including elementary schools; and, in 1823, he obtained permission from England to establish a Board of Education for the general superintendence of this system of education, and for the management of the university and school lands throughout the Province. The members of this Board, with Rev. Dr. Strachan at its head, as chairman, were: Hon. Joseph Wells, Hon. G. H. Markland, Rev. Robert Addison, Hon. J. B. Robinson, and Thomas Ridout, Esq. This Board prepared some general regulations in regard to the schools and proposed a plan by which to exchange 225,944 acres of the less valuable of the school lands for the more productive Clergy Reserve lands. The plan having been approved by the Home Government, was carried into effect by the Governor soon after. In 1824, the first attempts towards providing the public with general reading books, in connection with the Common and Sunday schools, were made. The sum of £150 was annually appropriated for this object, and authorized to be expended by the Provincial Board of Education in the purchase of "books and tracts designed to afford moral and religions instruction," and distributed equally among all the districts of Upper Canada.

Thus were presented the dim outlines of a system of public instruction which it was clear the necessities of the country required, but which for want of a vigorous and systematic supervision was gradually permitted to languish, and the legislative enactments themselves were suffered to become almost obsolete on the statute book.

In January, 1824, the Common School Act was made to apply "to all schools that are now or may hereafter be established and kept among the Indians who shall be resident within the limits of any organized county or township within this Province, excepting such schools as shall or may be otherwise provided for."[25] Provision was also made for the examination of Common School teachers by County Boards of Education.

STATE OF EDUCATION IN UPPER CANADA, 1827-1829, FROM THE OFFICIAL REPORTS, ETC.

The number and condition of the Common and other schools in Upper Canada in 1827 may be gathered from "An appeal to the Friends of Religion, and Literature, in behalf of the University of Upper Canada," published in London in 1827 (of which I have an original MS. copy). Dr. Strachan says:—

School in Upper Canada, 1827.—"In about 340 Common Schools in Upper Canada from 12,000 to 14,000 children are taught reading and writing, the elements of arithmetic, and the first principles of religion. The people, scattered as they are over a vast wilderness, are thus becoming alive to the great advantage of educating their children ... insomuch so, that schools supported by subscriptions are more in number than those established by law. Provision is made by statute for the translation of some of the more promising scholars from the Common to the District Schools, where the classics and practical mathematics are taught. In these schools (eleven in number) there are at present 300 young men acquiring an education to qualify them for the different professions....

Niagara District Board of Education, 1828.—"It must be admitted generally that after the approval and appointment of teachers by the Trustees the Board have not rejected teachers however incompetent, from a regards to the wishes of their employers, the terms for tuition being so very low as not to induce men of sufficient qualifications generally to engage in the humble and ill-requited duties.

Reading, writing and arithmetic have been uniformly taught in all schools. Grammar and geography in a few. Religious instruction has not been overlooked. Upon the whole, the system of education in this district may be considered as efficient as can be expected upon the footing on which it is placed."—*Rev. Thomas Creen.*

Provincial Board of Education, 1828.—The number of District Grammar Schools in operation in the Province is 11; pupils in attendance, 372. Number of Common Schools, 401; number of pupils in attendance, 10,712—increase over 1827 of nearly 2,000 pupils.

The President of the Board (Rev. Dr. Strachan) last summer visited in person all the districts of the Province, and not only inspected the grammar schools, but examined minutely the systems of management adopted by their respective teachers.

In order to produce a greater uniformity of the system to supply, in some measure, the want of experience to younger teachers, the President has submitted an outline of study for the grammar schools, the adoption of which, the board cannot but think would be highly beneficial, and produce a higher standard of education throughout the Province.[20]

In some places girls are admitted to the district schools, for want of good female schools, but the admission of female children interferes with the government which is required in classical seminaries.

In a population of nearly 200,000, at least one-fifth, or 40,000, is composed of children between the ages of 5 and 15 who should be going to school. Taking the number of those who are benefited in the Common and Sunday schools at 15,000, then the expense to the Province is about 3s. 9d. each. In some districts the salaries allowed to the schoolmasters of the Common Schools are exceedingly small. They range from £12 10s. downwards. In some little more than £5, and in one less than that trifling sum. Many schools continue only six months; others eight months in the year. The natural consequence of this state of things is that superior teachers desert the Common Schools as soon as they can procure any other employment, and many persons resort to the occupation of teachers merely as a temporary expedient. These latter are without experience, which is all-important to an instructor of youth and can have little desire to establish a reputation in an employment to which they have only recourse for present convenience.

In the sister Colony of Nova Scotia, the sum of £1,000 is annually appropriated to the Common Schools and divided among 12 counties, not equally, but in proportion to population. One law, by giving the same sum to each district, whether populous or not, in that particular requires alteration.

The Board would submit that in addition to the public allowance, a power should be given to the townships to assess themselves for the schools. In Nova Scotia it is provided in the statute that two-thirds of the freeholders may, under certain conditions, tax themselves according to their ability for the support of education, and that no school of 30 scholars shall be entitled to the stipulated aid of £20, unless the teacher receives *bona fide* from his employers £10, together with this sum, exclusive of and in addition to board, etc.; and that no school of 15 scholars shall be entitled to the stipulated sum of £15 unless the teacher receives from his employers £25 per annum as aforesaid. The Board had distributed to the Common Schools a large quantity of useful school books including Mavor's Spelling Book. They have also contracted for 2,000 copies of this excellent work to be executed on cards for the township schools. There appears to be a great scarcity of arithmetic books in the Province, and those in use are in general too difficult or deficient in matter, etc. The President has, therefore, undertaken to draw up a short manual on the subject, suitable to the state and business of the country.

Neither the sick nor the destitute have higher claims upon the public than the ignorant. The want of knowledge brings all other wants in its train; and if education be regarded as a charity, it is a charity of which the blessings are without alloy. It demands no jealous scrutiny of the claims of its applicants, nor does it require to be so stinted as not to multiply their number.—*Rev. John Strachan, President, York, 5th February, 1829.*

Midland District Grammar School, 1829.—It is to be lamented that so few of the wealthy farmers of the Midland District avail themselves of the means of giving their sons that degree of education which the public school can readily afford, which would qualify young persons to discharge the duties of the magistracy and other public situations with credit to themselves.

The trustees regret that no poor children are educated gratis under the patriotic and very benevolent provision of the statute, in consequence of no returns being made to them of the most promising scholars from the Common School. The trustees, therefore, submit, whether in order to encourage native genius in humble circumstances, some means might not be devised of maintaining all the 10 children whom the statute authorizes the trustee to select for gratuitous instruction.—*Rev. George O'Kill Stuart, Thomas Markland and John Macaulay, Kingston, December 30th, 1829.*

NOTE.—The local reports for the succeeding year are chiefly statistical and explanatory and contain no general remarks. From a report signed by the Rev. Dr. Strachan and Hon. Wm. Allan in 1839, it would appear that things had for years remained in *statu quo.* They say:—

"For many years elaborate reports were sent from this (Home District) Board of Education detailing what were believed to be the alterations necessary to render the present Common School Act efficient. In consequence of these, and like reports from other districts, a measure for the establishment of such schools has been for more than six years before the Legislature, which purposes to provide remedies for the defects which are met with in the working of the present system."

COURSE OF STUDY SUGGESTED BY REV. DR. STRACHAN AS SUITABLE FOR THE DISTRICT GRAMMAR SCHOOLS THROUGHOUT THE PROVINCE, 1829.

In a "letter from the Rev. Dr. Strachan to Rev. A. N. Bethune, Rector of Cobourg," dated October 6th, 1829, he thus sketched a course of study for Grammar Schools:

First Year—Boys from 7 to 9.

1st. *Latin.*—Eton Grammar; Vocabulary; Corderius; Selectæ e Profanis.

2nd. *English.*—Mavor's Spelling Book; Enfield's Lessons; Walker's Lessons; Murray's Lessons; Blair's Class Book; English Grammar; Writing; Arithmetic, chiefly mental.

Second Year—Boys from 9 to 11.

1st. *Latin.*—Grammar; Valpy's Delectas; New Testament; Daley's Exercises; Exampla Minora; Entropius; Phædrus; Cornelius Nepos.

2nd. *English.*—Grammar and Reading, as before; Writing and Arithmetic (mental and mixed); Geography; Civil and Natural History and Elocution.

3rd.—To commence French.

Third Year—Boys from 11 to 13.

1st. *Latin*—Grammar; Bailey's Exercises; Cornelius Nepos; Cæsar; Ovid's Metamorphoses; Nonsense Verses; Psalms into Latin Verse; Exampla Moralis; Versions or rendering English into Latin.

2nd. *Greek*—To commence about the middle of the third year: Eton Grammar, or Nelson's edition of Moore's Grammar; Greek Vocabulary; New Testament; Greek Exercises.

3rd. *English.*—Grammar; Writing; Elocution; Civil and Natural History; Geography, Ancient and Modern; English Composition.

4th. *Arithmetic.*—And to commence Algebra.

5th. *French.*

Fourth Year—Boys from 12 to 14.

1st. *Latin.*—Grammar; Terence Virgil; Horace; Sallust; Cicero; Livy; Latin composition, verse and prose; Grotius de Veritate Exampla Moralia.

2nd. *Greek.*—Eton Grammar; Græca Minora; Greek and Latin Testament; Xenophon; Homer.

3rd. *English.*—Grammar and Composition; Civil and Natural History; Geography, Ancient and Modern, use of the globes; construction of maps.

4th. *Mathematics.*—Arithmetic; Book-keeping; Algebra; Euclid.

5th. *French.*

Fifth Year—Boys from 14 to 16.

1st. *Latin.*—Virgil; Horace; Livy, Juvenal; Tacitus; Composition, in prose and verse.

2nd. *Greek.*—Græca Majora; Homer; Thucidides; Composition, in prose and verse.

3rd. *English.*—Grammar and Composition; Elocution; Civil and Natural History; Geography, Ancient and Modern; use of the globes; construction of maps.

4th. *Mathematics.*—Algebra; Euclid; Trigonometry, Application to heights and distances; Surveying; Navigation; Dialling; Elements of Astronomy, etc.

5th. *French.*

REV. DR. STRACHAN'S SYSTEM OF SCHOOL MANAGEMENT.

Rev. Dr. Scadding, in his sketch of Dr. Strachan, "The first Bishop of Toronto—a Review and a Study," says:

"The system pursued in Dr. Stachan's school at Cornwall and afterwards at York, exhibited features that would have gratified the advanced educationists of the present age. In that system the practical and the useful were by no means sacrificed to the ornamental and theoretical, or the merely conventional. Things were regarded as well as words.... In regard to things—the science of common objects—we doubt if in the most complete of our modern schools there was ever awakened a greater interest or intelligence in relation to such matters. Who, that had once participated in the excitement of its natural history class, ever forgot it? Or in that of the historical or geographical exercises? We venture to think that, in many an instance, the fullest experience of after life, in travel or otherwise, had often their associations with ideas awakened then; and often compared satisfactorily and pleasurably with the pictures of places, ani given, rudely it may be, in text books, ransacked and conned in a fervour of emulation then. The manner of study in these subjects was this: each lad was required to prepare a set of questions, to be put by himself to his fellows in the class. If a reply was not forthcoming, and the information furnished by the questioner was judged correct the latter 'went up' and took the place of the other. This process, besides being instructive and stimulating to the pupils, possessed the advantage of being, as it often proved, highly diverting to the teacher."

On this system Dr. Strachan himself remarks:

"The method of instruction by question and answer possesses many advantages over any other, and is not only the very best and shortest, but the most satisfactory. In this system the deficiencies of each scholar becomes manifest, and the teacher knows to what particular points he must direct his explanations. There is no time for inattention or wandering; the question and necessity for reply compel attention and recollection. The children, if the teacher proceed with conciliatory firmness, acquire lively interest in the lesson, for each is particularly addressed and brought forward with action."[27]

The late Bishop Fuller, who was also one of Dr. Strachan's pupils, also states that:—

"He had a remarkable talent for interesting boys in their work; and, by taking a deep interest in it himself, he led them to do the same. He was very original in many of his plans for promoting the good of his school. Amongst others, which I never met with elsewhere, was one of making the boys question one another on certain of the lessons. This made the boys quick at seizing on the leading points in the lessons, ready at shaping questions, and deeply interested in the questions and answers. The Bishop took as deep an interest in the questioning and answering of the boys as they did themselves; and thus this plan, whilst it was of great service to the boys in various ways, tended strongly to bind master and scholars together."[28]

As to his method of teaching arithmetic, he explains it in the following words:

"In a new country like this, a variety of branches must be taught in every respectable school. Young men ... are anxious to get forward as fast as possible, and even those destined for the learned professions are seldom allowed the time requisite for acquiring the knowledge previously necessary. These considerations induced me to turn my thoughts to the discovery of some sure, and at the same time, expeditious method of teaching arithmetic. This object I have accomplished with a much greater degree of success than I dared to promise myself.

"I divide my pupils into separate classes according to their progress. Each class has one or more sums to produce every day, neatly wrought upon their slates. The work is carefully examined, after which I command every figure to be blotted out, and the sums to be wrought under my eye. The one whom I happen to pitch upon first gives, with an audible voice, the rules and reasons for every step, and as he proceeds the rest silently work along with him figure for figure, but ready to correct him if he blunder that they may get his place. As soon as this one is finished, the work is again blotted out and another called upon to work the question aloud as before, while the rest proceed along with him in silence, and so on round the whole class…. This method of teaching arithmetic possesses this important advantage, that it may be pursued without interrupting the pupils' progress in any other useful study. The same method of teaching Algebra has been used with equal success. Such a plan is certainly very laborious, but it will be found successful, *and he that is anxious to spare labor ought not to be a public teacher*."[29]

Desiring to give a local interest to the exercises in his book, Dr. Strachan gave several examples from Canadian subjects. Thus a question is addition reads:—

"From Quebec to Montreal is 180 miles—from thence to Kingston 200—from thence to York 149—from thence to Niagara 78 miles—from thence to Detroit, 210. Required the distance from Quebec to Detroit. *Answer*—317 miles."

Again a question in multiplication reads:—

"The distance from Quebec to Montreal is 180 miles, supposing the road 17 yards broad, how many square yards does it contain? *Answer*—5,385,600 yards."

As to his diligence as a student, while yet a teacher. Dr. Fuller remarks:—

"The late Bishop said to me on one occasion: 'I had to study every night quite as hard as the boys; for I was not much in advance of the highest class in school. These and parochial duties demanded sixteen hours every day,—and yet these nine years were the happiest years of my life."

REV. DR. STRACHAN'S CAREER AS A TEACHER.

Having been appointed Minister at Cornwall in 1803, Dr. Fuller states that there he was:—

"Induced to resume his school, at the solicitation of the parents of those boys who had been in his school at Kingston, and of others, both in Lower and Upper Canada, who were desirous of placing their sons under a master so practical, wise and successful, as he had proved himself to be. Thus he commenced the school at Cornwall, which afterwards became so celebrated, and at which were educated the first men that Canada has produced, and of whom she may well be proud—such men as the late Sir J. B. Robinson, Judge Maclean, Sir J. B. Macaulay, Sir Allan MacNab, Judge Jones, Mr. Stanton, the Bethunes (Alexander, John and Donald), Sir James Stuart, and his brother Andrew Stuart, besides many others who have reflected credit on our country.

"The Bishop had a great faculty for not only attaching his scholars to him, but also for inducing them to apply themselves most assiduously to their studies. He told me he made it a rule, during the time he kept school, to watch closely every new boy, and at the end of a fortnight, to note down in a book his estimate of the boys who had passed through his hands.

"He was never afraid of having his dignity lowered by liberties taken with him, and he always felt every confidence in his position and entered warmly and personally into many of the boys' amusements, and thus gained an immense influence over them. The influence over his pupils has been shown in the fact, that almost all of them embraced his principles; and the love and affection for him of his celebrated Cornwall school was shown many years ago, when the surviving members thereof presented him with an address[30] and a most beautiful and costly candelabra. Nor did his more recent scholars entertain less affection for him, though they never proved it so substantially as did those of his Cornwall School.... He was an excellent teacher. His scholars were well grounded in their work. The grammar was well mastered, and every rule thereof deeply impressed on the memory. Every lesson was thoroughly dissected, and everything connected with it thoroughly understood, before we passed on to another lesson."[31]

MR. JOSEPH HUME'S ESSAY ON EDUCATION EDITED AS A CATECHISM BY MR. WM. LYON MACKENZIE IN 1830.

In 1830 Mr. Mackenzie republished at York (Toronto), in pamphlet form, the first part of a Catechism of Education, prepared by Mr. Joseph Hume, M.P., in England. The pamphlet in my possession is worn and weather-stained. It is inscribed to David Thorburn, of Queenston, and extends to 46 pages. In his preface Mr. Mackenzie says:

"To Mr. Joseph Hume.—The compiler is indebted for an Essay on Education, which lays down and explains principles of vital importance to the best interest of the Canadians, the perusal of which first suggested the design of this catechism.

"In the first parts, under the heads Domestic, Technical, Social and Political Instruction, it has been attempted to shew chiefly what the means are by which the human mind may be endowed with those qualities on which the generation of happiness depends."

VICISSITUDES OF EDUCATION IN UPPER CANADA, 1830-1839.

For many years subsequently spasmodic efforts were made from time to time by progressive and earnest men in the Legislature to establish a system of schools. Enquiries were instituted and reports made, chiefly but not wholly, by the House of Assembly. A vigorous contest was maintained between that body and the Legislative Council on the subject. Bills were passed by the Assembly and rejected by the Council. The contest continued until the Rebellion occurred, and this event turned all men's thoughts into another

74

channel for the time.

Of the able and zealous men who, almost single handed, fought the battle of elementary education in the Legislature, prior to the rebellion of 1837, I may refer to the efforts in this direction of Dr. Charles Duncombe and Mr. Malhon Burwell, who did good service in the cause, as also did Archdeacon Strachan, Hon. William Morris and others for higher education.

In the light of the growth and educational progress of to-day, the miserable condition of public education in the days of the educational pioneers to whom I have referred, can hardly be credited. And were it not on record in the proceedings of the Legislature, the statements there made would appear to apply to some other country rather than to ours.

There were in the House of Assembly in those days (as I have intimated) men of rare power and ability, who did noble service in the popular cause, and in behalf of general education. They passed school bills, founded on elaborate reports, year after year, only to see them defeated by a majority in the Legislative Council. This state of things continued for some years, and with disastrous effects on the intellectual life of the country. This fact is illustrated in the proceedings of the House of Assembly. For example: In a petition of the United Presbytery of Upper Canada, presented to the House in 1830, the signers say:—

"It is with deep regret that your petitioners (in their ministerial capacity, connected with a very large portion of His Majesty's subjects in this Province) are compelled to say that the state of education is, in general, in a deplorable condition."

The reason for this state of things is thus clearly set forth by the House of Assembly in an address to the Lieutenant-Governor, adopted in the same year:—

"We the Commons of Upper Canada, in Parliament assembled, most respectfully represent that there is in this Province a very general want of education; that the insufficiency of the school fund to support competent, respectable and well-educated teachers, has degraded common school teaching from a regular business to a mere matter of convenience to transient persons, or common idlers, who often teach school one season and leave it vacant until it accommodates some other like person, whereby the minds of our youth are left without cultivation, or, what is still worse, frequently with vulgar, low-bred, vicious or intemperate examples before them, in the capacity of monitors."

EDUCATIONAL EFFORTS OF MR. MAHLON BURWELL IN THE HOUSE OF ASSEMBLY, 1831-1836.

Few men exerted themselves more or to better purpose in the cause of education than did Mr. Burwell during the time he was a member of the old Upper Canada Legislature, in 1831-1838.[132]

Amongst the many motions relating to education which were moved by Mr. Burwell in the House of Assembly from time to time, was the following important one, which was concurred in by the House in February, 1831:—

> "That a standing committee be appointed on the subject of education generally in this Province....

> "That it be a principal duty and business of the committee to enquire whether an appropriation of 500,000 acres of land was not made, in virtue of a joint address of both houses of the Provincial Parliament, adopted at their session of 1797, or 1798, and whether the same is not subject to the control of the Legislature of this Province; to enquire if anything, and what, has been done with the lands or any part of them, and what is their present situation.

> "That the said committee do enquire in what way the several district schools of the Province can best be endowed with portions of the said lands, so as to render them more efficient and fitting for the improvement of the rising generation than they are at present."...

Such were the comprehensive terms of a motion which gave to the subject of education a status in the House of Assembly at the time by making a committee on the subject a Standing Committee of the House, and clothing it with important powers. Mr. Burwell also, of the same month, moved for the production of all the despatches, reports, and other documents relating to the royal grant of lands by George III. for grammar schools and colleges in Upper Canada. In response to this latter motion, the Lieut.-Governor, Sir John Colborne (Lord Seaton), sent down to the House a mass of papers of great value, showing what steps had been taken by the Imperial and Provincial Governments during the intervening years for the promotion of public education. These papers were printed at the time, but little is now known of their contents.

In April, 1831, Mr. Burwell, as chairman of the Quarter Sessions of the London District, presented to the Lieut-Governor a memorial setting forth the advantages to that locality of endowing a college at London. Amongst the reasons given are the following:—

> "Your memorialists are aware that education of a superior kind cannot be brought to every man's door, and that under any arrangements, the inhabitants of the Province generally must send their children a short distance from home; but such is the extent of the several districts, that the school can seldom be a day's journey from any part of them; and the scholars can return to their homes without expense during the holidays; and, if sick, they can be visited by their parents in a few hours, and removed to their habitations without difficulty. Added to all this the cheapness at which board can be obtained in country places, and the easiness with which, in most cases, it can be paid for by produce from their farms."

These reasons are somewhat primitive in their character; but they throw light on the social condition of the people in these days, and illustrate the common practice then of paying even for education "in kind," or by "produce from the farms." The object of the memorialists was to obtain such an endowment for the London District Grammar School—

"As shall render it efficient as a classical seminary, and a nursery (as such schools are intended to be) for the University of King's College....

"The endowment should be such a one as would furnish a good school-house, a commodious residence for the head master—to enable him to keep boarders and produce an income of four or five hundred pounds."

In the following June a similar, but a much longer and more strongly worded, memorial was presented to the Governor from the trustees of the Kingston "Royal Grammar School," protesting against the withdrawal from that school of an extra grant of £200 a year and giving it to Upper Canada College, thus reducing the rank of the Kingston "Royal Grammar School" to that of a district grammar school.

EFFORTS AT EDUCATIONAL LEGISLATION BY DR. CHARLES DUNCOMBE, 1831-1836.

As one of those who took a prominent part in the troublesome events of 1837-38, in Upper Canada, Dr. Duncombe acquired considerable notoriety. He was, nevertheless, a man of broad views, of comprehensive aims and large sympathies.[133]

From his first entry into the House of Assembly, Dr. Charles Duncombe, M.P.P. for the county of Norfolk, took up warmly the cause of popular education. In this he was actively supported by two other medical gentlemen —Dr. Thomas D. Morrison and Dr. Thomas Bruce—who were also members of the House of Assembly at that time.

Dr. Charles Duncombe's first motion in the House of Assembly (on the 13th December, 1831) was for an address to the Lieut.-Governor urging the setting apart of a sufficient quantity of the public lands of the Province to form a permanent fund for the support and maintenance of common schools. His motion was, however, defeated.

As Dr. Duncombe's motion is of historical interest, so far as the facts which it alleges are concerned, I give some extracts from it. The motion stated:—

"That there is in this Province a very general want of education; that the insufficiency of the Common School Fund to support competent, respectable and well-educated teachers, has degraded common school teaching from a regular business to a mere matter of convenience to transient persons, or common idlers, who often stay but for one season, and leave the schools vacant until they accommodate some other like person, whereby the minds of the youth of this Province are left without due cultivation, or, what is worse, frequently with vulgar, low-bred, vicious and intemperate examples before them in the persons of their monitors," (i.e., teachers).

The motion goes on to say that:—

"If provision were made for the liberal and punctual payment of common school teachers

... the teaching of common schools would soon become a regular and respectable calling, gentlemanly, well-educated persons would not be ashamed to take charge of youth, the schools would be no longer vacant, nor the scholars ignorant. Upper Canada would then form a national character that would command respect abroad and ensure peace, prosperity and happiness at home, perpetuate attachment to British principles and British institutions, and enable posterity to value, as they ought, the inestimable blessings of our glorious constitution."

The motion went on to urge the Lieut.-Governor to represent to the Colonial Secretary the important necessity—in view of the facts cited—of entreating

"That His Majesty, William IV., be graciously pleased to place at the disposal of the Provincial Legislature a portion of the waste lands of the Crown as a permanent fund for the support of common schools within the same."

Dr. Charles Duncombe, with a prescience of the future, and of the necessities of the case, (which were not then recognized, nor for many years afterwards,) strongly urged, as did other members of the Assembly, that at least one million acres of the "waste lands" of the Province should be set apart for the support of common schools.[34]

The motion was negatived. Dr. Duncombe was, however, determined not to be beaten. Mr. David Burn and other friends of his in the county of Oxford— no doubt on his suggestion—got up a petition to the Legislature on the subject, and on the 21st December—a week after his motion was defeated— Dr. Duncombe read this petition and had it referred to a select committee for report thereon.

On the 26th December an elaborate report on the petition was brought in by Dr. Duncombe himself, as chairman of the committee. In that report the whole subject was gone into fully, and a scheme elaborated by which the 1,000,000 acres of land were proposed to be hypothecated in advance, so that by the issue of debentures for $500,000, redeemable in ten, fifteen and twenty years, a sufficient sum would be at once realized on the prospective value of these lands to form a permanent fund for the support of common schools.

This report (as did the rejected motion) placed on record a few facts and principles which are interesting in the light of to-day. The report stated that—

"The common schools of this Province are generally in so deplorable a state that they scarcely deserve the name of schools."

It recommended that the common school law of the Province be so amended that hereafter the school grant be paid only to—

"Organized schools, taught by a person who had a certificate from the District Board of Education, or school inspector, of his or her ability to teach a common school."

It also urged that the Common School Fund should be large enough, with the local contributions, to provide an ample stipend for good teachers, instead of "transient persons" and "common idlers" then so often employed as teachers—

"So that common school teaching, instead of being a mere matter of convenience to transient persons, or common idlers, would become a regular, respectable business in the hands of gentlemanly, well-educated persons. For surely the foundation of the minds of our children (on which must depend the happiness or misery we are to enjoy with them) and their own success in life, is a business worthy to be respectable, worthy of the patronage of men in the highest walks of life."

The report then laid down an important principle in regard to the necessity for a certain and permanent endowment for public education. It said:—

"Funds and appropriation for the support of education should be permanent. They should not depend upon the annual vote of the Legislature, nor on any other casualty that might, by possibility fail, and thereby check the regular progress of education."

Dr. Duncombe, in stating this principle, had no doubt in view the example (then well known) of the fickleness of the Legislature in the matter of school grants. In 1816 the vote for the support of common schools was $24,000. In three subsequent years the same vote was repeated; but, in 1820, it was reduced to $10,000—closing schools here and there all over the Province, and inflicting grievous hardship on many worthy (and, in the language of the day and of the report, unworthy) teachers. This miserable state of things continued for many years, and, as I stated on this subject in 1863—

"Thus ebbed and flowed, without a master hand to stay the current, that tide which, in other lands, is regarded as the nation's life's blood; and thus was permitted to ensue that state of living death by which Upper Canada, in the significant and popular metaphor of the day was likened to a 'girdled tree,' destitute alike of life, of beauty, or of stately growth."[35]

No wonder that in these degenerate days the young men, with stirrings within them of noble impulses and patriotic devotion to their country, should have been compelled to depend upon themselves for intellectual enlightenment and advancement. The flippant sneer of many persons of to-day at such "self-made" men is unworthy of those who enjoy the advantages which these self-made men laboured to secure. They belonged to that noble band of pioneers, who achieved for us the civil and religious freedom which we now so richly enjoy. All honour to them, therefore!

CONTINUED EDUCATIONAL EFFORTS BY MR. BURWELL IN THE HOUSE OF ASSEMBLY.

In January, 1832, Mr. Burwell made a motion similar to the defeated one of Dr. C. Duncombe, which led to considerable discussion. It was as follows:—

"That this House do address His Majesty, humbly beseeching that His Majesty will be

In the same month Mr. Burwell introduced a bill "for the establishment and support of common schools throughout the Province." It was printed but was not proceeded with that session. Mr. Burwell's object clearly was to keep the subject before the House and to promote discussion on it. In this he succeeded. The House of Assembly was alive to the importance of the question, but the Legislative Council was obstructive in regard to the same subject.

In November, 1832, Mr. Burwell again had a committee of the House of Assembly appointed to enquire into the manner in which the King's wishes had been carried out in regard to the royal grant of lands for educational purposes in 1798. To expedite this enquiry the important despatches and reports formerly asked for by him and sent down to the House by the Governor, with others, were printed and distributed.

Mr. Burwell also introduced a bill "for the establishment, maintenance and regulation of common schools," in the Province. He made several motions, too, on the subject of the King's College charter and school lands. On the 21st November he submitted the first report of his "Select Committee on the Subject of Education." The historical part of this report being somewhat interesting in its statements, I quote it as follows:—

"The committee have been forcibly struck with the uniform anxiety which has been manifested at all times by the Legislature and Provincial authorities for the establishment of a university.

"It formed part of the prayer of both Houses in their address to the King in 1797.

"It was strongly recommended by the Executive Government, the judges, and law officers of the Crown, in 1798.

"In 1806 the Legislature, to show that something more was even then required than grammar schools, did all their limited means permitted, in providing a small apparatus for the instruction of youth in physical science, that they might enter the world with something more than a common district school education; such an institution was again noticed in 1820, and an earnest desire expressed by the Legislature, which knew best the wants of the Province, for its speedy establishment.

"In 1825 so many young men were found turning their attention to the learned professions that the Executive Government thought that the establishment of a university could be no longer delayed without the greatest detriment to the Province, and, therefore, applied to His Majesty for a Royal Charter, which was granted in 1827, in terms as liberal, it is said, as the then Government would allow; but such has proved by no means satisfactory to your Honorable House."[36]

About the middle of December, 1832, Mr. Burwell brought in the second and very elaborate report of the Select Committee on Education. This report was chiefly based upon the opinions of several witnesses examined by the committee on the subject of school lands, King's College charter, U. C. College, and education generally. The witnesses examined were Chief Justice Robinson, Archdeacon Strachan, Chairman, and the Hon. G. H. Markland, Secretary to the Provincial Board of Education; Hon. Joseph Wells, a member of the Board, and Treasurer of U. C. College; Rev. Dr. Joseph H. Harris, Principal of U. C. College; Rev. Dr. Thomas Phillips, Vice-Principal, and Mr. S. P. Hurd, Surveyor-General of the Province.

The general views of these noted men on the subject of education are both interesting and instructive in the light of to-day. The report itself deals with the then pressing question of the extension of educational facilities to the entire Province. It points out in strong language the undesirability of continuing a system of district, or grammar, schools which were quite adequate to the wants of the Province when the population was only 50,000, but which was not at all equal to the requirements of Upper Canada when that population had increased to nearly 300,000. These references show how wonderfully the Province has progressed in population and in its educational advantages since that time.

EARLY OPINIONS ON THE NECESSITY FOR MANUAL, OR INDUSTRIAL, EDUCATION.

The following passage from the report of 1832 is prophetical in its anticipation of the future. By way of illustration I may mention the fact that a somewhat similar utterance was made by Sir Lyon Playfair in his address as president of the British Association, at Aberdeen, in 1887. The passage in the report of 1832 is as follows:—

"That the situation of the Province in wealth and commerce, and in its demand for superior attainments in the various professions is very different from what it formerly was; and that unless opportunities are immediately furnished by the establishment of superior schools for the instruction of our youth in the higher branches of science, we must fall behind the age in which we live."

What was thus put forth as a local thought, but yet as an educational axiom, by these educational pioneers of Upper Canada, upwards of fifty years ago, is thus forcibly and beautifully amplified by the president of the British Association in 1887. Speaking generally, and contrasting the educational policy of the colonies and that of the mother country, he said:—

"The colonies, being young countries, value their raw materials as their chief source of wealth. When they become older they will discover it is not in these, but in the culture of scientific intellect, that their future prosperity depends.... Jules Simon tersely puts it:—'The nation which most educates her people will become the greatest nation, if not to-day, certainly to-morrow.' Higher education is the condition of higher prosperity, and the nation which neglects to develop the intellectual factor of production must degenerate, for it cannot stand still.... The illustrious consort of our Queen was not the first prince who saw how closely science is bound up with the welfare of states.... How unwise it is for England to lag in the onward march of science, when most other European powers are using the resources of their states to promote higher education and to advance the boundaries of knowledge. [She] alone fails to grasp the fact that the competition of the world has become a competition of intellect.... A nation in its industrial progress, when the competition of the world is keen, cannot stand still.... I contend that in public education there should be a free play to the scientific faculty, so that the youths who possess it should learn the richness of their possession during the educative process.... Science has impressed itself upon the age in which we live; and as science is not stationary, but progressive, men are required to advance its boundaries, acting as pioneers in the onward march of states. Human progress is so identified with scientific thought, both in its conception and realization, that it seems as if they were alternative terms in the history of civilization."

In giving these extracts so fully I have done so for two reasons: First, I desire to do honour to the zeal and to acknowledge the forethought and prescience of those members of the House of Assembly who, in 1832, placed so strong an emphasis upon the value of "the instruction of our youth in the higher branches of science;" and secondly, to point out, in the weighty words of Sir Lyon Playfair, the immense importance (in the light of past experience) which he and other leaders of thought in regard to England's industrial life and practical progress, attach to the teaching of elementary science in the schools. He touches upon this point in another part of his address, in pointing out the absurdity of requiring all pupils to study the same subjects. He says:—

"In a school a boy should be aided to discover the class of knowledge that is best suited to his mental capacities, so that in the upper forms of the school, and in the university, knowledge may be specialized in order to cultivate the powers of the man to the fullest extent.... The adaptation of public schools to a scientific age does not involve a contest as to whether science or classics shall prevail, for both are indispensable to true education. The real question is, whether schools will undertake the duty of moulding the minds of boys according to their mental varieties."

LATER OPINIONS ON THE NECESSITY FOR MANUAL TRAINING IN OUR SCHOOLS.

So deeply impressed was I of the immense importance of this subject, and of the necessity of providing in our school system for a practical solution of the question which was then, and is now, of pressing importance—viz., manual training in our schools—that in 1876 I prepared and delivered a lecture on the subject, in various parts of the Province. The lecture was founded on the industrial lessons taught to us so impressively at the Centennial Exhibition, Philadelphia, in 1876. These lessons, in their educational aspects, were even more forcibly impressed upon me at the great Industrial Exhibition held in New Orleans, in 1885. Having been there six weeks, as an Educational Juror, on behalf of the United States Bureau of Education, I had abundant and admirable facilities for studying the whole question, and for seeing how it was being worked out (more or less effectually) in the various national school systems which came under review during that enquiry—especially in France. Thus the French school law of 1882 provides that "primary education includes [among other things] the elements of the natural, physical and mathematical sciences, and their application to agriculture, to hygiene, and to the industrial art; manual work, and the use of tools of the principal trades, the elements of drawing, modelling, etc." Apprenticeship schools have also been established, the object of which is to form workmen, as distinguished from foremen, and in which various trades are taught. An official report, published by the United States Bureau of Education in 1882, states that the apprentices of these schools "find employment readily after they have left the workshops, at wages, it is said, varying from five to even as much as eight francs per day."

In discussing this question in the lecture to which I have referred, these passages occur:—

"It is not assumed that every pupil in our schools is qualified, or that he should be compelled, as a matter of course, to engage in the study of elementary science or practical drawing. Far from it. But what I do say is, that those pupils who exhibit a taste for any of the various subjects of natural history, elementary science or practical mechanics, should have an opportunity in the Public and High Schools (of cities and large towns) of learning something about them. In an address by Mr. Gladstone on this subject, he stated that the boys of the English schools, and it is so in our schools, had not yet had fair play in the study of elementary science and natural history....

"There are few schools in which there are not boys possessing talent scientific, inventive, or industrial talent, or constructive genius, which are never evoked, much less aroused or stimulated. As to the question whether for the few the country should be put to the expense of their special training, I answer it in the words of Professor Huxley, who says:—

"To the lad of genius, even to the one in a million, I would make accessible the highest and most complete training the country could afford. Whatever it might cost, depend upon it the investment would be invaluable. I weigh my words when I say: that if the nation could purchase a potential Watt, or Davy, or Faraday, at the cost of a hundred thousand pounds down, he would be dirt cheap at the money.... It is a mere commonplace and an every-day piece of knowledge to say that, what these three men did, (in their special departments of practical science), has produced untold millions of wealth for England and the world, speaking in its narrowest economical sense of the word."

The educational mind of the United States, as well as Europe, is being constantly directed to the consideration of this interesting practical subject. Magazines and reviews, as well as educational journals, freely discuss it. One of the most useful articles on "Manual Training in the Public schools," will be found in the *Andover Review* for October, 1888. The United States Bureau of Education has also published various reports and papers on the subject. One of the most valuable is an elaborate report on *Industrial Education in the United States*, published in 1883. Some of the more important railways in that country have also established training schools for their employés.

FURTHER EDUCATIONAL EFFORTS IN THE HOUSE OF ASSEMBLY, 1835, 1836.

For the four years during which Dr. Duncombe was a member the Legislature of Upper Canada, his efforts to promote the cause of education were unceasing. With the exception of Mr. Burwell, who devoted himself almost entirely to the interests of education in the House, none excelled Dr. Duncombe in his zeal for the cause of public education. His efforts were chiefly directed to awaken an interest amongst his fellow members in the subject generally, and especially on behalf of the education of the deaf and dumb, in asylums for the insane, in prison discipline and similar matters. At length his efforts in the session of 1835 culminated in the appointment, by resolution of the House of Assembly, of Doctors Charles Duncombe, Thomas D. Morrison and William Bruce, Commissioners, to enquire, amongst other things, into "the system and management of schools and colleges" in the United States and elsewhere. Two of these commissioners deputed their colleague, Dr. Duncombe, to "go on a journey to the United States, or elsewhere, to obtain such information as is desired by a resolution" of the House of Assembly in that behalf. Six hundred dollars were granted by the House to defray the expenses of this enquiry.

Late in 1835 Dr. Duncombe went on his mission of enquiry to the United States, and visited literary institutions in the Western, Middle, Eastern and some of the Southern States of the Union. He also obtained detailed information as to education in England, France and Prussia, and embodied the result in an elaborate report of nearly sixty pages and an appendix of one hundred and sixty pages. To this report he annexed the draft of a School Bill, extending to twenty-two pages, with a variety of forms and instructions appended. The whole document embraced two hundred and sixty pages of printed matter. The report is minute and exhaustive in its treatment of the subject in hand, although somewhat discursive and speculative in many parts. It is, nevertheless, in the light of to-day, both interesting and instructive. It presents a vivid picture, and not a very flattering one, of the condition of education in the United States and in Europe. Its discussions of special subjects—such as female education, classical studies, the management of colleges and universities, etc., etc.—are fair and enlightened, and, on the whole, intelligent and practical in their character.

It is clear that the Legislative Council of the day did not sympathize with Dr. Duncombe and his colleagues in their zeal for popular education.

The bill which he had so carefully prepared, although adopted by the House of Assembly by a vote of 35 to 10, early in 1836 failed to receive the sanction of the Council. His proposition to increase the common school grant from $22,600 to $80,000 per annum was considered too great a step in advance, and was not therefore pressed to a vote in the House of Assembly. He, however, got two influential committees appointed to deal with the questions of public education and school lands. These committees were subsequently united and enlarged. They did good service and kept public interest awakened as to the value of the important subjects entrusted to them.

ANALYSIS OF DR. DUNCOMBE'S REPORT ON EDUCATION, 1836.

The report, be it remembered, speaks of events and educational facts of more than fifty years ago. They are of special interest to us of to-day, since they form the background, so to speak, of our own educational history and progress. I shall make a few extracts from the report:—Dr. Duncombe says:—

> "The first principles of the system recommended in this report with regard to common schools, schools for the education of the poorer classes, and for the education of teachers (or the normal schools) made their appearance almost simultaneously in Great Britain and on the Continent, as appears by the voluminous reports of Lord Brougham ... and by Mr. Dick's very able and splendid report upon the common schools ... of Scotland, and by M. Cousin's reports of the schools in Prussia and Germany, and Bulver's observations upon education as a prevention of crime in France.... The glimmering of this beacon light was soon seen across the ocean, and lighted up a similar flame in the United Slates. Commissioner after commissioner was sent to Scotland and to England by the authority of their State Legislatures to light their lamps at the fountain of science, that the whole continent of America might be ignited by the flame."

Dr. Duncombe's observations in regard to the state of education in the United States are interesting, as by contrast they illustrate the remarkable progress made in that country during the last half century in the matter of public education. He says:—

> "In the United States, where they devote much time and expense towards the promotion of literature, they are equally destitute of a system of national education with ourselves: and although by their greater exertion to import the improvements made in Great Britain and on the Continent, and their numerous attempts at systematizing these modern modes of education ... they have placed themselves in advance of us in their common school system. Yet, after all, their schools seemed to me to be good schools on bad or imperfect systems; they seem groping in the dark, no instruction in the past to guide the future, no beacon light, no council of wise men to guide them, more than we have, upon the subject of common schools. Our schools want in character, they want respectability, they want permanency in their character and in their support.... It should be so arranged that all the inhabitants should contribute something towards the [maintainance of the school fund], and all those who are benefited directly by it should pay, in proportion to such benefit, a small sum, but quite enough to interest them in the prudent expenditure of their share of the school moneys."

The objection to a liberal education being too freely given for the benefit of the learned professions seems to have been urged even in these days. Dr. Duncombe answers it in the following language:—

"It has been supposed that there are too many in the learned professions already, and that, therefore, there are too many who obtain a liberal education. But this opinion is founded upon two errors: One is, that every liberally educated man must be above manual labor, and must, therefore, enter one of the learned professions; and the other is, that all who do enter these professions do it, and have a right to do it, from personal and family interests, and not for the public good—whereas a liberal education ought not to unfit a man, whether in his physical constitution or his feelings, for active business in any honest employment; and neither ought men who enter any of the learned professions to excuse themselves from labor and privation for the good of the world. There is a great and pernicious error on this subject."

The question of free education is thus discussed by Dr. Duncombe:—

"Nothing is more important in the formation of an enterprising character than to let the youth early learn his own powers; and in order to this, he must be put upon his own recourses, and must understand, if he is ever [to be] anything, he must make himself, and that he has within himself all the means for his own advancement. It is not desirable, therefore, that institutions should be so richly endowed as to furnish the means of education free of expense to those who are of an age to help themselves; nor is it desirable that any man, or any society of men, should furnish an entirely gratuitous education to the youth of the Province. All the necessary advantages for educating himself ought to be put within the reach of the young man, and if, with these advantages, he cannot do much towards it he is not worthy of an education."

After discussing several other topics in his report, Dr. Duncombe made a striking forecast of the educational future of Upper Canada. He said:—

"Was there ever a more auspicious period than the present for literary reform? If I rightly understand the signs of the times, we stand upon the threshold of a new dispensation in the science of education, and especially in the history of common schools, colleges and universities in this Province. The flattering prospects of our being permitted legally to dispose of the school lands of this Province, so long dormant—the sale and appropriation of the clergy reserves for the purposes of education, and, above all by our having control of the other natural resources of the Province, we shall be enabled to provide respectably and permanently for the support of literary institutions *in every part of the Province*, while by remodelling the charter of King's College, so as to adapt the institution to the present state of science of education, and the wishes and wants of the people of this Province.... With such charming prospects before us, with what alacrity and delight can we approach the subject of education to make liberal, permanent and efficient provision for the education of all the youth of Upper Canada, to cause 'the blind to see, the deaf to hear and the dumb to speak,' and, above all, to make certain and extensive provision for the support of schools for teachers and tutoresses."...

It is sad to think that to the writer of these cheering, hopeful words, the future so vividly pictured by him became suddenly darkened, and the pleasant hopes in which he then indulged were never realized by him, or by many of those who, more than half a century ago, were like him so active in promoting the great cause of popular and collegiate education in this Province. Within one year Dr. Duncombe was a "proscribed rebel," as were many others who with him saw as in a vision the future which, he then pictured for Upper Canada.

SUMMARY OF, AND REFLECTIONS ON, THESE EDUCATIONAL EFFORTS,

FROM 1830 TO 1839.

During the next session of the Legislature, in the winter of 1836, Mr. Burwell sought to give effect to Dr. Duncombe's liberal resolution of the preceding session, viz., to provide, out of the public in revenue, a grant of $80,000 a year for support of the common schools. He proposed two resolutions: one was to the effect that $40,000 a year be granted out of the public revenue for the support of these schools; the other was as follows:—

> "That the sum of ten thousand pounds ($40,000), be raised annually by assessment, by order of the Quarter Sessions in the several districts on the ratable property of the inhabitants, in aid of the Provincial grant for the common school fund, in the same manner as other assessments are now made."

When the matter came before the House of Assembly in February, 1837, the committee of supply reported a grant of only $22,400 for the year. The assessment proposition was not adopted, as the question of local taxation for school purposes though often before it had not yet been practically entertained by the Legislature.

Next year, however, another effort was made to provide somewhat liberally for the common schools. But as the Bill as passed by the House of Assembly, embodied in it the principle of local taxation for schools for the first time, it was not concurred in by the Legislative Council. That body proposed a conference to explain the reason, and appointed the Honorable Messrs. Allan and Hamilton as its conferees. The House of Assembly nominated Messrs. Boulton, Cartwright, Thompson and Rykert as its representatives at the conference.

The Legislative Council stated that:—

> "It could not pass the Bill, because it proposes to levy an assessment at the discretion of the Justice of the Peace, to the extent of $1\frac{1}{2}$d. [3 cents] in the £ [$4] to support Common Schools; and as acts have lately passed imposing rates on the inhabitants of several of the districts, for the purpose of defraying the expense of building jails and court-houses and for the construction of macadamized roads, the Council fear that the proposed assessment for common school education might be burthensome," etc.

Thus, because jails, court-houses and roads were considered more necessary and important than schools, the last Act for the promotion of education ever passed by the Upper Canada House of Assembly was rejected by the Legislative Council! Such was the untoward state of affairs when the Legislative Union of Upper and Lower Canada took place in 1840.

EXTRACTS FROM OFFICIAL REPORTS ON EDUCATION IN UPPER CANADA IN 1838.

I shall now give a few extracts from official returns illustrative of the state of education in the Province in 1838 and 1839, while these efforts of improvements were being made. They also show how entirely practical were the views of those who took an active part in educational affairs of the time, how keenly alive they were to the educational deficiencies of those days.

Other extracts from official reports and proceedings of the House of Assembly might be given to illustrate this part of the subject, but they would make this retrospect too long. They are all of a most interesting and instructive character, and well deserve publication in a connected form. They throw a vivid light upon the educational chaos which existed at the time. They also show how enlightened comparatively, as well as how darkened also, were the views of those who took part on both sides in the educational debates and proceedings of those years—especially during 1830,—1836, 1838 and 1839. What were then problematical theories and merely tentative schemes, are to-day educational truisms and successful fields of operation.

The growth of the schools under the fitful system which prevailed in Upper Canada from 1816 to 1842 was painfully slow. The number of what was called "schools" was small, and the quality of them, with rare exceptions, was exceedingly inferior. Anything beyond the three R's was generally taught by itinerants. Dr. Ryerson mentions in an autobiographical letter, as an example, that his knowledge of English grammar was derived entirely from the "lectures" of a peripatetic teacher of that subject. He also mentions several of his after contemporaries who acquired a knowledge of grammar and other special subjects in the same way. No one, as he said to me, ever heard in these days of the possibility of a "royal road to learning." It was hard work, of the hardest kind, and few ever dreamt of reaching a higher eminence than that of mastering the first two R's—Reading and 'Riting. Arithmetic was approached with caution, and its higher "developments" with consternation. How could such a state of things be otherwise when "transient persons" and "common idlers" were with rare exceptions, the kind of "teachers" employed. Education had no money value then, except in so far as it receded from a rate of payment to that of a day laborer or a pensioner.

The following are the extracts from the official reports:—

INFLUENCES BY AMERICAN TEACHERS AND SCHOOL BOOKS DEPRECATED.

Schools in the Home District—No United States books permitted.—The schoolmasters, with the exception of two Americans who have been long in the Province, are all British subjects—that they have all taken the oath of allegiance—that during the last year the salary allowed was £10 (ten pounds each), and no books from the United States are permitted to be used in the schools.—*John Strachan, Wm. Allan, Toronto, 8th March, 1839.*

Schools in the Eastern District—Transitory Teachers.—Were the allowance to be increased teachers would come forward better prepared and be induced to remain. Many at present seem to continue for a few months, as a matter of convenience, and to assist themselves in following other occupations, which greatly retards the improvement of the children.—*Joseph Aderson, D. McDonell, Cornwall, 9th May, 1839.*

Schools in the Western District: Their State and Suggestions for Improvement.—The situation of the school houses is not always judiciously chosen, it being situated often more for the convenience of some one influential person than for that of the inhabitants generally of the settlement.

The school-house is often a wretched log hut, or a ruinous building altogether unfit for the purpose—especially in the winter season.

In too many cases the teachers are badly qualified for the task which they undertake; and some of them having taken up the profession more from necessity than choice are seldom permanent, and consequently very ineffectual teachers.

The remuneration which the teachers of common schools receive for their services are by no means sufficient to induce respectable and well qualified teachers to undertake the irksome and laborious task.

Hints for the Improvement of the Schools of the Province (condensed).—1. The school should be erected in a dry and healthy situation if possible, and situated so as to suit the majority of the inhabitants of the settlement in which it is erected. It should be a neat and commodious building, sufficiently large to render it airy and healthy in the summer season and well finished inside and out to cause it to be comfortable in the winter.

2. A comfortable dwelling should be erected for the accommodation of the teacher and his family.

3. Teachers throughout the Province might be divided into three classes, allowance from Government to be not less than £100, £75 and £50 respectively.

4. Every teacher, previous to receiving any appointment, should be examined as to his literary acquirements, his political opinions and his moral character.

5. A uniform set of elementary books should be compiled and published for

the use of the common schools of the Province, and those republican productions that tend to poison the minds of the youth of the country should be driven out of the Province.

6. A discreet and competent person should be appointed by his Excellency the Lieutenant-Governor to visit the schools in each district eight, or at least four, times in the year to examine the scholars and the internal economy of the schools and to report thereon—*W. Johnson, Sandwich, 21st February, 1839.*

Schools in the London District—"Boarding Round"—American Books.— The Board of Education cannot abstain from remarking upon a system commonly practiced by teachers and generally encouraged by the employers in the country, of receiving the teachers as members or lodgers with each family who are subscribers to the school in succession for the period of engagement, which in its influence and consequence has not hitherto been productive of good; and more especially in cases where the teachers have been Americans, a system than which none can be more mischievous in its effects, added to which the circumstance, as will be seen by reference to the books used in the schools, that a portion of American books, particularly geographies, have been permitted to be used (notwithstanding the Board have the power to order the discontinuance of such) because others could not be procured in the country, nor has any provision been made by the legislature for the formation of depots where proper books could be had.—*John B. Askin, London, 12th February, 1838.*

Names of text-books used in the common schools of Upper Canada in 1838, viz.:—

Old and New Testaments.

Readers—English, Murray's, Canadian and Reading Made Easy.

Spelling Books—Mavor's, Cobb's, Webster's, Graham's, Universal.

Grammars—Murray's, Lennie's, Kirkham's, McCulloch's.

Arithmetics—Walkingame's, Gray's, Dillworth's, Daboll's, Watson's, Pike's, Adams', Morrison's, Hutton's, Rogers', Bailey's, Hall's, Joyce's, Keith's, Allison's, Bonnycastle's.

Geographies—Goldsmith's, Hutton's, Olney's, Woodbridge's, Willett's, Evans', Stewart's, Parley's, Elvey's.

History—English, Goldsmith's, Tytler's, Hume's, Simpson's.

Geometry and Euclid—Ingram's, Hutton's.

Dictionaries—Walker's, Cobb's, Walker Johnson's.

Miscellaneous—Dillworth's Teachers' Assistant, Burham's Primer, Mason's Primer, Child's A, B, C, Scott's Lessons, Morrison's Book-keeping, Blake's Natural Philosophy, Blair's Rhetoric.

Number of schools in Upper Canada in 1838 (estimated), 835.

EXTRACTS FROM THE REPORT OF A COMMISSION APPOINTED TO ENQUIRE INTO THE SUBJECT OF EDUCATION IN UPPER CANADA IN 1839.

The Commissioners appointed to conduct this enquiry were the Rev. Dr. McCaul, Rev. H. J. Grasett and S. B. Harrison, Esq. James Hopkirk, Esq., was appointed Secretary. The following are the extracts:

Preliminary Educational History.—In 1797 both Houses of the Legislature petitioned the King for an appropriation of waste lands of the Crown to form a fund for the support of a Grammar School in each district and a College or University for instruction in the different branches of a liberal education. In 1807 an Act, limited to four years, was passed granting £800 for the support of eight district Grammar Schools. In 1808 the limiting clause (to four years) was repealed. In 1816 an Act establishing common schools was passed and £6,000 were granted for their support. In 1819 an amending Act was passed requiring annual examinations in the schools; that reports to the district Board of Education should be made each year; that "ten children of the poorer inhabitants," to be selected by ballot, should receive free tuition in each Grammar School, and that trustees should give certificates to teachers. In 1820 the grant to common schools was reduced from £6,000 to £2,500 per annum. In 1824 £150 per annum was granted for the supply of common schools, with books, tracts, etc., and that teachers must be examined and licensed by the District Board of Education, one member of which might certify as to the ability of the teacher before the payment to him of the public grant. In 1833, the annual grant to common schools was increased from £2,500 to £5,650. No grants to a teacher is to be made "unless the trustees shall make it appear that they have made provision for his support so as to secure him for his services in a sum at least equal to double the amount which may be allotted by the Board of Education from the public money." No school legislation took place during the years from 1833 to 1841.

District Grammar Schools.—The Commissioners made several recommendations for the improvement of the schools, viz:—1. Uniformity in the system applicable to all the schools. 2. Examination of teacher, so as to test his qualification for the office of teaching. 3. Assistant in each school where there are 30 pupils. 4. School-house built on a uniform plan. 5. Admission of a certain number of free pupils. 6. Quarterly reports from each school and systematic inspection of them.

Common Schools.—The Commissioners also made recommendation for the improvement of these schools, viz.:—1. That there should be a model school with two rooms in each township, and at least two acres of land attached thereto for the use of the master. 2. In each of these schools there should be a male and female teacher (married desirable), and, in addition, other "teachers licensed to itinerate through the township, beyond the sphere of the permanent school," say at places "more than two miles distant from it." "Thus provision is made for one permanent and four occasional schools in each township." 3. Fees to be $2 per quarter, while one pupil in five might be admitted free. 4. The subjects of the instruction should be: Spelling, reading, writing, the Holy Scriptures, geography, history, arithmetic, book-keeping, mensuration, and in girl's school sewing and knitting. 5. Books should be provided at a cheaper rate from Britain, or a series of compilations, or republications should be prepared and printed here, and that they should be appointed to be used in all the schools of the Province. 6. The general control of the schools should be vested in a Board of Commissioners, with a secretary at Toronto. One of the Board should be chairman and inspector general of the schools—having control over the Grammar and Common Schools, and should be the medium of communication between the District Boards and the Council of King's College. 7. There should be elected township director of schools. The Commissioners add:—

Normal School.—"No plan of education can be efficiently carried out without the establishment of schools for the training of teachers." They, therefore, recommended that the Central School of Toronto should be a Normal School—others to be added afterwards.

Grants.—The Commissioners recommend that £21,410 be granted for District Grammar Schools—£12,000 from the sale of Grammar School lands, and £24,300 for Common Schools—£15,000 of the latter to be raised by taxation at the rate of $\frac{3}{4}$d. in the £.

EDUCATIONAL OPINIONS OF PROMINENT PUBLIC MEN IN 1839.

Hon. G. S. Boulton.—In his replies to the Commissioners, he said:—Teachers should be British subjects and should be examined by the Board of Education and approved previous to appointment. Each teacher should receive at least $20 per annum, exclusive of fees from pupils.... I recommend the passage of an Act appropriating 500,000 acres of land for the support of Common Schools, as proposed in the last session of the Legislature by a joint committee of both Houses."

Hon. Wm. Morris, in his reply to the Commissioners, said:—The hundreds of the youth of the country who, for want of convenient institutions of learning, have been sent to and educated in the neighboring Republic, where, if they have not imbibed a predilection for that form of government, have been greatly exposed to the danger of losing that attachment to monarchical government, and the principles of the British Constitution, which is the essential duty of those who administer the affairs of this colony to cherish in the minds of the rising generation.

Hon. James Crooks.—The system of Common Schools, although in some instances abused by the employment of improper persons, indeed sometimes aliens, as teachers, yet, on the whole, I think highly beneficial; perhaps were the system of parochial schools, as established in Scotland, with such modification as would be necessary under the different circumstances of this Province, engrafted upon the Common School system, it might be found to work well.

Hon. P. B. De Blacquiere.—The present condition of teachers is truly wretched, and reflects great disgrace upon the nation, and what but the actual results can or could be expected? I think a difficulty will arise as to finding inspectors properly qualified, or who, in the present state of the country, can be trusted....

Rev. Robert McGill.—I know the qualifications of nearly all the Common School teachers in this (Niagara) District, and do not hesitate to say, that there is not more than one in ten fully qualified to instruct the young in this the humblest department. I should doubt, therefore, whether the money granted to them being an equivalent good, or whether the state of education in this Province would be worse were those funds entirely withdrawn.

Rev. Robert Murray.[37]—The great difficulty attending any change in the present wretched system of education in the Province is to ensure the efficiency of that scheme which may be adopted in its room. To leave the supervision in the hands of the electors in each district, or to a few individuals appointed by them, probably themselves without education, would certainly tend to perpetuate the system of gross oppression to which teachers have been subjected, and to disappoint the reasonable expectations of the Government.... It appears absolutely necessary to ensure the efficiency of a system (as suggested) that men of education, who themselves have had large experience in the education of youth should be appointed to superintend the whole system of operation....

Malhon Burwell, Esq.—I cannot conceive anything more wanting in efficiency than our present system for Common School education. I annex for the notice of the Commission of Investigation a copy of a Common School bill, which I have several times endeavored to get passed through the House of Assembly.

(NOTE.—See Bishop Strachan's estimate of this bill in next extract.)

Right Rev. Bishop Strachan.—The Common School Bill, drawn up by Mr. Burwell, appears to be an able performance; it has several times been entertained by the House of Assembly, and once passed that body, but was unfortunately lost in the Legislative Council. It is based on true principles, and contains within it the power of expansion as new townships, counties and districts are organized. It may, perhaps, admit of a few modifications, but is, on the whole, by far the best measure for the establishment of common schools which I have seen.

SEPARATE EDUCATIONAL FORCES SHAPING THEMSELVES IN UPPER CANADA.

I will now take up the thread of the historical narrative of education in Upper Canada from page — of this Retrospect.

During the early settlement period, and that preceding the union of Upper and Lower Canada in 1840, two social forces (which took an educational form later on), were slowly shaping themselves into an antagonism to each other which culminated in the events or political crisis of 1837-38. This was apparent from the position which the representatives of these forces assumed on the religious, political and other questions of the day. As yet the question of an educational system for the Province—beyond that of a University and district Grammar Schools—had, down to 1836, taken no definite shape in the public mind. Indeed, such a thing, as we now regard it, was not deemed practical, except by a few leading men, as I have shown, who were years in advance of their times.

NOTED REPRESENTATIVE EDUCATIONAL LEADERS—DR. STRACHAN AND DR. RYERSON.

It will simplify my statement of the case if I revert back to the transition period between the establishment of the district Grammar Schools in 1809 and the university charter of 1827; and from thence take a somewhat prospective view of events in the order in which they afterwards transpired. For convenience I would, therefore, select two noted men of their times as representatives of the two social forces to which I have referred, and of the opposite opinions on education and other subjects which then prevailed.

The first was the Rev. Dr. Strachan (afterwards first Church of England Bishop of Toronto), and the other was the Rev. Dr. Ryerson, the representative and trusted leader of the members of the Methodist Church in the Province.

Dr. Strachan was the undoubted representative of the English and particularly the Scotch views on educational matters. Dr. Ryerson, on the other hand, was the equally true and faithful exponent of the British Colonial, or United Empire Loyalist, views and opinions on the same subject. What these latter views and opinions were may be gathered from a reference to the educational chapter in the colonial history of the thirteen colonies, as given in an earlier portion of this Retrospect.

THE EDUCATIONAL EFFORTS OF THE U. E. LOYALISTS AND THE RULING PARTY.

The first settlers of Upper Canada were "exiled tories," so called, from the revolted colonies. In that, and in the other Provinces, they were warmly received and welcomed as the heroic defenders of the royal cause. They sacrificed everything but their principles and their honor in maintaining "the unity of the Empire." Even after the struggle was ended, they adhered to the "lost cause" with the same devotion as they had shown in following the royal standard, not only to victory, but even to disaster and defeat. They were men of wonderful resolution and daring, as well as of superior intelligence. Such were the first settlers of Upper Canada.

Soon after the arrival of the "U. E. Loyalists" in Upper Canada, a tide of emigration set in, chiefly from the three kingdoms. These immigrants brought with them the feelings and habits of home life in the old world, with the opinions and prejudices of their class, illustrating the truth of the old Latin quotation, "*Cælum, non animum, mutant qui trans mare currunt.*"

By degrees portions of the U. E. Loyalists and of these immigrants, whose views on "Church and State" coincided, united their forces and formed a powerful and dominant party. They ruled the Province with a high hand for many years. From their social position and frequent intermarriage they became a compact and exclusive party, and were distinguished by the *sobriquet* of the "Family Compact." Against this powerful party was arrayed many of the U. E. Loyalists and their descendants, and the entire liberal and progressive party.

It is sufficient to say in this connection that under the skillful leadership of Dr. Ryerson and other prominent men of moderate views who acted with him, the power of the Family Compact was broken, the compact itself was gradually dissolved. Its opponents became in turn the ruling party in this Province, a position which their legitimate successors still occupy.

The Family Compact party, in the heyday of their power and influence, were not averse to education. Far from it; for they were men of education themselves. But it took the form of zeal for higher education and for the higher classes. Rev. Dr. Strachan, who was the most energetic and powerful leader of this party, occupied a seat in the Legislative Council (Senate) by appointment of the Governor. He devoted all his energies to the establishment of a university, with district classical schools as feeders. He practically ignored elementary schools, or rather made no provision for them; and it was not until nine years after these district classical schools were established that the U. E. Loyalists, (combined with the progressive party of which it formed no inconsiderable portion), were able to get a measure passed by the Legislature for the establishment and maintenance of common schools.[38]

AN EDUCATIONAL GLANCE BACKWARDS.

But in order to understand more fully the sequence of events which led to the development of the educational spirit in this Province, it will be necessary to give a condensed summary of the facts. With this historical background in prospective view, the distinguishing features of that comprehensive system of education which, in later years, Dr. Ryerson was privileged to found, can be more clearly seen.

The U. E. Loyalists removed to British America in 1783, the year of their exile. Most of them settled in Upper Canada, along the north shore of the Upper St. Lawrence, and the corresponding margin of Lakes Ontario and Erie. They brought with them from the old colonies their educational traditions and their devotion to the flag of the Empire. Those of them who had settled along the Bay of Quinté, united in 1789, in framing a memorial to Governor-General Lord Dorchester (Sir Guy Carleton), in which lamenting the educational privations which they had endured since their settlement in Canada, they prayed the Governor to establish a "seminary of learning" at Frontenac (Kingston). Their prayer was granted, so far as the setting apart of lands for the support of the seminary was concerned, as well as the support of schools wherever the expatriated colonials had settled, or might settle, in the country.

Immediately after the passing of the Constitutional or Quebec Act, of 1791, by which, among other things, Upper Canada was separated from Quebec, the Governor of the new Province (J. Graves Simcoe), sought the co-operation of the Church of England Bishop (Mountain), of Quebec, who had ecclesiastical jurisdiction over both Provinces, in urging upon the Home Government the necessity of providing for a University and for classical schools in Upper Canada. Provision for elementary schools formed no part of this scheme. The British Colonial idea of providing for such schools never crossed the minds of the leaders of public opinion in these days nor that of the bishop. They were chiefly Englishmen, with the old-fashioned English ideas of those times, that the education of the masses was unnecessary, for it would tend to revolution and the upsetting of the established order of things.

In April, 1795, Governor Simcoe addressed a letter to the Protestant Episcopal Bishop of Quebec—then having jurisdiction in Upper Canada—urging him to seek to promote the establishment of a "Protestant Episcopal University" in Upper Canada. The reasons which he gave for this appeal were characteristic of the English Churchmen and of the times, and reveal somewhat of the social and religious state of the colony. They showed, too, that he was a statesman as well as a Churchman. He said:

> The people of this Province enjoy the forms as well as the privileges of the British constitution. They have the means of governing themselves; and, having nothing to ask, must ever remain a part of the British Empire, provided they shall become sufficiently capable and enlightened to understand their relative situation and to manage their own power to the public interest. Liberal education seems to me, therefore, to be indispensably necessary; and the completion of it by the establishment of a university in the capital of the country, * * * would be most useful to inculcate just principles, habits, and manners into the rising generation; to coalesce the different customs of the various descriptions of settlers * * * into one form. In short, from distinct parts and ancient prejudices to new-form, as it were, and establish one nation, and thereby strengthen the union with Great Britain and preserve a lasting obedience to His Majesty's authority.

> I naturally should wish that the clergy requisite for offices in the university, in the first instance, should be Englishmen, if possible. * * * I most earnestly hope that * * * by giving the means of proper education in this Province, both in its rudiments and in its completion, that from ourselves we may raise up a loyal, and in due progress, a learned clergy, which will speedily tend to unite not only the Puritans within the Province, but the clergy of the Episcopal Church, however dispersed * * * and on all sides, to bring within the pale [of the Episcopal Church] in Upper Canada a very great body of sectaries, who in my judgment, as it were, offer themselves to its protection and re-union.

> These objects would be materially promoted by a university in Upper Canada, which might, in due progress, acquire such a character as to become the place of education to many persons beyond the extent of the King's dominions. * * * The Episcopal clergy in Great Britain, from pious motives as well as policy, are materially interested that the Church should increase in this Province. I will venture to prophesy its preservation depends upon a university being erected therein. * * * I have not the smallest hesitation in saying that I believe if a Protestant Episcopal university should be proposed to be erected (even in the United States) the British nation would liberally subscribe to the undertaking. * * * The universities of England, I make no doubt, would contribute to the planting of a scion from their respectable stock in this distant colony.

There are two or three things worth noticing in this vigorous letter of the Governor:—

(1) Among the objects sought to be attained by the establishment of a university was the conservation of "the privileges of the British Constitution"; (2) the fusing of the various nationalities represented in the colony; (3) the

absorption of "Puritans" and "sectaries" into the Episcopal Church; (4) the growth and spread of loyalty to the King's authority.

Two things also are noticeable: First, the Governor did not ignore, or underestimate, the necessity of popular education, or "education in the rudiments;" second, he gives no hint of a desire to appropriate the public domain to the building up of an "Episcopal university." On the other hand, he assumes that, if done at all, it is to be aided by contributions from England. I call attention to these two points, from the fact that they were quite lost sight of by those who afterwards took up the cause of university education in Upper Canada where he had left it.

PROVISION FOR HIGHER EDUCATION IN U. C. BY THE IMPERIAL GOVERNMENT.

Governor Simcoe, having received a higher appointment in the colonial service, left soon after. The Bishop of Quebec, however, acted upon his suggestion and wrote to the Colonial Minister on the subject, in June, 1796. In November, 1797, the Legislature of Upper Canada addressed a memorial to King George III, asking:

"That His Majesty would be graciously pleased to direct his Government in this Province to appropriate a certain portion of the waste lands of the Crown as a fund for the establishment and support of a respectable grammar school in each district thereof, and also of a college, or university, for the instruction of the youth in the different branches of liberal knowledge."

To this memorial the King directed a gracious answer to be sent. The duke of Portland, Colonial Minister, therefore instructed the acting Governor, President Russell, to give practical effect to the prayer of the petitioners. In doing so he used the following language:

[His Majesty] being always ready ... to assist and encourage the exertions of his Province in laying the foundation for promoting sound learning and a religious education, has condescended to express his [desire] to comply with the wishes of the Legislature ... in such a manner as shall be judged to be most effectual—

First, by the establishment of free grammar [classical] schools in those districts in which they are called for, and—

Secondly, in due process of time, by establishing other seminaries of a larger and more comprehensive nature, for the promotion of religious and moral learning, and the study of the arts and sciences.

Such were the terms in which the King, through his Colonial Minister, intimated his desire that classical and university learning should be promoted in this Province. The very comprehensiveness and express terms of the duke of Portland's dispatch on this subject gave rise to a protracted controversy in after years, especially as the controverted expressions were embodied in substance in the royal charter for a university obtained in 1827 by Rev. Dr. Strachan (afterwards first Church of England Bishop of Toronto). Around the expressions—"religious education," "religious and moral learning," and "other seminaries of a larger and more comprehensive nature," etc., a fierce war was waged for many years, which, though virtually over now, has yet left traces of the bitter conflict.

The result of the instructions to President Russell was, that 549,217 acres of crown lands was set apart for the twofold purpose set forth in the Colonial Minister's dispatch. Of these acres, 225,944 were, in 1827, devoted to the university that was virtually established, on paper, in that year, and by royal charter in 1828.

As these lands thus set apart were, in those early days, unproductive of revenue, nothing could be done to give practical effect to the gracious act of the King. A principal for the proposed university was, however, selected in Scotland. The position was first offered to the afterwards justly celebrated Rev. Dr. Thomas Chalmers, but declined. It was then offered to a successful parish schoolmaster, Mr. (afterwards so distinguished in this Province as the Rev. Dr.) Strachan.

THE REVEREND DOCTOR STRACHAN AS AN EDUCATOR.

Rev. Dr. (afterwards Bishop) Strachan, though not a versatile man, was in many respects a many-sided one. In his day he had to do with all of one great public questions which came before the country. On many of them (and in their settlement), he has left the impress of his active mind and persistent will. This was particularly the case in regard to those questions which more deeply touched the best interests of Canadian life, in its religious and social aspects. And it was a singular yet characteristic fact, that the more he was opposed by those who differed *in toto* from the policy of his acts, the more strenuously he persevered in his purpose—even against the wiser counsels and calmer judgment of many leading public men of his time. But this opens up a question which it is not my purpose to discuss.

Dr. Strachan, as I have said,—although not versatile,—was a many-sided man. And this was quite true in regard to that department of his career which I desire to illustrate. He was both an educator and an educationist. In the former capacity he was successively the parish schoolmaster, near St. Andrew's, and at Kettle, (Scotland). He had there as a pupil the afterwards celebrated Sir David Wilkie. In Canada, he was first a tutor in the family of the Hon. Richard Cartwright, at Kingston; then master of the Cornwall Grammar

School, at which most of the distinguished public men of the Bishop's later years were educated. Subsequently he was Chairman of the Provincial Board of Education at York. He was named by the late Hon. Peter McGill as first Principal of McGill College, Montreal—although he never was in a position to undertake its duties. He was afterwards President of King's College, Toronto, and subsequently President of Trinity College University.

In his capacity as an educator, Dr. Strachan was considered one of the most successful teachers which this Province has yet produced. His aim was to call into active play the varied mental powers of his pupils, and to stimulate any desire which they had to excel in knowledge and virtue. One of his earliest *brochures* is *a Letter to his Pupils*, and is in the nature of an appeal on behalf of the Christian religion. This, he inscribed, "as a mark of esteem to Mr. Andrew Stuart and Mr. James Cartwright, students-at-law." This letter was printed at Montreal, in 1807, in the quaint old type of the time. It is evidently a warning appeal against the infidelity and excesses of the French revolutionists.

Dr. Strachan's early and practical experience as a teacher gave to him an additional and keen sense of the educational wants of the country. His success as an educator proved to him what could be done in that direction. It also enlisted his feelings and fired his ambition to be the founder of an institution of superior learning, in which the young men of the Province could be thoroughly educated. The education of the masses was not provided for by him, but in an Act passed in 1819 and relating to classical schools (which he promoted), it was agreed—

> That in order to extend the benefits of a liberal education to promising children of the poorer inhabitants, trustees [of common schools wherever established] shall have the power of sending scholars, not exceeding ten in number, to be chosen by lot every four years, to be taught gratis at the [classical] schools.

Thus, in this exceptional manner, provision was made so that, should a limited number of the children of the poorer inhabitants develop ability or taste for learning, they should not be wholly excluded from the privileges so liberally provided for children of the richer classes. These class distinctions have, happily, forever disappeared from our statute book. They were no doubt conceived in a benevolent spirit, and were characteristic of the social ethics of the times, but they were pernicious as a principle to embody in a school law.

In his "Appeal" in behalf of a university in Upper Canada, published early in 1827, Dr. Strachan gave a fuller expression to this idea of providing education only for the wealthier classes. He said:—

> It is indeed quite evident that the consequences of a university ... possessing in itself sufficient recommendations to attract to it the sons of the most opulent families, would soon

be visible in the greater intelligence and more confirmed principles of loyalty of those who would be called to various public duties required in the country—*i.e.*, the governing classes.

In justice to Dr. Strachan, it is proper to state that a few years afterwards (in reply to a question put to him by a committee of the House of Assembly) he laid down a broader, a nobler and a more comprehensive principle in regard to a system of national education. He said:—

The whole expense [of education] in a free country like this should be defrayed by the public; that promising boys, giving indication of high talent, though poor, might have an opportunity of cultivating their faculties, and, if able and virtuous, taking a lead in the community.

LACK OF COMPREHENSIVENESS IN THE EDUCATIONAL POLICY OF THE TIMES.

The policy of the country in regard to education in these early times was further marked by a lack of comprehensiveness in its aims.

The framework of the educational system, then projected, was constructed on a principle the very reverse of natural. And this fact led to the existence, subsequently, and for many years, of a singular anachronism as the result of its application of that principle. Thus, in 1797, lands were set apart in Upper Canada by the Crown for the establishment of district grammar schools and a university. But no provision was thought of for the establishment of elementary schools. These grammar schools were first established in 1807— eight in all, viz., at Sandwich, Townsend (London District), Niagara, York, Cobourg, Kingston, Augusta (District of Johnstown), and Cornwall. But no provision was made for elementary schools (and then only for four years) until 1816—nine years after the district grammar schools were established.

Dr. Strachan's feelings in this matter were evidently in harmony with this spirit of the times, and he directed his efforts exclusively to the establishment of these higher institutions of learning. He never lost sight, however, of the crowning institution of all—the university. His speeches and addresses on education all pointed to "this consummation, devoutly to be wished."

Referring to this educational anomaly, or anachronism, of establishing higher institutions of learning before providing for elementary schools, an English resident in a book entitled "Three Years in Canada," and published in 1839, thus forcibly points out the singular want of foresight in this matter. He says:—

"The Provincial Board of Education either assumed that elementary education in Upper Canada had attained its zenith or deemed it better to begin at the apex and work downward to the base of the structure they were called upon to rear than to follow the old-fashioned custom of first laying the foundation and then working upwards."

The fact was, and the chief reason for the perpetration of this educational anachronism was, that the friends of popular education, while all-powerful in the House of Assembly, were few and consequently uninfluential in the Legislative Council. They were, therefore, not able at all times to influence that body so as to secure its assent to the elementary education bills passed by the popular branch. We have seen that, in 1838, the Council refused to concur in the Common School Bill passed in that year by the House of Assembly. Before another School Act was introduced, both Houses had ceased to exist in the Union of the two provinces in 1840.

REV. DR. STRACHAN'S REASONS FOR ESTABLISHING A UNIVERSITY IN UPPER CANADA.

The reasons which Dr. Strachan gave for urging the early establishment of a Provincial University were reasonable and weighty in themselves, had the other necessary kind of school been established and provided for. I shall give these reasons in Dr. Strachan's own words. They are characteristic of the Bishop's own feelings in regard to American institutions and their influence on the young. He said:—

> "There is not in either province any English seminary ... at which a liberal education can be obtained. Thus the youth of 300,000 Englishmen have no opportunity of receiving instruction within the Canadas in law, medicine or divinity.

> "The consequence is that many young men ... are obliged to look beyond the province for the last two or three years of their education—undoubtedly the most important and critical period of their whole lives ... The youth are, therefore, in some degree, compelled to look towards the United States, where means of education, though of a description far inferior to those of Great Britain, are yet superior to anything within the province, and a growing necessity is arising of sending them to finish their education in that country."

Dr. Strachan then proceeds to point out in his own graphic language, the peculiarly adverse influences to which loyal Canadians from youth were then subjected while attending schools and universities in the United States. He says:—

> "Now, in the United States a custom prevails unknown to or unpractised in any other nation; in all other countries morals and religion are made the basis of public instruction, and the first books put into the hands of children teach them the domestic, the social and religious virtues; but in the United States politics pervade the whole system of education; the school books, from the very first elements, are stuffed with praises of their own institutions, and breathe hatred to everything English."

Dr. Ryerson came to the same conclusions as did Dr. Strachan in regard to the character of American school books. Speaking on the same subject, twenty years afterwards, he said:—

> "With very few exceptions American school books abound in statements and allusions

prejudicial to the institutions and character of the British nation."

Dr. Strachan still further refers to the anti-British influences of education obtained by Canadian youth in the United States. He said:—

"To such a country our youth may go, strongly attached to their native land ... but by hearing its institutions continually depreciated, and those of the United States praised ... some may become fascinated with that liberty which has degenerated into licentiousness, and imbibe, perhaps unconsciously, sentiments unfriendly to things of which Englishmen are proud."

Dr. Strachan then proceeded to point out the advantages of having the youth of the province "carefully nurtured within the British Dominions." He said:—

"The establishment of an university at the seat of Government will complete a system of education in Upper Canada from the letters of the alphabet to the most profound investigations of science.... This establishment, by collecting all the promising youth of the colony into one place, will gradually give a new tone to public sentiment and feelings ... producing the most beneficial effects through the whole province. It is, indeed, quite evident that the consequences of an university ... possessing in itself sufficient recommendations to attract to it the sons of the most opulent families would soon be visible in the greater intelligence and more confirmed principles of loyalty of those who would be called to various public duties required in the country."

From these wise and practical remarks, it will be seen how truly Bishop Strachan estimated the great advantages to the youth of the country of university training obtained within our borders. In this view he was far-seeing enough. But yet his range of vision, as to its beneficial effects, did not extend beyond "the sons of the most opulent families"—which was another indication of the prevailing feeling of the times, that higher education in the form of university training was not thought of even for "the promising children of the younger inhabitants." Happily our public men, and the Bishop himself, outgrew this narrow feeling and social prejudice. He even lived to see, and with great satisfaction as to the results, that, under the fostering care of men of large sympathies and more generous impulses, the doors of the educational institutions of the country, from the highest to the lowest, were thrown wide open to every boy, rich and poor, high and low, and to all the youth of the province, without distinction of race, or creed, or social rank.

Rev. Dr. Strachan succeeded in getting a Royal Charter for the university in 1828. This charter virtually placed the proposed university under the control of the Episcopal Church. When its terms were known in Upper Canada it was fiercely assailed. The charter was subsequently modified, in deference to public opinion; but it was not until many years afterwards that the university was, by statute, declared to be free from denominational control. Out of the controversy which the Duke of Portland's despatch and the charter caused, arose other colleges and universities, viz, Victoria and Queen's.

REV. DR. STRACHAN, THE FOUNDER OF TWO UNIVERSITIES IN TORONTO.

In the Rev. Dr. Scadding's most interesting sketch of the "First Bishop of Toronto,—a Review and a Study"—occurs the following striking passage in regard to the founding of the "Twins of Learning" in Toronto:—

The results of the life of the first Anglican Bishop of Toronto are tangible realities.... He built the principal church edifice appertaining to his own communion four times.... "Twins of Learning" witness for him; he founded two universities in succession (1842 and 1852), both invested with the character borne by such institutions as originally instituted, by Royal charter —procured in both instances by his own personal travail; the later of the two by an individual and solitary effort, to which it is not easy to find a parallel. He saw both of them in operation, investigating, conserving and propagating truth, on somewhat different lines indeed, but probably with co-ordinate utility, as things are. The very park, with its widely renowned avenue, the Champs Elysées of Toronto, in which the bourgeoisie of the place love to take their pastime, are a provision of his—that property having been specially selected by him, as President of King's College, with the same judiciousness and the same careful prescience of the need of amplitude for such purposes which guided him also in choosing the fine site and grounds of Trinity College.

THE UNIVERSITY OF TORONTO.

This university was originally established under the charter obtained by Rev. Dr. Strachan in 1828. But it only existed on paper until 1842-43.

In April, 1842, the corner-stone of the new institution was laid by Governor-General Sir Charles Bagot, (M.A. of Christ Church, Oxford). In June, 1843, it was opened under the style and title of the "University of King's College," Toronto, by the Right Rev. John Strachan, D.D., LL. D., President of the University. In October of that year, an effort was made by Hon. Attorney-General Baldwin to introduce a comprehensive scheme of university reform, but it was defeated in the Legislature. In 1845 and 1847 other abortive attempts were made to "reform" the university; but in 1849 a comprehensive measure was introduced into the Legislature and passed into a law, by which it was reincorporated under the name of the "University of Toronto," and made a purely provincial institution, by placing it under the sole control of the Government, and of a senate and officers appointed by the Government.

In 1853 another Act was passed, under which the University was constituted with two corporations, "The University of Toronto," and "University College," the functions of the former being limited to the examination of candidates for degrees in the several faculties, or for scholarships and honors, and the granting of such degrees, etc.; those of the latter being confined to the teaching of subjects in the Faculty of Arts.[39] By this Act certain institutions, from which students might be examined, were affiliated with the University.

In 1873 further amendments were made in the constitution of the University. The Chancellor was made elective for a period of three years by Convocation, which was then re-established. By this Act the powers of the Senate were extended to all branches of knowledge, literature, science and arts, and also to granting certificates of proficiency to women; the power of affiliation was likewise extended; the Senate was also empowered to provide for local examinations.

Latterly, the faculties of law and medicine have been restored and other extensions of the University course have been made.

THE UNIVERSITY OF VICTORIA COLLEGE, COBOURG.

The Rev. Dr. Ryerson, who was the founder of this University, thus speaks of its early history, in an address to the students when he was appointed its first principal in 1841. He said:—

His late Most Gracious Majesty William IV., of precious memory, first invested this institution, in 1836, with a corporate charter as the Upper Canada Academy—the first institution of the kind established by Royal Charter unconnected with the Church of England, throughout the British colonies. It is a cause of renewed satisfaction and congratulation that, after five year's operation as an academy, it has been incorporated as a university and financially assisted by the unanimous vote of both branches of the Provincial Legislature—sanctioned by more than an official cordiality, in Her Majesty's name, by the late lamented Lord Sydenham, Governor-General, one of whose last messages to the Legislative Assembly was a recommendation to grant £500 as an aid to the Victoria College.... We have buoyant hopes for our country when our rulers and legislators direct their earliest and most liberal attention to in literary institutions and educational interests. A foundation for a common school system in this Province his been laid by the Legislature, which I believe will, at no distant day, exceed in efficiency any yet established on the American continent;[40] and I have reason to believe that the attention of the Government is earnestly directed to make permanent provision for the support of colleges also, that they may be rendered efficient in their operation and accessible to as large a number of the enterprising youth of our country as possible.

This institution originated with the Wesleyan Methodists in 1828-30. The conference in the latter year agreed to establish it as an Academy, and the following year, Dr. Ryerson, in the *Christian Guardian* newspaper, of which he was then editor, issued a strong appeal in behalf of the proposed institution on the 21st April, 1831. On the 7th June, 1832, the foundation stone of the Academy was laid; and on the 18th June, 1836, it was formerly opened under the designation of "Upper Canada Academy." In the previous year Dr. Ryerson was deputed to go to England to collect subscriptions on behalf of the institution. He was there enabled to obtain a Royal Charter for the Academy and a grant of $16,400 from the Local Legislature.

Amongst the last public acts performed by Lord Sydenham was the giving of the Royal assent to a Bill for the erection of the Upper Canada Academy into a College with University powers. This he did on the 27th August, 1841. Dr. Ryerson thus refers to the event, in a letter written from Kingston on that day:—

The establishment of such an institution by the members of the Wesleyan Methodist Church in Canada attests their estimate of education and science; and the passing of such an Act unanimously by both Houses of the Legislature, and the Royal assent to it by His Excellency in Her Majesty's name, is an ample refutation of recent statements and proceedings of the Wesleyan Committee in London ... while the Act itself will advance the paramount interests of literary education amongst Her Majesty's Canadian subjects.... For the accomplishment of this purpose, a grant must be added to the charter—a measure ... honorable to the enlightened liberality of the Government and Legislature. When they are securely laying a broad foundation for popular government, and devising comprehensive schemes for the development of the latent resources of the country, and the improvement of its internal communication, and proposing a liberal system of common school education, free from the domination of every church, and aiding colleges which may have been established by any church, we may rationally and confidently anticipate the arrival of a long-looked for era of civil government and civil liberty, social harmony, and public prosperity.

The Academy was thus incorporated as a University, in August, 1841. In October, 1841, Rev. Dr. Ryerson was appointed the first president of the University, a position which he held until he was appointed Chief Superintendent of Education for Upper Canada in 1844. He was succeeded by the Rev. Dr. Macnab, now rector of Darlington. In 1850 the late accomplished president (Rev. S. S. Nelles, D.D., LL.D.) was appointed. He had been a pupil under Dr. Ryerson, but finished his university education at the Wesleyan University, Middletown, Conn., and graduated there. He received the degree of D.D. from the Queen's University, Kingston, and that of LL.D. from his own university. His career was an unusually long and prosperous one; and under his administration the university has taken high rank amongst the sister universities of Ontario.[41]

In the original appeal made by Dr. Ryerson in England on behalf of the Academy (in 1835), he stated the "specific objects of the institution" to be as follows:—

1. To educate, upon terms equally moderate with similar institutions in the neighboring republic of the United States, and with strict attention to their morals, the youth of Canada generally.

2. To educate for common school masters, free of charge, poor young men of Christian principles and character, and of promising talent, who have an ardent thirst for knowledge.

3. To educate the most promising youth of the recently converted Indian tribes of Canada as teachers to their aboriginal countrymen.[42]

These extracts are highly interesting, as showing the noble and comprehensive aims, in these early days of educational effort, which Dr. Ryerson had in view in founding this valuable institution of learning. He goes on then (apart from these objects) to show the grave necessity which existed for the early establishment of such an institution. He said:—

For want of such an institution upwards of sixty of the youth of Canada are now attending seminaries of learning, under a similar management, in the United States, where nearly two hundred Canadian youth have been taught the elementary branches of a professional education during the last eight years. There is good reason to believe that nearly, if not quite, all the Canadian youth now being taught in the United States seminaries of learning, will return to Canada as soon as this institution shall have been brought into operation....

In behalf, therefore, of this institution—most important to the best interests of a healthy, fertile and rapidly improving British colonial possession, the inhabitants of which have in this, as in other instances, shown the strongest desire to help themselves to the utmost of their very limited means—a respectful and earnest appeal is made to British liberality, an appeal which it is devotedly hoped will be responded to in a manner that will contribute to draw still closer the bonds by which the loyal Province of Upper and the British population of Lower Canada are united to the Mother Country.

This appeal was endorsed by the Governor of the Province, Sir John Colborne (afterwards Lord Seaton), in the following terms:—

The Rev. Egerton Ryerson proceeds to England ... to solicit subscriptions ... to enable [the conference here] to bring into operation a seminary established at Cobourg, in Upper Canada.... As I am persuaded this colony will derive the greatest advantage from the institution and from the exertions of the conference to diffuse religions instruction, I cannot but strongly recommend that it may receive encouragement and support from all persons interested in the welfare of Upper Canada.

The "appeal" was also heartily endorsed by the Hon. Peter McGill, founder of McGill College University, Montreal, and by other distinguished gentlemen and merchants in Montreal. In his letter Mr. McGill referred to Dr. Ryerson as "a gentleman who has distinguished himself in Upper Canada by his writings in defense of religion, order, and good government."

After much delay and great discouragement, Dr. Ryerson succeeded in the objects of his mission—money and a royal charter; but at the close of his mission he writes to the Academy Committee as follows:—

Thus terminated this protracted [business], ... though I had to encounter successive, discouraging and almost insurmountable difficulties [in obtaining the charter]. Not having been able to effect any loan ... on account of the agitated state of the Canadas, and being in suspense as to the result of my application to the Government, I was several months pressed down with anxiety and fear, by this suspense and by reason of the failure of my efforts to obtain relief. In this anxiety and fear my own unassisted resolution and fortitude could not sustain me. I had to rely upon the unfailing support of the Lord my God.

I have given these particulars somewhat in detail, as they afford a striking narrative illustration of the almost insurmountable difficulties which the early pioneers of education in this Province encountered in endeavoring to found these valuable institutions which have been so useful to this country, and which have shed such lustre upon their founders' names. It is also due to Victoria University, and (as I shall show) to Queen's University also to state these particulars, from the fact that the first practical, yet entirely abortive, attempt to make King's College a provincial university, was made in 1843, two years after the Methodists and Presbyterians had, in self-defence, been compelled to found universities of their own. This they did at a great sacrifice.

By the time that the liberation of King's College took place, in 1849-'53, the really provincial universities at Cobourg and Kingston had become recognized as most important factors in our educational system; and from them alone, up to that time, could students of all denominations obtain a university education.

In connection with the university, Faraday Hall, or School of Practical Science, was erected in 1877. It is a handsome and spacious building, and is admirably fitted up for the purpose of science teaching.

THE QUEEN'S COLLEGE UNIVERSITY, KINGSTON.

As early as 1829 it was felt among the members of the United Presbytery of Upper Canada that a seminary, or college, for the training of their ministers was highly desirable. As the management of King's College at Toronto was in the hands of the adherents of the Church of England, it was felt that such an institution could not be made available for Presbyterian theological instruction. A committee of the British House of Commons, to which had been referred petitions from Canada in 1828 and 1830 against the exclusive character of the charter of King's College, Toronto, were disposed to solve the difficulty by suggesting that two theological chairs be established in King's College (and did so recommend)—one for students of the Churches of England and Scotland, respectively. Nothing, however, of the kind was done; nor was there any arts college then open on equal terms to all the youth of the country. The Presbyterians, like the Methodists, had, therefore, to found an institution of their own. Steps were taken by the synod of the Church in 1831 and 1839 to found such an institution. At a meeting held in Hamilton, in November, 1839, the commission appointed for that purpose prepared the draft of a charter for the proposed college. Kingston was selected by the synod as the site for the new institution.

An Act embodying the charter was passed by the Provincial Legislature in February, 1840, incorporating the "University of Kingston." The Act was, however, disallowed by the imperial authorities, on the ground that it conflicted with the royal prerogative of granting charters. A royal charter was, however, issued in 1841, incorporating the institution under the name of Queen's College, with "the style and privileges of a university."

The opening of Queen's took place on the 7th of March, 1842. Rev. Thomas Liddell, D.D., of Edinburgh, was the Principal and Professor of Divinity, and Rev. P. C. Campbell, of Brockville, Professor of Classics. Rev. James Williamson, D.D., LL.D., in 1842, became Professor of Mathematics and Natural Philosophy. He is, therefore, the oldest college professor in

Ontario.

After the opening of King's College, Toronto, in 1843, an agitation commenced with the view to unite the three universities then in operation into a single provincial institution. Many plans were proposed, and several measures tending to that end were introduced into Parliament and fully discussed. In 1843 the Hon. Robert Baldwin introduced a university bill, which, though it presented many popular features, was strongly objected to by the churches named and others also, because it was deficient in providing for religious instruction.

A bill was introduced by Hon. W. H. Draper, in 1845, to amend the law so as to make it more generally acceptable to the religious bodies of the country; and in 1847 the late Hon. John Hillyard Cameron introduced a measure in which it was proposed to devote a large part of the endowment to increased support of high schools and also to largely subsidize the denominational colleges. The measure failed to carry in Parliament, however, and this practically ended the agitation for the union of colleges for many years.

In 1846 Dr. Liddell resigned his position as Principal and returned to Scotland. Rev. J. Machar, D.D., was next appointed Principal, and under his administration there was slow but real improvement.

Rev. Dr. Cook, of Quebec occupied the position of Principal for a time, but he refused to accept the position permanently. Rev. Dr. Leitch was next appointed, but his early death deprived the institution of his services. He was followed by the Rev. Dr. Snodgrass, and on his retirement the Rev. George Monro Grant, D.D., of Halifax, was appointed. Dr. Grant entered on his arduous duties with his accustomed energy, and occupies that position with great acceptance. He is an able speaker and a wise administrator. Queen's College has now faculties of arts, theology, and law, and there are affiliated with it the Royal College of Physicians and Surgeons, also in a prosperous condition, and the Kingston Women's Medical College.

In 1869 it was resolved to make an appeal to the country for aid. The people of Kingston raised about $25,000, and the result of the whole effort was that about $103,000 was raised for the equipment of the college.

In 1878 Principal Grant made the proposition to raise $150,000, in order to provide new buildings, additional professors, and apparatus. The appeal was successful; additional ground of about twenty acres was at once purchased—a site of rare beauty and convenience—and the present noble building was erected.

THE UNIVERSITY OF TRINITY COLLEGE, TORONTO.

The immediate cause of the founding of this College and University was the suppression, in 1849, of the Faculty of Divinity in King's College, now the University of Toronto. In consequence of this the Right Rev. J. Strachan D.D., Bishop of Toronto, issued in February, 1850, a pastoral appeal to members of the Church of England for funds to enable him to establish a Church University and College. In response to this pastoral, the Bishop succeeded in raising a large endowment from voluntary subscriptions from churchmen in Canada, England, and the United States, so that on April 30, 1851, the foundation stone of the college building was laid, and on January 15, 1852, the work of instruction was begun, the staff consisting of four professors in arts, besides those in the faculties of law and medicine. During the last thirty years the endowment has been largely increased by liberal contributions made from time to time, so that the original amount is now about trebled. In 1878 a large and handsome convocation hall was erected, and in 1884 a long felt want was supplied by the erection of a finely proportioned and beautiful chapel.

The University of Trinity College at present consists of the faculty of arts and divinity, of an affiliated Medical School with a commodious building and a large staff of professors, and an affiliated Women's Medical College. Provision is also made for the higher education of women in connection with the Bishop Strachan School in Toronto, and connected with the University is a large school for boys at Port Hope.

The R. C. University College at Ottawa.

The College (or University) of Ottawa is under the direction of the Roman Catholic Church. It was founded in 1848 by the Right Reverend Joseph Eugene Guignes, O.M.I., D.D., first R. C. Bishop of Ottawa. In 1856, the Bishop confided the direction of the college to the "Society of the Oblate Fathers of Mary Immaculate." The total value of the college building and grounds is about $75,000. It has also a good library and cabinet of natural philosophy (or physics), and of chemistry and natural history. The college obtained university powers in 1866. It confers degrees in arts, science, and literature—B. A., B. Sc., B. L., as well as M. A.

The Western University, London.

This institution, in connection with the Church of England in Canada, was incorporated in 1878, with power to affiliate with Huron Theological College and to confer Degrees in Arts, Divinity, Medicine and Law. The affiliation between that College and the University took place in 1881, and the

University was inaugurated in the month of October of that year. The object of its establishment was, as a Church of England Institution in the Diocese of Huron, to obtain the same power of conferring Degrees as was possessed by the sister University of Trinity College; also, that a liberal Education in Arts, Science and Literature might be extended to that extensive portion of the Province of which London is the geographical centre.

THE MCMASTER UNIVERSITY.

By the munificence of the late Hon. Wm. McMaster, McMaster University is being established on a sound financial basis. McMaster Hall, Woodstock College and Moulton College (for ladies) are affiliated institutions.

UPPER CANADA COLLEGE.

Upper Canada College was founded in 1828 upon the model of the great public schools of England, and was endowed with a grant of 66,000 acres of public lands, from which it now derives an annual income of $15,000, in addition to its building and grounds in the city of Toronto. It is governed by a committee of the senate of the Provincial University. The curriculum extends over a six years' course of study in the same number of forms, and embraces the usual subjects.

In other forms, known as the lower and upper modern, commercial and scientific training can be obtained. Scholarships may be established by the different county councils, while four exhibitions have been founded out of the University funds. This college and the high schools constitute the principal feeders of the Collegiate Institutes and provincial University.

ALBERT COLLEGE, BELLEVILLE.

This institution, founded in 1854, was the product of the zeal of the Methodism of that early day. Accordingly, the General Conference of the Methodist Episcopal Church, in 1854, adopted a scheme—initiated in the Bay of Quinté Conference in the preceding year—for the erection and maintenance of an educational institution of high grade in Belleville. Having been chartered by Parliament in 1857 as "Belleville Seminary," it was opened in July of the same year, and entered upon its work under very favorable auspices.

In the year 1886, by Act of Parliament, the name was changed to "Albert College," and a senate created with ample powers. By the terms of the union of the Methodist Churches of Canada, Albert College was retained in Belleville, and adopted by the General Conference of the United Church as a church school. The charter was amended and the college was affiliated to the Victoria University, Cobourg. The senate has full powers to examine, grant prizes, scholarships, medals, honor certificates, and diplomas in music, fine arts, commercial science, collegiate courses, etc.

WOODSTOCK COLLEGE.

Woodstock College, formerly "The Canadian Literary Institute," was founded in 1867, principally through the exertions of the late R. A. Fife, D.D. Under his presidency, ably assisted for eighteen years by Prof. J. E. Wells, M.A., the school constantly increased in efficiency and power, until from a small beginning it has attained its present large proportions and wide influence.

THE SCHOOL OF PRACTICAL SCIENCE, TORONTO.

Prior to the year 1871 there was no institution in the Province for practical instruction in the industrial sciences. In 1870 the Government of the Province issued a commission to Dr. Hodgins, Deputy Superintendent of Education, and to Dr. Machatt of London, directing them to proceed to the United States for the purpose of inspecting and reporting upon any Technical or Science Schools or Colleges there established, as to their buildings, departments of study and general appliances. On their return a report was submitted to the Government, with full details as to the cost of the proposed institution. The Government acted upon the information contained in their report, and with a grant of $50,000 established a "College of Technology" in Toronto. In 1877 the name was changed to the School of Practical Science, and the Hon. Adam Crooks, Q.C., Minister of Education, had a suitable building for it erected close to the Provincial University, four of the University Professors are engaged in Departments of the School. The new building was opened for students in September, 1878.

VARIOUS OTHER COLLEGES AND SCHOOLS, ETC.

There are numerous superior colleges and schools for boys and colleges for ladies in Ontario, but the limits of this paper forbids a further reference to them, or to the other numerous educational institutions—theological, literary and commercial—in the Province.

Rev. Dr. Ryerson's Advocacy of Popular Rights, 1827-1841.[43]

During all this time the friends of popular education were not idle. From 1827 and for many years Dr. Ryerson was engaged in waging war with the opponents of liberal institutions and religious equality. His chief antagonist was Dr. Strachan. The subjects in dispute related to a dominant church, the application of clergy-reserved lands to the purposes of education, and the liberation of the provincial university from exclusive control under the presidency of Dr. Strachan, first as archdeacon and afterwards as bishop. Not being eligible to the popular branch of the Legislature (being a minister), Dr. Ryerson had to develop his powers of resistance to the dominant and ruling party in other directions; and this he did with wonderful success. As a writer and debater few equalled him in his presentation of facts, and in his skill in detecting the weak points of his adversary's position or argument. As a controversialist and pamphleteer he had confessedly no rival. He, therefore, was able to furnish his friends in the House of Assembly with facts and arguments which were irresistible. They passed resolutions and school bills time and again, but could not always induce the Legislative Council (Senate) to concur in their adoption. This state of things continued for many years, and with disastrous effects on the intellectual growth and well-being of the province. This fact is attested by indubitable witnesses, and is recorded in the proceedings of the House of Assembly of the time, as is shown in the extracts from its proceedings which I have already given.

Educational Legislation in the United Parliament of 1841 and 1843.

In 1840 the House of Assembly and Legislative Council of Upper Canada ceased to exist, and the two Provinces of Upper and Lower were united under one Legislature.

The momentous political events which preceded this union, and which led to the total disruption of all political parties and combinations, were very salutary in their effects. Under the liberal policy pursued by the Home Government, after the publication of Lord Durham's report, grievances were redressed, and a broad and comprehensive scheme of popular government inaugurated. The result was that the wise and statesmanlike measures, designed to promote public tranquility and local self-government, were proposed to and adopted by the Legislature.

Amongst these was a measure providing for the establishment of a municipal council in each local division of the Province of Upper Canada (and partly so in Lower Canada) for the regulation of internal matters.

In recommending the scheme of Common School Education to the favorable consideration of the first Parliament of United Canada, in 1841, Lord Sydenham, the first Governor-General, used the following language:—

> A due provision for the education of the people is one of the first duties of the State, and, in this province especially, the want of it is grievously felt. The establishment of an efficient system, by which the blessings of instruction may be placed within the reach of all is a work of difficulty, but its overwhelming importance demands that it should be undertaken. I recommend the consideration of that subject to your best attention, and I shall be most anxious to afford you, in your labours, all the co-operation in my power. If it should be found impossible so to reconcile conflicting opinions as to obtain a measure which may meet the approbation of all, I trust that, at least, steps may be taken by which an advance to a more perfect system may be made, and the difficulty under which the people of this province now labor may be greatly diminished, subject to such improvements hereafter as time and experience may point out.

The enlightened expectations of the Governor-General were, happily, realized. But so diverse were the populations of the two Canadas thus united, and so different were their social conditions, that the School Act then passed was repealed two years afterward (in 1843), and a school bill for each Province was passed by the Legislature in that year. Provision for Roman Catholic and Protestant Separate Schools was made in both Acts.[44]

On this system was ingrafted, by means of a separate Act applicable to the whole Province, a scheme of public education, with a liberal provision ($200,000 per annum) for its maintenance.

ORIGIN OF THE ANNUAL GRANT OF $200,000 FOR THE COMMON SCHOOLS IN 1841.

In a letter to the writer of this Retrospect, from the Hon. Issac Buchanan, dated 11th April. 1883, in reply to some enquiries in regard to the appointment of Dr. Ryerson, Mr. Buchanan thus related the circumstances under which the munificent sum of $200,000 a year was granted by the Legislature in 1841 for the support of the then newly-established Common Schools in Upper and Lower Canada. He said:—"This first attempt of mine to get an endowment for education (out of the Clergy Reserve Fund), failed as there was no responsible government then. But five years afterwards when my election for Toronto had carried Responsible Government, and before the first parliament met, I was talking to the Governor-General (C. Poulett Thompson, Lord Sydenham). He felt under considerable obligation to me for standing in the breach when Mr. Robert Baldwin found that he could not succeed in carrying Toronto.... He spoke of Canada as 'a drag upon the mother country.' I replied warmly ... for I felt sure (as I told him), that if we were allowed to throw the affairs of the Province into regular books ... we would show a surplus over expenditure. His Excellency agreed to my proposal, and I stipulated that, if we showed a yearly surplus, one half would be given as an endowment for an educational system. Happily we found that Upper Canada had a surplus revenue of about £100,000 ($400,000), one half of which the parliament of 1841 laid aside for education, the law stipulating that every District Council getting a share of it would tax locally for as much more, and this constituted the fund of your educational system."

EDUCATIONAL EFFORTS OF DR. RYERSON UP TO THIS TIME.

Up to this time Dr. Ryerson's energies, as I have shown, were wholly engrossed in contending for the civil and religious rights of the people. He had also, ten years before, projected and collected money for the establishment of an academy or college for higher education at Cobourg, on the north shore of Lake Ontario. His efforts in this, and in the establishment of the Victoria College at Cobourg, as a university, in 1840, aroused a widespread interest in education generally, which bore good fruit afterward. This university has now been in operation forty-eight years, and from it the first arts graduate in Upper Canada was sent forth in 1846. Its first president was the Rev. Dr. Ryerson; the second was the Rev. Dr. Macnab, now of Bowmanville. Its late distinguished president, the Rev. Dr. Nelles, was Dr. Ryerson's pupil. He held his position with honor to himself for thirty-six years, and died in October, 1887, deeply and universally regretted by the entire community.

FIRST APPOINTMENT OF A SUPERINTENDENT OF EDUCATION FOR UPPER CANADA.

In the *Canada Gazette* of May, 1842, the following announcement was made:—

"SECRETARY'S OFFICE, KINGSTON, 11th May, 1842.

"His Excellency the Governor-General has been pleased to make the following appointments:—

"The Honorable Robert Sympson Jameson, Vice-Chancellor, to be Superintendent of Education, under the Provincial Act, 4th and 5th Victoria, chapter 18.

"The Reverend Robert Murray and Jean Baptiste Meilleur, Esquire, to be Assistant Superintendents of Education for Western and Eastern Canada, respectively.

"By command,
"S. B. HARRISON, Provincial Secretary."

Had the Governor-General, Lord Sydenham, not met with the fatal accident which terminated his life, in September, 1841, the Rev. Dr. Ryerson would, without doubt, as I have shown in "The Story of my Life," have been appointed in that year. Mr. Murray, who was neighbor and friend of the Hon. S. B. Harrison, of Bronte, near Oakville, then Provincial Secretary, was nominated by him, and received his appointment from Lord Sydenham's successor, Sir Charles Bagot.

In point of fact, the appointment was first spoken of to Dr. Ryerson by Lord Sydenham himself, in the autumn of 1841. The particulars of that circumstance are mentioned in detail in a letter written by Dr. Ryerson to T. W. C. Murdoch, Esq., Private Secretary to Sir Charles Bagot, on the 14th January, 1842. Dr. Ryerson said:—

"In the last interview with which I was honoured by [Lord Sydenham], he intimated that he thought I might be more usefully employed for this country than in my present limited sphere; and whether there was not some position in which I could more advantageously serve the country at large. I remarked that I could not resign my present official position in the Church, with the advocacy of whose interests I had been entrusted, until their final and satisfactory adjustment by the Government, as I might thereby be represented as having abandoned or sacrificed their interests; but that after such adjustment I should feel myself very differently situated, and free to do anything which might be beneficial to the country, and which involved no compromise of my professional character; that I knew of no such position likely to be at the disposal of the Government except the superintendency of Common Schools (provided for in the Bill then before the Legislature), which office would afford the incumbent a most favorable opportunity, by his communications, preparation and recommendation of books for libraries, etc., to abolish differences and jealousies on minor points; to promote agreement on great principles and interests; to introduce the best kind of reading for the youth of the country; and the not onerous duties of which office would also afford him leisure to prepare publications calculated to teach the people at large to appreciate, upon high moral and social considerations, the institutions established amongst them; and to furnish, from time to time, such expositions of great principles and measures of the administration as would secure the proper appreciation and support of them on the part of the people at large. Lord Sydenham expressed himself as highly gratified at this expression of my views and feelings; but the passing of the Bill was then doubtful, although His Lordship expressed his determination to get it passed if possible, and give effect to what he had proposed to me, and which was then contemplated by him."

"What afterwards grew to be the Department of Education was (under the first general school law, passed in 1841, for the whole of the Province of Canada) originally a subordinate branch of the Provincial Secretary's office at Kingston. That for Upper Canada was managed by Assistant Superintendent Rev. Robert Murray, M.A., and one clerk (Mr. Robert Richardson). The nominal Chief Superintendent, as above noted, was the Hon. Vice-Chancellor Jameson. On the repeal of the General School Act of 1841 and the passing of a separate Act for each province in 1843 the Education branch of the Provincial Secretary's office was divided and reconstructed. The divisions then made were designated respectively "Education Office (East) and Education Office (West)."[45]

APPOINTMENT OF REV. DR. RYERSON AS SUPERINTENDENT OF EDUCATION.

In 1844 Mr. Murray was made Professor of Mathematics in the University of King's College, and the Rev. Dr. Ryerson was appointed as Superintendent of Schools in his place. The announcement of this appointment appeared in the CANADA GAZETTE of October, 1844, as follows:—

"SECRETARY'S OFFICE, MONTREAL, 18th October, 1844.

"His Excellency the Governor-General has been pleased to appoint:—

"The Reverend Egerton Ryerson, D.D., to be Assistant Superintendent of Education for that part of the province formerly Upper Canada, in place of the Reverend Robert Murray, appointed a Professor in the University of King's College, and all communications connected with the Education office for Upper Canada are to be addressed to him at Cobourg.

"By command.
"D. DALY,
"Secretary of the Province."

Dr. Ryerson was notified of the appointment by letter in September, 1844, but was not gazetted until the 18th of the next mouth. It was my good fortune to be associated with him from the time of his appointment in 1844 until he retired from office in 1876.

DR. RYERSON'S REPORT ON A SYSTEM OF PUBLIC INSTRUCTION FOR UPPER CANADA.

Immediately after his appointment Dr. Ryerson went to Europe, and remained away for over a year in familiarizing himself with the systems of education there. On his return he published an elaborate report on his projected scheme of "Public Instruction for Upper Canada." That report was approved by the Governor-General in Council, and he was directed to prepare a bill to give effect to his recommendations, which he did in 1846. A brief analysis of that report may be interesting:—It is divided into two parts: 1. Principles of the system and subjects to be taught; 2. machinery of the system.

After defining what was "meant by education," the principles of the system were laid down as follows:—

1. It should be universal.

2. It should be practical.

3. It should be founded on religion and morality.

4. It should develop all the intellectual and physical powers.

5. It should provide for the efficient teaching of the following subjects: Biblical history and morality, reading and spelling, writing, arithmetic, grammar, geography, linear drawing, vocal music, history, natural history, natural philosophy, agriculture, human physiology, civil government, political economy. Each of these topics was fully discussed and illustrated in the first part of the report.

The second part explained the machinery of the system, which was summarized as follows:—

1. Schools—their gradation and system.

2. The teacher and his training.

3. The text-books recommended.

4. Control and inspection on the part of the Government.

5. Individual and local efforts.

These several topics wore also fully discussed and illustrated, so that the whole comprehensive scheme of education proposed by Dr. Ryerson was clearly and fully understood. The report occupied nearly 200 pages.

The school law founded upon this report provided, amongst other things, for—

1. A general Board of Education for the Province, to take charge of a normal school, and to aid the Chief Superintendent in certain matters.

2. A normal school, with practice or model schools attached.

3. The regulation of school libraries.

4. Plans of school houses.

5. Appointment of district, instead of county and township, school superintendents.

6. Apportionment of school moneys to each school according to the average number of children in each school district, as compared with those in the whole township.

7. Levy of a school rate by each district (county) municipal council, of a sum at least equal to the legislative grant to each such district.

8. The collection, by the local school trustees, of the balance required to defray the expenses of their school, in any way which the school ratepayers (at the annual meeting) might determine.

9. The recommendation of a uniform series of text books, with the proviso that no aid would be given to any school in which books disapproved of by the general Board of Education might be used.

10. The establishment of district model schools (reënacted from the Act of 1843).

11. Examination and licensing of teachers.

12. Visitation of schools by clergymen, magistrates, municipal councillors, etc.

13. Protection of children (reënacted from the Act of 1843) from being "required to read or study in or from any religious book, or join in any religious exercise or devotion, objected to by parents."

14. Establishment (reënacted from the laws of 1841 and 1843) of Roman Catholic Separate Schools, where the teacher of the locality was a Protestant, and *vice versa*. (These schools received grants in accordance with their average attendance of pupils.)

15. Levy of rates by district municipal councils, at their discretion, for the erection of school houses and teachers' residences.

Such were the principal provisions of the first School Act, proposed and adapted from other school laws by Dr. Ryerson in 1846, so far as rural schools were concerned. In the following year he prepared a comprehensive measure in regard to schools in cities, towns and incorporated villages.

CHIEF FEATURES OF DR. RYERSON'S FIRST REPORT AND SCHOOL BILL OF 1846.

In sending his draft of School Bill to the Government, early in March, 1846, Dr. Ryerson, in a private letter to Hon. Attorney General Draper, dated

30th of that month, thus explained its general features:—

"I thank you sincerely for your kind favor of the 23rd instant, and feel not a little gratified that you approve of the draft of Bill which I had prepared for your consideration. I feel the justice of the high ground on which you place the moral qualifications of teachers and their duties....

"That to which I attach the highest importance in the measure is the authority of trustees to levy a rate-bill upon all the inhabitants of a school section. The rate-bill will thus be a second edition of the school tax imposed by the District Council. The principle, once established, it will be seen after a while that the Council may as well impose the whole of the school tax at once as to have the imposition of it divided between the Council and the trustees....

"I attach the greatest importance to the Normal School. I have no doubt the Legislature will be disposed to support it when once established.... I hope, however, that you will have in view the providing for it hereafter, and some appropriation for school libraries ... from which an offer to a district or township, five pounds for example, upon the condition that it would also contribute so as to purchase books from a list recommended by the Provincial Board of Education, and, therefore, the most suitable for the young and grown-up people of the country....

"It has been mentioned to me, and I have thought that the term inspector, instead of superintendent, would be the better designation of the District overseer of Schools....

"I this day transmit to Mr. Secretary Daly my 'Report on a system of Elementary Instruction for Upper Canada.'... I have introduced no debatable topics, except that of Christianity, the principle of maintaining which as the basis and cement of a system of public instruction, I have discussed at large. On the defective modes of teaching those branches (viz., reading, writing, arithmetic, grammar and geography), which are taught in the Common Schools, I have also dwelt at some length in order to furnish District Superintendents and other persons concerned with a proper standard of teaching and examination, and in order to inculcate the true principles of teaching which are applicable to all subjects. I hope the Report will be the means of laying a good foundation in the leading minds of the country on the great work of public instruction.

"I should add in respect to my Report that, in pointing out defects in systems of instruction and modes of teaching, I have almost invariably quoted American authors, and have thus incidentally exposed the defects of almost every part of the American system, and have practically shown that every redeeming feature of the American school system has been or is being borrowed from European governments."

OBJECTIONS TO DR. RYERSON'S SCHOOL BILL OF 1846 ANSWERED.

In a private letter to Hon. Attorney-General Draper, dated 20th April, 1846, Dr. Ryerson replies to several objections made in the House of Assembly and by the press to his first School Act of 1846. I quote the following:—

"The Montreal *Pilot* objects to appointing trustees for three years. This is one of the improvements adopted in the New York law of 1843. The superintendents, in their reports, speak largely of the evils of the annual system, and strongly on the advantages of the triennial one. The opposition to the Bill seems to be based on notions derived from what the State of New York system was several years ago. The opponents do not seem to be aware that it was amended in 1841, and amended again in 1843. Messrs. Price, Roblin, etc., seem to be where the Americans were ten years ago.

"I anticipate the objection to the rate-bill clause. I look upon that above all others to be the poor man's clause, and at the very foundation of a system of public education. It is objected to by precisely the class of persons or rather by the individuals that I expected. I have heard of one rich man objecting to it, who educates his own children at colleges and ladies' seminaries, but who looks not beyond his own family. He says, I am told, that 'he does not wish to be compelled to educate *all the brats* in the neighborhood.' Now, to educate 'all the brats in every neighborhood' is just the very object of this clause; and, in order to do so, it is proposed to compel selfish, rich men to do what they ought to do, but what they will not do voluntarily.[46]

"Mr. Gowan's statements as to the evils of not extending the period of keeping a school open in each district beyond three months of the year are substantially what have been communicated to me in many reports and letters. In several of the annual district reports which I have received, it is stated that giving public money to districts in which a school is not taught more than three months of the year is an actual injury rather than a benefit, and an abuse of the intentions of the Legislature."

FIRST AND SECOND COUNCILS OF PUBLIC INSTRUCTION, 1846 AND 1850.

Dr. Ryerson was assisted in his important work by an able council of representative men, who were appointed in 1846. The members of this first council were as follows:—

Rev. Egerton Ryerson, D.D., Chief Superintendent of Schools; Right Rev.

Michael Power, D.D., Roman Catholic Bishop of Toronto; Rev. Henry James Grasett, M.A., Rector of Toronto; Hon. Samuel Beaty Harrison, Q.C., Judge, County of York; Joseph Curran Morrison, Q.C., M.P.P.; Hugh Scobie, Esq., Editor of the *British Colonist*; James Scott Howard, Esq., Treasurer, County of York.

Dr. Ryerson proposed to Bishop Strachan that he should represent the Church of England on the new Board. The Bishop was quite pleased at his request, and so expressed himself. He declined, however, on the ground that he feared his appointment might embarrass, rather than aid, in the promotion of the new scheme of education. He suggested that Rev. H. J. Grasett be appointed in his place.[47] He also gave friendly advice to Dr. Ryerson to be careful not to recommend a personal enemy for appointment on such a board.

Two more members were added in 1850, viz., Rev. John Jenning, D.D., Presbyterian Minister; Rev. Adam Lillie, D.D., Congregational Minister. Not one of the gentlemen named survive; but, in their day, they rendered effective service to the country as members of the first and second Councils of Public Instruction.

The Hon. S. B. Harrison (afterwards Judge of the County of York) was nominated by Rev. Dr. Ryerson, as Chairman of the reconstructed Board of Education in 1850 (then named the Council of Public Instruction), as successor to the lamented Bishop Power, who died in 1847.[48] Mr. Harrison held that position until his death, in 1862.

Dr. Ryerson did not enter practically upon the duties of his office until about the middle of 1846. In the meantime, the correspondence and routine duties of the Education Office were (on Dr. Ryerson's suggestion) placed in the hands of his friend, the Rev. Alexander MacNab, D.D., now Rector of Darlington (Bowmanville).

RELIGIOUS INSTRUCTION IN THE COMMON SCHOOLS, 1846.

Among the first duties of the new Provincial Board of Education was the establishment of a Normal School, the authorization of a series of text-books, and the preparation of regulations for the government of the Common Schools. The most important of these regulations was the one relating to religious instruction in the schools. Before submitting it to the Board for adoption Dr. Ryerson consulted various representative persons on the subject. In a private letter to Hon. Attorney-General Draper, dated December 17th, 1846, Dr. Ryerson thus explained his proceedings in regard to the preparation of the clause in the new regulations relating to religious instruction in the schools. He said:—

"I submitted the clause first to Rev. Mr. Grasett. He quite approved of it, as he felt exceedingly anxious that there should be such an explicit recognition of Christianity in our school system. I then waited on the Roman Catholic Bishop, who examined it and concurred in it…. I showed it also to the Bishop of Toronto. After he had read the section he said he believed I had done all that could be done on that subject, and that … he would write a circular to his clergy, recommending them to act as school visitors, and to do all in their power to promote the efficiency and usefulness of the Common Schools."

In his report for 1847, Dr. Ryerson stated that he consulted other ministers on the subject. The Hon. Mr. Draper, in a private note to Dr. Ryerson, dated 1st January, 1847, said:—

"I am more gratified than I can express that you have so successfully met the difficulty about the religious instruction of children in Common Schools. You (to whom I expressed myself about three years ago on the subject of the importance of not dividing religion from secular instruction) will readily understand the pleasure I feel that in Common Schools at least the principle and promoted application of it, for mixed schools, has been approved by the Bishop of my own Church and by the Roman Catholic Prelate."

In a letter to the late Hon. Robert Baldwin, written in 1849, Dr. Ryerson thus refers to the question of religious instruction and the Bible in school: "Be assured that no system of popular education will flourish in a country which does violence to the religious sentiments and feelings of the churches of that country. Be assured, that every such system will droop and wither which does not take root in the Christian and patriotic sympathies of the people—which does not command the respect and confidence of the several religious persuasions, both ministers and laity—for these in fact make the aggregate of the Christianity of the country."

Speaking in a subsequent letter of another feature of the question of the Bible in schools, Dr. Ryerson says: "The principal opposition which, in 1846 and for several years afterwards, I encountered was that I did not make the use of the Bible compulsory in the schools, but simply recognized the right of Protestants to use it in the school (not as an ordinary reading book), as it was not given to teach us how to read but to teach us the way to Heaven), as a book of religious instruction, without the right or the power of compelling any others to use it. The recognition of the right has been maintained inviolate to the present time; facilities for the exercise of it have been provided, and recommendations for that purpose have been given, but no compulsory authority assumed, or right of compulsion acknowledged; and the religious exercises in each school have been left to the decision of the authorities of such school, and the religious instruction of each child has always been under the absolute authority of the parents or guardian of each child."

To the objection urged against the reading of the Bible in the schools because "a majority of the teachers are utterly unfit to give religious instruction," Dr. Ryerson replied: "The reading of the Bible and giving religious instruction from it are two very different things. The question is not the competency of teachers to give religious instruction, but the right of a Protestant to the reading of the Bible by his child in the school as a text-book of religious instruction. That right I hold to be sacred and divine."

STATE OF COMMON SCHOOL EDUCATION IN UPPER CANADA, 1845.

From the reports then made to him by the County Superintendents of Schools, I select the following extracts, showing what was the actual state of education in the province when Dr. Ryerson commenced his labors as Superintendent of Education.

Mr. Hamilton Hunter, Superintendent of Schools in the Home District (County of York), in his report for 1845, says:—

"There is one fact with which I have been forcibly struck, in my visits to the schools, which shows, in the clearest manner, the great necessity that existed in this Colony for the establishment of a system of Common School education. It is this: That in our schools the amount of attainment, on the part of the pupils, is generally in an inverse ratio to their size and age, after they have reached their twelfth or thirteenth year. The largest scholars that attend our schools are by far the lowest in point of attainment, which shows how sadly the education of that portion of the community, now about to attain the years of manhood and womanhood has been neglected. In many of our country schools, it is a very common thing to find persons advanced to the age of young men and women commencing to learn the first rudiments. The mind feels pained upon contemplating this; but it is gratifying to think that a remedy has been provided against it in the establishment of our Common Schools, by which the elementary branches of education are brought within the grasp of all. It leads us to reflect upon the melancholy state of ignorance that must have existed at no distant period in this Province had no means been provided other than those which formerly existed for placing the elements of knowledge within the reach of the rising generation."

Hon. Hamnett Pinkey, Superintendent of Schools in the District of Dalhousie (Carleton, etc.), in his report, says:—

"The Common Schools are very indifferently conducted, and the masters in general very inadequately perform the duties required of them; a reform is expected from the establishment of the District Model School."

Rev. Alexander Mann, M.A., Superintendent of Schools in the Bathurst District (Lanark, etc) says:—

"In existing circumstances I have declined giving a regular certificate to any teacher.... I made an effort on my own responsibility, and at my own expense to improve teachers, by opening a private school, solely for their benefit, but as I did not meet with proper encouragement I was obliged to relinquish my purpose."

Richey Waugh, Esq., Superintendent of Schools in the Johnstown District (Leeds and Grenville), says:—

> "The trustees of many schools employ teachers only for whatever time the school fund will pay their wages, and they receive but little benefit from the public money thus expended."

Patrick Thornton, Esq., Superintendent of Schools in the Gore District (Wentworth, etc.), says:—

> "It is a matter of regret that the old parrot system of repeating words without attaching ideas to them, does still in too many instances prevail; and the dregs must remain till some of the old formal teachers are off the field."

Rev. Newton Bosworth, F.R.S., Superintendent of Schools in the Brock District (Oxford, etc.), says:—

> "The diversity of books and modes of teaching referred to in my last report, still exists, nearly to the same extent; and in the qualifications of teachers also, as great a variety was observable as before.... It appears to me that parents should be impressed, to a much greater extent than at present, with a sense of the necessity and importance of education for their children."

George Duck, jr., Esq., Superintendent of Schools in the Western District (Kent, etc.), says:—

> "In many townships little or nothing was raised by rate-bill. In many places the poverty of the settlements prevented it; and the only school that was kept open in these districts was just during the time that the allowance from the aggregate fund was sufficient to pay the teacher. This course is, in fact, of very doubtful benefit, as the school is seldom kept open for more than three months in the year, and the children lose so much benefit continuous education produces."

School Houses and School Teachers in 1845-1850.

The Rev. Dr. Ryerson, in his report for 1845-46, speaking of school houses in the Province, says:—

"With a few exceptions, the school houses are deficient in almost every essential quality of places adopted for elementary instruction. Very few are furnished with any thing more than desks and forms of the most ordinary kind, and have no apparatus for instruction, nor appendages, or conveniences either for exercise or such as are required for the sake of modesty and decency."

In his annual Report for 1847, Dr. Ryerson incidentally refers to the character of teachers in some districts. He says:—

"In one district, where intemperance heretofore prevailed to a considerable extent, even among school teachers, the Superintendent gave notice that he would not give a certificate of qualification to any but strictly sober candidates, and that, at the end of six months he would cancel the certificates of all teachers who suffered themselves at any time to become intoxicated.... I know of two other districts in which the Superintendents have acted thoroughly on the same principle, with the same happy results.... In a note in reference to it in the printed Form of Regulations, I remarked that 'no intemperate or profane person should be intrusted with the instruction of youth.'... No one will doubt that there are fewer unqualified and immoral teachers employed now than there were before the passing of the present School Act (of 1846)." Pages 8 and 9.

In his circular issued to the newly formed County Boards of Examiners, dated 8th October, 1850, Dr. Ryerson thus referred to this matter:—

"Many representations have been made to this Department respecting intemperate and profane and Sabbath-breaking teachers.... I cannot but regard it as your special mission to rid the profession of common school teachers of unworthy character, and ... to protect the youth against the poison of a vicious teacher's example." *Report for 1850, pages 305, 306.*

DR. RYERSON'S PRACTICAL AGENCIES TO GIVE INFORMATION AND REMOVE PREJUDICE.

It will thus be seen from the foregoing, that at this time educational affairs were at a low ebb. Dr. Ryerson, therefore, sought in every practical way to overcome this educational apathy and inertia. His pen and personal effort were freely used. The first circular to municipal councils—prepared by him—was issued by the new Provincial Board of Education in August, 1846. This he followed up by one from himself addressed to county councils, in which he explained fully and at length the scope and objects of the new scheme of popular education. This was done under three heads:—1. That it was "based upon the principles of our common Christianity." 2. That "upon the duty of educating the youth of our country there exists but one opinion, and, therefore, there should be but one party." 3. That "the system of elementary education is public, not private."

Another agency Dr. Ryerson sought to employ to aid the Department in its great work. And by it he hoped to educate and rightly influence public opinion in favor of the new departure then in progress. The plan he proposed to the Government in 1846, to authorize the issue, under his direction, of a departmental *Journal of Education*, "to be devoted," among other things, to the exposition of every part of our school system," then new to the people, ... "and to the discussion of the various means of promoting the efficiency of the schools." This the Government felt unwilling at the time to do. He, therefore, undertook the expense and responsibility of the publication himself in January, 1848. And it was not until years had demonstrated the practical value and success of the proposed agency that the expense of the publication was provided for by an annual vote of the Legislature.

A third agency which Dr. Ryerson successfully employed to aid the Department was that of personally holding county school conventions. In explaining this project to the Government in 1846, he said:—

"I propose ... to visit and employ one or two days in school discourse and deliberation with the Superintendent, Visitors, Trustees and Teachers in each of the several Districts of Upper Canada. I know of no means so effectual to remove prejudice, to create unanimity of views and feelings, and to excite a general interest in the cause of popular education," etc.

This project was concurred in by the Government, on condition that the expense of the proposed nearly three months' visitation "should not exceed £75."

Thus was inaugurated, in 1846, a series of county school conventions which, at intervals of about five years each, were held all over the country. The early ones involved travelling in all kinds of weather and in all kinds of conveyances, so as to keep engagements made weeks before. They were, however, of immense service to the Department in removing prejudice, settling difficulties and solving doubts as to the practicability of plans proposed for improving the condition of the schools and raising the intellectual and social status of the teacher.

COMBINED OPPOSITION TO THE PROJECTED SYSTEM OF EDUCATION.

It was not to be expected that so comprehensive a scheme of education as that proposed by Dr. Ryerson in 1846 and 1847 would meet with general acceptance. The very reverse was the fact. It was assailed as revolutionary and oppressive. It certainly was revolutionary in the best sense; but not oppressive, for it was largely permissive and wholly tentative. And, for many years the Town of Richmond, in the County of Carleton, refused to establish schools under its provisions. The new measures were so far revolutionary that they differed almost wholly from the former projected school acts. The system proposed was composite. Its machinery was adopted chiefly from the State of New York. The principle upon which the schools were to be supported was taken from New England—Normal schools, from Germany, and the uniform series of school books, from Ireland. All were, however, so blended together and harmonized, to meet the requirements and circumstances of the country that they became, in Dr. Ryerson's moulding hands, "racy of the soil."

Up to this time no one but Dr. Ryerson had been able to give a practical turn to the rather crude theories which had been held on the subject of popular education. He, however, had to pay the penalty of all such reformers; but yet he lived to see the fuller details of his system of education worked out on his own lines.

It is needless to say that Dr. Ryerson's scheme was assailed as impracticable. This I have explained. It was held to be too comprehensive for the country. Even his reference to the compact and systematized plan adopted in Prussia was seized upon as an indication of his covert design to introduce the baneful system of so-called "Prussian despotism." His commendation of "free schools," as a prospective feature of our educational system was denounced as an attempt to legalize an "outrageous robbery," and as communistic "war against property." As an example of the injustice of these criticisms on Dr. Ryerson's scheme of education, he said in a lecture on education in 1847:—

"I have seen in certain of the public prints, a provision of our school law ascribed to Prussia, which was borrowed from the school law of the City of Buffalo; and another provision declared to be incompatible with the rights of man which forms the basis and glory of the common school system of Massachusetts."

Although opposition to Dr. Ryerson's educational plans, as embodied in his school acts, was somewhat general, yet it was singularly illogical. The sore point was that it touched men's pockets in the form of school rates.

EDUCATIONAL PROCEEDINGS OF DISTRICT COUNCILS IN 1847, 1848.

An influential district council in the West sought to influence all of the others against the new system, especially against the establishment of a Normal School. In a memorial to the Legislature (which it sent broadcast), dated Hamilton, 10th November, 1847, and signed by James Little, Chairman of the Education Committee, John White and Francis Cameron, and adopted by the Gore District Council, the following passages occur:

> "With respect to the necessity of establishing a Normal, with Elementary Model Schools in this Province, memorialists are of opinion that, however well adapted, such an institution might be to the wants of the old and densely populated countries of Europe, where services in almost every vocation will scarcely yield the common necessaries of life, they are, so far as this object expected to be gained is concerned, altogether unsuited to a country like Upper Canada.... Nor do your memorialists hope to provide qualified teachers by any other means, in the present circumstances of the country than securing as heretofore, the services of those whose physical disabilities from age render this mode of obtaining a livelihood the only one suited to their decaying energies, or by employing such of the newly arrived emigrants as are

qualified for common school teachers year by year as they come amongst us, and who will adopt this as a means of temporary support, until their character and ability are known and turned to better account for themselves."

This memorial having been sent to each of the district councils in Upper Canada for their concurrence, and with a view to procure the repeal of the School Act, 9 Vic., ch. 20, the Colborne District Council not only refused to concur in it but subjected it to severe criticism. In regard to the foregoing extract from the Gore District Memorial, the Colborne Council (now Peterboro' and Victoria) in its report on that memorial said:

"That the moneys required to pay for the establishment and support of Normal and Model Schools are little less than a waste of so much of the Legislative grant, is an opinion in which your committee are so far from concurring, that they believe it is from these sources must mainly arise the instrumentality through which the friends of education can alone hope for the first considerable amelioration of the evils they lament…. Nor can your committee reconcile it either with their just expectations, or their sense of duty to rest satisfied with the services of those whose physical disabilities from age and decaying energies render them unfit, or of those 'newly arrived emigrants,' whose 'unknown character and abilities' render them unable to procure a livelihood by any other means than by becoming the preceptors of our children; the dictators of their sentiments and manners; the guardians of their virtue; and in a high degree the masters of their future destinies in this world and the next."

This report was prepared by Mr. Thomas Benson, Chairman of the Education Committee, and Warden of the District (father of Judge Benson of Port Hope). It was adopted by the Colborne District Council in February, 1848.[49]

The Western District Council, in its memorial to the Legislature against the School Act, represented that "spite, hatred and malice between neighbors and friends," existed, and was "occasioned by the present School Act." It added:

"So numerous are the petitions on the subject that more than half of the time of the Council is taken up in endeavoring to settle the differences, but unfortunately without any beneficial effect."

The Chief Superintendent, in his report, referring to this statement says:

"Now, in examining the printed report of the committee, to whom all these petitions were referred, I find that of the twenty-nine petitions presented to the Council, one prayed for the establishment of a female school in one of the sections (which was granted); one prayed for a local school tax in a section; two related to the formation of new school sections, and the remaining twenty-five related to the disputes as to the boundaries of school sections and the non-payment of school moneys by township superintendents. Thus not one of these disputes could have arisen out of the School Act, but must have all been caused by an improper division of the school sections, either by the township superintendents under the late Act, or by the Council under the present statute."

In this (Western) District the Council says:

"We well know that a very large number of the trustees can neither read nor write, and, therefore, it must be obvious that the greater part of the requirements of the law remain undone."

On this statement the Chief Superintendent remarks:

"In other districts where the trustees can read and write, and where the councillors an correspondingly intelligent and discreet in their school proceedings, no disputes or inconvenience have, as far as I am aware, occurred on this subject."

In the District of Dalhousie, the Chief Superintendent states:

"Still greater dissatisfaction and confusion were created by the mode of proceeding adopted by the council. Before the passing of the present School Act the council of this district never imposed a school assessment.... The introduction of a district assessment (under the new Act) would naturally excite some dissatisfaction, and especially in a district bordering on counties in Lower Canada where the school assessment had been resisted.... In addition the Chief Superintendent adds:

"The Council in the autumn of 1847 passed a by-law to this effect:

"Whereas the school section division mode by this Council at its last session, are in many instances, discordant to the convenience and wishes of the inhabitants, and that to correct them satisfactorily this present session is impracticable. The District Superintendent is empowered and required to make a distribution of the school fund (legislative grant and county assessment) 'share and share alike,' among qualified teachers without reference to the number of scholars under their tuition, but in proportion to the time such teachers may have been teaching, etc."

Thus the Superintendent remarks, "this by-law contemplated the abolition of the statute requiring the school grant to be distributed according to the school population of each section. It made no distinction between the able teacher who taught sixty scholars and the young one who taught twenty; it had no regard to the engagements which may have been made by trustees according to law; it required of teachers conditions which the law had not enjoined, and proposed to deprive many of them of advantages which the law had conferred.... Of course I pointed out the illegality and injustice of the by-law and it was not acted upon. At the session of the Council lately held, a resolution was adopted praying the Governor-General to dissolve the Council that the sense of the inhabitants of the Dalhousie District might be taken on the school law.... It is doubtless probable that many of the inhabitants have not distinguished between the provisions of the law and the proceedings of their own Council—attributing to the former what has been occasioned by the latter."[50]

Contrast the enlightened discussion of such questions to-day with the ignorant dogmatism of that day, and you can form some idea of the magnitude of Dr. Ryerson's labors,—not only in laying broad and deep the foundations for his superstructure, but in seeking to overcome the deep-rooted and unreasoning prejudices of those days—days indeed of anxiety and toil and fierce opposition, which I so well remember.

ESTIMATE OF LORD ELGIN'S CHARACTER BY THE HON. W. H. DRAPER.

On the arrival in Canada of Lord Elgin, as Governor-General, Dr. Ryerson wrote confidentially to Hon. Attorney-General Draper (on the 16th February, 1847), asking him for his "opinion of the new Governor-General." Mr. Draper replied on the 22nd as follows:—

"As far as my opportunities of judging go, I think Canada will find cause of satisfaction in having Lord Elgin for a Governor. He is industrious in habit, pleasing in manner, extremely courteous and affable in bearing. I find him also diligent and shrewd in inquiry; and the observations which fall from him show that he has studiously kept pace with the great questions of the day (I do not mean our Canadian politics simply), and besides the cultivation of classical education in its broader sense, he possesses a mind stored with facts bearing on and illustrative of those questions. In these respects, or more correctly speaking in the latter, and as regards trade and finance, he reminds me more of Lord Sydenham than any other governor of my time. I think he possesses also caution and firmness;—that he will not resolve hastily, that he may not have to change his resolves. He has large ideas of the capabilities and resources both of Canada and of the British North American Provinces, and, as it strikes me, without any reference to a political union of these provinces, thinks that a course might be taken to develop the whole, by separate parts taking a common course in matters in which they have a common interest— internal communication, favorable to our European commerce and connections will serve as an illustration of the sort of questions to which I allude.... All this, of course, is mere opinion, but such are my first impressions, and as such, and no more, I readily give them to you in reply to your enquiry, etc."

Subsequently, Dr. Ryerson met Lord Elgin in Montreal, and, in a letter to me, dated 24th July, 1847, he says:—

"At his own request I have had an interesting interview with Lord Elgin. He is exceedingly well versed in systems of education, and is a thoroughly practical man on the subject."

INVALUABLE ASSISTANCE GIVEN TO DR. RYERSON BY LORD ELGIN.

It was fortunate that just at this crisis Canada was favored with the presence of one of the most accomplished, in every sense of the term, of the Queen's representatives, the Earl of Elgin and Kincardine.

That distinguished statesman, who afterwards filled with great dignity the highest post in the civil service of Great Britain, that of Governor-General of India, reached Canada at a critical transitional period in our history. Few can recall the incidents of those days without a feeling of admiration for the fearlessness, tact, and ability with which he discharged the delicate and difficult duties of his high office.

When Lord Elgin arrived in Canada in 1847, and when he removed to Toronto, after the riot and burning of the Parliament House in Montreal in

1849, educational affairs were fiercely discussed and were yet almost at the low ebb at which Dr. Ryerson had found them. Not that they had previously reached a higher plane and had gradually settled down to a lower one. The reverse was the fact, but the question of education had only then (in Dr. Ryerson's hands) begun to attract serious public attention. It was, however, as I have explained, in an adverse direction, for the whole subject, in the advanced form in which it was presented by Dr. Ryerson, was unpopular. It involved taxation and other unpalatable "burdens," as its opponents averred. Notwithstanding the zeal and ability with which Dr. Ryerson had collected and arranged his facts, analyzed the various systems of education in Europe and America, and fortified himself with the opinions of the most experienced educationists in these countries, the system which he projected, and the school law which embodied it, continued to be fiercely assailed by a portion of the press, and by hostile politicians. This hostility culminated in an event which brought things to a crisis in 1849.

At this time, an administration was in office, one or two members of which were personally unfavorable to Dr. Ryerson's continuation in office. One of these, a prominent and popular member of the cabinet (Hon. Malcolm Cameron, who afterward became a warm friend of Dr. Ryerson) induced his colleagues to assent to the passage of a school bill which practically legislated Dr. Ryerson out of office, besides being objectionable in other respects. He at once tendered his resignation. The Hon. Robert Baldwin, Attorney-General, declined to recommend its acceptance. By advice of the Cabinet, the operation of the bill was suspended until a new one, framed by Dr. Ryerson, could be prepared and passed. The result was the passage of the School Act of 1850—popular in its character and comprehensive in its provisions. It now forms the broad basis of the present school system of Ontario.

It was at this period of our educational history that Lord Elgin first came into official contact with our educational system. Being familiar with the Scottish parochial school system, he soon mastered the whole subject, and perceived the great importance to the whole country of the question which was then being so fiercely discussed.

Being in England in 1853, Dr. Ryerson wrote to me there:—

"I was glad to learn that Lord Elgin was to go in the same steamship with you from Boston. I have no doubt it will have proved interesting to him as well as to you, and perhaps useful to you. I miss you very much from the office, but I do not like to employ any more aid without sanction of the Government, though I could get no one to take your place. I would wish you to write me what Lord Elgin may have thought or have said as to our doings and plans of proceeding. If the library plan succeeds, it will achieve noble results.[51] I feel that our success and happiness in the Department are inseparably united."

It was indeed fortunate for my mission that I was on the same Cunard steamer to England with His Excellency the late lamented Lord Elgin, to whom I entered into full detail in regard to the objects of that mission. Before leaving the steamer, Lord Elgin most kindly promised to aid me in every way he could while in England, and wrote me his address as "Broom Hall, Dumfermline," in case I should have occasion to refer to him. He also added the following paragraph to the letter of your instructions and authority, which, in more than one instance, I found to be of essential service to me:—

> "I believe the object of Mr. Hodgins' mission to be most important to Canada, and I trust that he will meet with all support and encouragement.
>
> (Signed) "Elgin and Kincardine,
"Governor-General.
>
> "September, 1853."

One of my letters, reporting to Dr. Ryerson as far as I had gone, my proceedings in England, having been enclosed to the Hon. Mr. Hincks, he said in reply:—"I return you Mr. Hodgins' interesting letter, with thanks for its perusal. It was fortunate he went by the same steamer as Lord Elgin. I am much interested in the success of your libraries, which is beyond my most sanguine expectations.

I recall with pleasure the great services which Lord Elgin then rendered to the cause of education at a critical period of its history in this Province. His speeches and addresses on the subject at that time had a wonderful effect in moderating the opposition which Dr. Ryerson received while laying the foundations of our system of education. They had also the potent effect of popularizing that system in the estimation of the people which it was designed to benefit. That popularity has, happily, continued to this day, thanks in a great degree to the dignity imparted to the subject by the persuasive eloquence of Lord Elgin. His eminence as a distinguished graduate of Oxford, and his general knowledge of European systems of education, enabled him to speak with a precision and certainty which few could gainsay. It was a gratifying fact that he identified himself personally, as well as officially, throughout the whole of his seven years' administration, with the general education and intellectual improvement of the people of Canada. The first bill to which His Excellency assented in the Queen's name was the School Act of 1850, to which I have referred.

PROCEEDINGS OF THE FIRST COUNCIL OF PUBLIC INSTRUCTION—THE NORMAL SCHOOL.

One of the first and necessary acts of the Provincial Board of Education, or first council of public instruction, was the adoption of a uniform series of text-books—one only on each subject. Those chosen were the Irish National Series, with two additions. The next important step taken by the Board was the establishment, in November, 1847, of a Normal School, with the necessary adjunct of a Model School. The old Government House was fitted up as a Normal School, and the stable connected with it was renovated and converted into a Model School, or school of practice for teachers-in-training. [52] On the removal of the seat of government to Toronto, in 1849, the Normal School was held in the Temperance Hall, and other arrangements were made.

So successful were these schools in raising the status of the teaching profession that the government of the day—the memorable Baldwin-Lafontaine administration—willingly listened to a proposition of the Provincial Board of Education to grant funds for the purchase of a site and the erection of suitable buildings for these schools. The Hon. Francis Hincks, who was Inspector General, had (upon Dr. Ryerson's estimate) a proposed grant of £15,000 put in the estimates of 1850 for the purposes named. A site of seven acres and a half of land was purchased from the estate of the Hon. Peter M'Gill. The writer of this retrospect had the pleasure (in the absence of

Dr. Ryerson in Europe) of signing the cheque for the purchase money, £4,500, and of seeing that the deed was duly made out in the name of Her Majesty the Queen and her successors, and transferred for safe keeping to the Crown Lands Department.

After the plans for the buildings had been approved, certain important additions were considered desirable (chiefly a theatre, or central lecture hall, etc.). As the grant already made was quite insufficient for the proposed additions, Mr. Hincks was once more appealed to. He responded very promptly and heartily, and recommended to his colleagues that a further grant be made, which was done, and an item of £10,000 additional was placed in the estimates of 1851 and concurred in by the Legislature. The work then proceeded and near the close of the second year it was brought to a conclusion.

So carefully had these two grants been husbanded that when the buildings were completed and furnished, there was a balance left over of £90. With this sum the expense of fitting up the Departmental Library was defrayed. The result was highly gratifying to Mr. Hincks, and he so expressed himself at the opening of the buildings in the following year.

LAYING THE CORNER STONE OF THE NORMAL SCHOOL BUILDING, 1851.

On Wednesday, the 2nd of July, 1851, the imposing ceremony of laying the corner stone of the new edifice took place. The guard of honor was the 71st Highlanders, under Sir Hew Dalrymple. Ministers of both Houses of Parliament, the city corporation, etc., attended. The inscription on the brass plate—I quote from the original, as written by Dr. Ryerson—was as follows:

> "This Institution, Erected by the Enlightened Liberality of Parliament, is Designed for the Instruction and Training of School Teachers upon Christian Principles."

Right Rev. Bishop Charbonnell, to whom was assigned the duty of presenting the Governor-General with the silver trowel, spoke with great cordiality, and with French grace and eloquence. He said:

> "MONSEIGNEUR,—Je suis très heureux et très honoré d'avoir èté choisi par le Conseil de l'Instruction Publique, dont votre Excellence a daignè me faire membre, pour lui prèsenter cette truelle d'argent aux industrieuses emblèmes du blazon des Bruces.
>
> "L'etablissement dont votre Excellence va poser la pierre angulaire, Monseigneur, sera un des plus glorieux monuments de tout ce que son libéral gouvernement aura fait pour la prospérité, de ce pays: *ad œdificationem.*"

This in substance is as follows:—

"My Lord,—I am very happy and am highly honored to have been chosen by the Council of Public Instruction—of which your Excellency has condescended to make me a member—to present to you, on their behalf, this silver trowel emblazoned with the industrial emblems which form the arms of the Bruces.

"The institution, of which your Excellency is about to lay the corner stone, is destined to be, my Lord, one of the most glorious monuments amongst all of those which your liberal administration has devised for the welfare of this country."

In laying the corner-stone, Lord Elgin was particularly happy in his reply to these remarks, and to the address of the newly-constituted Council of Public Instruction. He said, addressing Dr. Ryerson:—

"It appears to me, sir, ... that this young country has had the advantage of profiting by the experience of older countries—by their failures and disappointments, as well as by their successes; and that experience, improved by your diligent exertions and excellent judgment ... and fortified by the support of the Council of Education, and the Government and Parliament of the Province, has enabled Upper Canada to place herself in the van among the nations in the great and important work of providing an efficient system of general education for the whole community.... I do not think that I shall be charged with exaggeration when I affirm that this work is *the* work of our day and generation—that it is the problem in our modern society which is most difficult of solution.... How has Upper Canada addressed herself to the execution of this great work?... Sir, I understand from your statements—and I come to the same conclusions from my own investigation and observation—that it is the principle of our educational system that its foundation be laid deep in the firm rock of our common Christianity.... Permit me to say, both as an humble Christian man and as the head of the Civil Government of the Province, that it gives me unfeigned pleasure to perceive that the youth of this country, ... who are destined in their maturer years to meet in the discharge of the duties of civil life upon terms of perfect civil and religious equality—I say it gives me pleasure to hear and to know that they are receiving an education which is fitted so well to qualify them for the discharge of these important duties; and that while their hearts are yet tender ... they are associated under conditions which are likely to provoke amongst them the growth of those truly Christian graces—mutual respect, forbearance and charity."

One of His Excellency's last acts in Toronto, when about to leave the country, was to visit those buildings and express his satisfaction with the several departments of the system therein conducted.

The County Model Schools of 1843-1850.

The necessity of these schools was felt more than forty years ago, and provision was then made for their establishment. Thus, in the first School Act passed in 1843 to regulate Common Schools in this province, section 57 of that Act declares:—

"That it shall and may be lawful for the court of wardens of any county in Upper Canada ... to raise and levy by county rate a sum not exceeding £200 ($800), and to appropriate and expend the same for the maintenance of one or more *County Model Schools*, within such county and to constitute, by by-law, or by-laws, to that effect, any township, town, or city school, or schools within the county, to be, for any term not less than one year, such County

Model School or Schools," etc.

"A sum not less than £40" was appropriated to each such school towards 'the payment of the teachers and the purchase of books and apparatus.' The 66th section of the same Act also declared:—

"That in every such township, town or city Model School gratuitous instruction shall be given to teachers of Common Schools within the township, town or city, wherein such Model School may be established during such periods and under such regulations of the township, town or city superintendent may from time to time direct."

"Again, in the first Common School Act prepared by Dr. Ryerson, and passed in 1846, after providing for the establishment of District Model Schools—it was declared (sec. 40):—

"That at every such District Model School gratuitous instruction shall be afforded to all teachers of Common Schools within the district in which such Model School may be established during such period and under such regulations as the district superintendent may from time to time direct."

These County Model Schools (as will be seen) had higher functions than have the County Model Schools of the present day. They were designed to afford instruction to persons who were already teachers, and were thus in Dr. Ryerson's views constituted local Normal Schools for that purpose. So much importance did Dr. Ryerson attach to the value of training institutions for teaching, and so much did he anticipate a demand for them that on page 162 of his "Report on a System of Public Elementary Instruction," published in 1845, he said:—

"As soon as examples of the advantages of trained teachers can be given, I believe the ratio of demand will increase faster than that of supply, and that an additional Normal School will soon be required in each of the most populous districts."

Then again so jealously was the efficiency of these District or County Model Schools guarded that in the same Act, 9 Victoria, chapter 20, it was provided that no teacher could be appointed to such school without the approval in writing of the district superintendent, and unless he held a certificate from the Normal School (which was established in 1847). In addition to these requirements power was given to the district superintendent to suspend or dismiss Model School teachers and to appoint others in their places, in case the local trustees neglected or refused to do so. This district superintendent was also authorized to examine (as they often did at the Model School) all "candidates for teaching in Common Schools" and to give them certificates of qualification, special or general, at his discretion.

The question may here be asked, "Of what practical value were these County Model Schools in the work of training school teachers, and did they at all discharge the higher functions to which reference is made?"

It was clear that these schools were regarded in those early days as a necessary adjunct to our system of education, for the very purpose of aiding teachers in their professional work. Thus, Mr. Hamilton Hunter, in his report as School Superintendent of the Home District for the year 1844 says:—

"The deficiency in the qualification of teachers could be remedied by establishing in each district a Model School upon a good scale, and having it under the management of a superior teacher or teachers.... The School Bill makes provision for this, etc."

In his report for 1847 Dr. Ryerson thus speaks of the operation and success of these schools wherever they had been established:—

"The School Superintendent of Dalhousie District says: 'In this [County Model School] I have there held public examinations of Common School teachers; and on some occasions, when reluctant to give them certificates, I have sent them to the Model School Master for information and examination.... [These teachers] did not make any permanent stay except one, merely learning the mode of instruction, the value of the studies and discipline of the school.'... The Superintendent of the Johnstone District says: — ... 'Much good has been done by the establishment of the Model School in this district. Several teachers, whose education was by no means good, have acquired a sound knowledge of the subjects which are required to be taught in the Common Schools.' The Superintendent of Schools in the Midland District says:—'Almost every teacher who has attended the Model School for any length of time is now teaching with good success.'"

In the Act which was hurriedly passed in 1849, but which, by Order-in-Council, never went into operation, provision was made to establish, or continue the County Model Schools "in any township, town, or city," and granting to each of them "£25 over and above the sum to which such schools would be entitled as a Common School

... which sum shall be expended in the payment of a teacher or teachers, and for

no other purpose."

In the Act of 1850, provision for the establishment and maintenance of Township Model Schools was made. Township councils were authorized to raise a special tax for the support and efficiency of these schools; and it was "provided likewise, that tuition to student-teachers in such Model Schools should be free."

The reason why Township Model Schools were substituted for county ones, is given by Dr. Ryerson in his circular to town reeves, dated 12th August, 1850. Other reasons contributed to this change, but the circular gives the chief reason.

"The attempts of district councils to establish Model Schools have thus far proved entire failures...: The late district councils have in every instance, except one, abandoned the attempt.... To the success and usefulness of a Model School, a model teacher, at any expense, is indispensable, and then a Model School-house, properly furnished, and their judicious and energetic management."

In addition, I may say that the causes of failure of these valuable training institutions in 1850, may be incidentally learned from the very words here used by Dr. Ryerson by way of suggestions to town reeves. These schools had neither model teachers, nor were the buildings "model school-houses." Besides, the district superintendents of that day, and after them, the township superintendents, had, as a rule, no experience as trained teachers themselves.

By the Act of 1871, the status and qualifications of these most important officers were raised to their present high standard. The very name was changed, and that of inspector was substituted.

It was felt by Dr. Ryerson that until these new officers had secured some degree of popular favor, and had proved their efficiency as organizers of schools, and as practical judges of the necessary qualifications of teachers, it would be useless for him to attempt the re-establishment of the County Model Schools. Before that time had fully arrived he retired from office—leaving this important and necessary duty to be undertaken (as it was efficiently) by his successor, Hon. Adam Crooks, as Minister of Education.

FUNDAMENTAL PRINCIPLES OF DR. RYERSON'S SCHEME OF EDUCATION.

In founding the system of public instruction for Upper Canada, Dr. Ryerson wisely laid down certain fundamental principles which he believed to be essential to the success and stability of that system. These general principles may be thus summarized:

1. That the machinery of education should be in the hands of the people themselves, and should be managed through their own agency; they should, therefore, be held, be consulted, by means of public meetings and conferences, in regard to all school legislation. This he himself did every few years.

2. That the aid of the Government should only be given where it could be used most effectually to stimulate and assist local effort in this great work.

3. That the property of the country is responsible for, and should contribute toward the education of the entire youth of the country; and that, as a complement to this, "compulsory education" should necessarily be enforced.

4. That a thorough and systematic inspection of the schools is essential to their vitality and efficiency.

These and other important principles, Dr. Ryerson kept steadily in view during his long administration of the school system of his native Province. He was not able to embody them all at once in his earlier school bills, but he did so in the final legislation on the subject with which he was connected in 1870-1874. Their judicious application to the school system contributed largely, under the Divine blessing, which he ever sought, to the wonderful success of his labors.

CAN UPPER CANADA EMULATE THE STATE OF NEW YORK IN EDUCATIONAL MATTERS?

In his "Address to the People of Upper Canada" on school affairs in 1850, Dr. Ryerson thus answers this question:—

"Another ground of encouragement in our country's educational work is the practical proof already acquired of the possibility of not only improving our schools, but of successfully emulating our American neighbours in this respect. Often have we heard this, both publicly and privately, pronounced utopian; and often have we sought in friendly discussion to prove that it was neither impracticable nor extravagant to aim in rivalling our New York neighbours in our Common Schools."—*Journal of Education for Upper Canada*, vol. 3, page 2.

In his report for 1851, Dr. Ryerson returns to this subject. He says:—

"The period is very recent when the [subject of educational comparison with the State of New York] would have been an absurdity—when the word 'contrast' must have been employed instead of the word 'comparison,' when not a few of our fellow countrymen, and some of our public men, considered the project, or the idea of emulating the Common School doings of our New York neighbours, as presumptuous and chimerical. I have not viewed the noble and patriotic exertions of the American people in any spirit of jealousy.... I hold up their example to the admiration and imitation of the people of Canada; but I have not despaired of, much less depreciated my own country; and have had, and have still in a higher degree than ever, a strong conviction that there are qualities in the people of Upper Canada, which, under a proper and possible organization, and with judicious counsel, would place schools and education in this country upon more than a level with what we have witnessed and admired in the State of New York. It is true our American neighbours have had more than thirty years the start of us; but I am persuaded we shall not require half that time to overtake them—profiting, as we have done, and doubtless will do, by their mistakes and failures, as well as by their ingenuity and success. To rebuke an unpatriotic spirit of Canadian degradation in which some Canadians indulge,[53] and to animate the hopes and exertions of the true friends of our intellectual and social progress, I will show what has already been accomplished in Upper Canada in respect to Common Schools by a comparison, in a few particulars, with what has been done in the State of New York." (The particulars which Dr. Ryerson points out are seven in number).—*Report for 1851*, (written in 1852), page 17.

In his reply to a complimentary letter from the Municipal Council of the County of Norfolk, in 1851, Dr. Ryerson thus referred to this subject:—

"No person who has at all studied the subject of comparative school legislation between Canada and other countries, can fail to observe that there is an extent of local discretion and power in each of our School and County Municipalities not found in any one of the neighbouring States, while there are other elements incorporated into our school system, which secure to the remotest municipality of Upper Canada the information and facilities which can alone be acquired and provided by a Public Department. But the rational conviction and voluntary co-operation of the people themselves have been relied upon and appealed to as the basis of exertion and the instrument of success. When, therefore, steps were taken to improve the text-books of the schools, a set of the books recommended was procured and furnished to each County Municipality in Upper Canada, that the people might examine and judge of the desirableness of the books proposed, in regard to both excellence and cheapness. In promoting an improvement in the condition and character of school-houses, plans and illustrations of school-houses and premises were procured and placed in the hands of the local councils, and several of them were published in the *Journal of Education*. The same course has been adopted in respect to School Maps, etc. And in pressing upon the public mind the necessity and advantage of duly qualified School Teachers, an institution has been established to train them; and the specimens of Teachers thus trained (though but partially trained in most instances, from the short period of their training) have excited a desire and demand for improved teachers in every County in Upper Canada. I trust this year will witness the introduction of Libraries—thus completing the establishment of every branch of our school system.

"In all this there has been no coercion—but a perfect blending of freedom and unity, of conviction and action; and the entire absence of any opposition to the school system during the recent elections throughout Upper Canada, shows how general and cordial is the conviction of the people as to its adaptation to their circumstances and interests.

"I have the deepest conviction of the strong common sense and patriotism of the Canadian people at large—a conviction founded on long observation and comparison between the people of Canada and those of many other countries; and I have a faith, little short of full assurance, as to the advancing and glorious future of our country. With this conviction and faith, and animated with the consciousness of general approval and co-operation on the part of the people, I shall renew my humble contributions of labour to the common treasury of Canadian progress and civilization."

ESTABLISHMENT OF THE EDUCATIONAL DEPOSITORY, AND ITS RESULTS.

In 1850-51, Dr. Ryerson, while in England, made arrangements for establishing a library, a prize book and an apparatus and map depository, in connection with his Department. His reasons for doing so may be thus briefly stated:

1. He felt it to be practically useless to train teachers in the best methods of imparting instruction, and in the use of apparatus and other school appliances in the normal school and not provide for them, when in charge of schools, a constant and abundant supply of these necessary appliances at the very cheapest rates.

2. He held it to be equally necessary that the pupils, who had acquired a taste for reading and knowledge in the schools, should have an equally abundant and perennial supply of the best and purest literature as it is issued from the press; otherwise they would be sure to procure reading matter (often pernicious, as he had painful proof) for themselves.

3. He could see no distinction, and therefore could not admit of any, in the principle of providing such a two-fold supply of school material and reading matter, and in that of providing trained teachers and skilled inspectors at the expense of the Province, as well as a money bonus to aid in maintaining the schools in a state of efficiency.

4. He further felt that it was immaterial whether the money voted by Parliament was expended in one direction or the other, so long as in each department of the system the best interests and necessities of the schools were consulted, and the symmetry and efficiency of the school system, as a whole,

were preserved and promoted.

5. He projected this plan of supply on a purely commercial basis, and so arranged and successfully carried out his scheme that while there was distributed nearly a million dollars' worth of school material and books up to the time when the depository was closed, it did not cost the country anything for the expenses of its management, as it more than paid its way. An elaborate report on this subject was prepared by Mr. James Brown, an experienced accountant, under the direction of Hon. Adam Crooks, the first Minister of Education. It more than sustained the statement here made. The particulars are as follows:—

ABSTRACT OF DEPOSITORY SCHEDULE PRESENTED TO THE LEGISLATURE IN 1877.

Total amount of legislative grants to the depository for all purposes, viz.:

(1) Purchase of stock, and (2) Salaries and the entire cost of management, etc., 1850 to 1875 inclusive	$811,523 72
Total value of books, maps and apparatus despatched from the depository, 1850 to 1875 inclusive	803,067 86
Difference to be accounted for	8,455 86
Net value of the stock on hand at the end of 1875, after paying all expenses of management, etc	79,509 41
Deduct the difference to be accounted for (as above)	8,455 86
Grand total of profits made by the depository after paying all charges, as above, during the years 1850-1875	71,054 55

DR. RYERSON A COMMISSIONER ON KING'S COLLEGE, ETC., NEW BRUNSWICK IN 1854.

On the 1st of May, 1854, the Legislature of New Brunswick passed an Act empowering the Lieutenant-Governor to appoint a Royal Commission:—

"To enquire into the present state of King's College, its management and utility, with a view of improving the same, and rendering that institution more generally useful, and of suggesting the best mode of effecting that desirable object," etc.

In accordance with this Act, Sir Edmund Head, the then Lieutenant-

Governor, in August, 1854, appointed the following gentlemen as commissioners, viz.:—Hon. John Hamilton Gray, (late Judge of the High Court of British Columbia), Rev. Dr. Egerton Ryerson, John William (now Sir Wm.) Dawson, Hon. John Simcoe Saunders, and Hon. James Brown.

In accepting the position of commissioner, Dr. Ryerson, at the close of his letter to Provincial Secretary Partelow, said:—

"When I mentioned to the head of the Canadian Administration the request which had been made to me from New Brunswick, and the probability that a compliance with it would cause my absence for two or three weeks from the duties of my department, he thought I ought, by all means, to go—that it was part of my appropriate work, and that we should regard each Province of British North America as a part of our own country.

"New Brunswick is so to me, in a peculiar sense, as the birth-place of my sainted mother and my elder brothers and sisters."

The commission met first at Fredericton, and afterwards at Toronto. To Dr. Ryerson was entrusted the principal duty of drawing up the elaborate report, and in Hon. J. H. Gray's letter as chairman, accompanying the report in December, 1854, he says:

"I beg to express, with the full concurrence of my fellow commissioners, our acknowledgements of the very valuable assistance afforded us by Dr. Ryerson. His great experience and unquestioned proficiency on all subjects connected with education, justly entitle his opinion to great weight."

Sir Wm. Dawson, in a letter to Mr. Gray, thus summarizes the contents of the report:—

"1st. The improvement of the College course of instruction and its extension by the introduction of special courses. 2ndly, The definition of the true place of the Provincial College in its relations to the other educational institutions of the Province, and to the religious beliefs of the people; and 3rdly, The union of all the educational institutions in a Provincial university system, under official supervision."

A change in the Government of New Brunswick in 1854, prevented the report being considered in the Legislature at that time. In a letter from Mr. Gray to Dr. Ryerson, dated May 15, 1855, he says:—

"The change of Government prevented our report being adopted and acted upon, but it met with universal approbation, and from every portion of the Province the voice of praise has gone up. I give you credit for it all; and in my remarks in the House, I made my acknowledgements publicly to you and Mr. Dawson."

In a confidential letter to me, on Separate School matters, from Dr. Ryerson, dated Quebec, January 30, 1858, he said:—

"Sir Edmund Head (now Governor-General), highly approved of my Report, etc., on the New Brunswick College question and has sent it to the authorities of McGill College to see if they cannot adopt something of the same kind."

Mr. Gray had hoped that the comprehensive bill proposed by the commission in 1854, and to give effect to their recommendations relating to King's College, Normal and Model Schools, and a Chief Superintendent of Education, would be passed in the following year, 1855. In this he was disappointed, for the bill did not pass until 1860. In a letter to Dr. Ryerson from the Hon. Charles Fisher, dated Fredericton, 14th May, 1860, he said:—

"After years of controversy and difficulty we have passed an Act to remodel King's College on the plan proposed by your commission, under the title of the University of New Brunswick. We have not connected the College or the head of it with the other educational interests in the Province, but confined him to the University, and he must be a layman. This provision was inserted to prevent difficulty."[54]

PARTIAL CHRONOLOGICAL SKETCH OF DR. RYERSON'S EDUCATIONAL WORK, 1855, ETC.

I will now give a brief summary, in chronological order, of the successive steps which Dr. Ryerson took to develop the system of education which he had founded.

In 1855 Dr. Ryerson established meteorological stations in connection with twelve selected county grammar schools, ten following the coast line of the lakes and on the large rivers, and two entirely inland. In this he was aided by Colonel now General Sir (J. H.) Lefroy, R.E., for many years director of the Provincial (now Dominion) Magnetical Observatory at Toronto. Sets of instruments, having been purchased in London and tested at the Kew Observatory, were sent out to the twelve stations, duly equipped and provided with all necessary appliances.

In 1857 Dr. Ryerson made his third educational tour in Europe, where he procured, at Antwerp, Brussels, Florence, Rome, Paris and London, an admirable collection of copies of paintings by the Old Masters, statues, busts, etc., besides various other articles of a typical character for an educational museum in connection with the Department. In 1867 I was deputed to largely add to this museum collection, which I did in Paris, London, etc., especially in the direction of Egyptian and Assyrian antiquities, busts, casts, fictile ivory, etc.

In 1858-61 Dr. Ryerson took a leading part in a protracted public discussion before a committee of the House of Assembly, in favor of grants to the various "outlying" denominational universities, chiefly in terms of Hon. Robert Baldwin's liberalized University Act of 1853. He maintained that these colleges "did the State some service," and that it was right that their claims should be recognised in a substantial manner, as colleges of a central university. He deprecated the multiplication of universities in the Province, which he held would be the result of a rejection of the proposed scheme. His plan was not adopted, and universities were increased from five to eight subsequently. Twenty-five years after the close of that discussion a scheme for the confederation of these colleges was again considered but without much effect.

In 1862, Dr. Ryerson addressed a circular to boards of trustees in cities and towns, deploring the "numbers of children in these centers of population, growing up with no other education than a training in idleness, vagrancy and crime." He added: "I have, at different times, submitted three propositions or plans for the accomplishment of the object of free schools in cities and towns. First, that as the property of all is taxed for the common school education of all, all should be compelled to allow their children the means of such education at either public or private schools. Or, secondly, that each municipality should be empowered to deal with the vagrancy of children of school age, or the neglect of their education, as a crime, subject to such penalties and such measures for its prevention as each municipality, in its own discretion, might from time to time adopt. Or, thirdly, that the aid of religious benevolence should be invoked and encouraged to supplement the agency of our present school system."

Before bringing the matter again before the Government, Dr. Ryerson solicited the opinion and suggestions of the school boards on the subject.

BISHOP FRASER'S ESTIMATE OF THE U. C. SYSTEM OF EDUCATION IN 1863.

In 1863, Rev. James (afterwards Bishop) Fraser (of Manchester), was appointed a Royal Commission to enquire into the American and Canadian systems of education. From his report, published after his return to England, I quote the following passages:—

"The Canadian system of education, in those main features of it which are common to both Provinces, makes no pretence of being original. It confesses to a borrowed and eclectic character. The neighboring States of New York and Massachusetts, the Irish, English and Prussian systems, have all contributed elements, which have been combined with considerable skill, and the whole administered with remarkable energy, by those to whom its construction was confided. It appears to me, however, that its fundamental ideas were first developed by Mr. (now, I believe, Sir Arthur) Buller, in the masterly report on the state of education in Canada, which he addressed in the year 1838 to Lord Durham, the then Governor-General, in which he sketched the programme of a system, 'making,' as he candidly admitted, 'no attempt at originality, but keeping constantly in view, as models, the system in force in Prussia and the United States, particularly the latter, as being most adapted to the circumstances of the colony.'

"As a result of Mr. Buller's recommendations, (not, however, till after the legislative union of the Provinces which Lord Durham had suggested, as the best remedy for the various political ills under which they severally laboured,) a law was passed in 1841, covering both Provinces in its range, for the establishment and maintenance of public schools. It provided for the appointment of a Superintendent of Education for the whole Province, with two Assistant Superintendents under him, one for each of the sections. A sum of $200,000 was appropriated for the support of schools, which was to be distributed among the several municipal districts, in proportion to the number of children of school age in each of them; $80,000 being assigned to Upper and $120,000 to Lower Canada, such being the then ratio of their respective populations.

"The circumstances of the two sections, however, particularly in the proportions of Roman Catholics to Protestants in each, and the extent to which the Roman Catholic religion may be said to be established in Lower Canada, were soon found to be so different that insuperable difficulties were encountered in working a combined system under one central administration, and in 1845 the law was changed. The nominal office of Chief Superintendent was abolished, and the entire executive administration of the system was confined to the sectional superintendents, and the Provinces, for all educational purposes, again became separated. The law itself was thoroughly revised and adapted to the peculiar wants of each Province, as ascertained by experience; and ever since there have been two systems at work, identical in their leading idea, differing, sometimes widely, in their details, administered by independent executives, and without any organic relations at all.

"Before we proceed to observe the manner and record the results of its practical working, it is proper to premise that it is a purely permissive, not a compulsory system, and its adoption by any municipality is entirely voluntary…. Entering a Canadian school, with American impressions fresh upon the mind, the first feeling is one of disappointment. One misses the life, the motion, the vivacity, the precision—in a word, the brilliancy. But as you stay, and pass both teacher and pupils in review, the feeling of disappointment gives way to a feeling of surprise. You find that this plain, unpretending teacher has the power, and has successfully used the power, of communicating real, solid knowledge and good sense to those youthful minds, which, if they do not move rapidly, at least grasp, when they do take hold, firmly. If there is an appearance of what the Americans call "loose ends" in the school, it is only an appearance. The knowledge is stowed away compactly enough in its proper compartments, and is at hand, not perhaps very promptly, but pretty surely, when wanted. To set off against their quickness, I heard many random answers in American schools; while, per contra to the slowness of the Canadian scholar, I seldom got a reply very wide of the mark. The whole teaching was homely, but it was sound. I chanced to meet a schoolmaster at Toronto, who had kept school in Canada, and was then keeping school at Haarlem, New York, and he gave Canadian education the preference for thoroughness and solid results. Each system—or rather, I should say, the result of each system—seems to harmonize best with the character of the respective peoples. The Canadian chooses his type of school as the Vicar of Wakefield's wife chose her wedding-gown, and as the Vicar of Wakefield chose his wife, "not for a fine, glossy surface, but for such qualities as will wear well." I cannot say, judging from the schools which I have seen —which I take to be types of their best schools—that their choice has been misplaced, or that they have any reason to be disappointed with the results. I speak of the general character of education to which they evidently lean. That the actual results should be unequal, often in the widest possible degree, is true of education under all systems, everywhere.

"One of the most interesting features in the Canadian system is the way in which it has endeavored to deal with what we find to be one of our most formidable difficulties, the religious difficulty. In Canada it has been dealt with by the use of two expedients; one, by prescribing certain rules and regulations, which it was hoped would allow of religious instruction being given in the schools without introducing sectarianism or hurting consciences; the other, by permitting, in certain cases, the establishment of "separate," which are practically denominational, and in fact Roman Catholic schools.

"The permission under certain circumstances to establish separate, that is, denominational schools, is a peculiar feature of the system both of Upper and Lower Canada. Dr. Ryerson thinks that the admission of the principle is a thing to be regretted, though at the same time he considers that the advantages which it entails entirely rest with those who avail themselves of its provisions, and he would not desire to see any coercion used either to repeal or modify them.

"Such, in all its main features, is the school system of Upper Canada. A system, in the eyes of its administrators, who regard it with justifiable self-complacency, not perfect but yet far in advance, as a system of national education, of anything that we can show at home. It is indeed very remarkable to me that in a country, occupied in the greater part of its area by a sparse and anything but wealthy population, whose predominant characteristic is as far as possible removed from the spirit of enterprise, an educational system so complete in its theory and so capable of adaptation in practice should have been originally organized, and have been maintained in what, with all allowances, must still be called successful operation for so long a period as twenty-five years. It shows what can be accomplished by the energy, determination and devotion of a single earnest man. What national education in Great Britain owes to Sir James Kay Shuttleworth, what education in New England owes to Horace Mann, that debt education in Canada owes to Egerton Ryerson. He has been the object of bitter abuse, of not a little misrepresentation; but he has not swerved from his policy or from his fixed ideas. Through evil report and good report he has resolved, and he has found others to support him in the resolution, that free education shall be placed within the reach of every Canadian parent for every Canadian child. I hope I have not been ungenerous in dwelling sometimes upon the deficiencies in this noble work. To point out a defect is sometimes the first step towards repairing it; and if this report should ever cross the ocean and be read by those of whom it speaks, I hope, not with too great freedom, they will perhaps accept the assurance that, while I desired to appreciate, I was bound, above all, to be true; and that even where I could not wholly praise) I never meant to blame. Honest criticism is not hostility."

In a letter addressed to Dr. Ryerson in 1875, the Bishop says:—

"I take it very kindly in you that you remember an old acquaintance, and I have read with interest your last report. I am glad to observe progress in the old lines almost everywhere. I was flattered also to find that some words of mine, written in 1865, are thought worthy of being quoted.... It is pleasant to find a public servant now in the thirty-second year of his incumbency, still so hopeful and so vigorous. Few men have lived a more useful or active life than you, and your highest reward must be to look back upon what you have been permitted to achieve."

Speaking of the character of Dr. Ryerson's educational work and of the way in which he met difficulties in accomplishing it, Mr. J. Antisell Allen, of Kingston, in his paper on "*Dr. Ryerson, a Review and a Study,*" says:—

"There is hardly a foot-length of our civilization on which he has not left his mark. For those who believe that, on the grounds of expediency, a government is justified in interfering with the ordinary working of the great human life-struggle, and so, in taking one man's money to benefit another man's children, that is to a majority so overwhelming as to come almost under the category of universal, as to be every one's belief—what system of general education can recommend itself more fully, or work more smoothly, than does his? In his struggles in this direction, neither seduced by friends, nor cowed by enemies, nor damped in his ardour by the vastness of the undertaking—turning neither to the right hand nor to the left—he has raised to himself a "*monumentum perennius ære,*" and has bequeathed to us and posterity a system of public and high school education second to none anywhere, and, making some deduction for possible mistakes incident to our weak humanity, a system almost as perfect as we in this generation are perhaps capable of generally acquiescing in."

In 1867 Dr. Ryerson made his fourth and final educational tour in Europe and America. On his return he submitted to the Government a highly valuable "Special Report on the Systems and State of Popular Education in the several countries in Europe and the United States of America, with practical suggestions for the improvement of public instruction in Upper Canada." He also made a separate and interesting "Report on the Institutions for the Deaf and Dumb in various countries." A few years afterwards he had the happiness of seeing institutions of a similar kind in successful operation in this Province.

CHARACTER OF THE IMPORTANT SCHOOL LEGISLATION OF 1871.

The fifth and last series of conventions was held in 1869, and on the results of the consultations and deliberations of these conventions, Dr. Ryerson framed that crowning measure of his administration, which received the sanction of the legislature in 1871—twenty-one years after the first great departure in school legislation—that of 1850.

For the various objects which he had recommended during the years from 1850 to 1871, liberal grants were made by the Legislature. The policy of the Government during those years was to sustain Dr. Ryerson and to second his efforts to build up and consolidate the system of public instruction which he had taken such pains to establish. The result was that our school system expanded and grew in every direction, and became firmly rooted in the affections of the people. In this way it came to be regarded as one of the most successful and popular systems of education on the continent. And yet, as I have shown, he was continually suggesting improvements in it, for he always held that there was room, as well as a necessity, for them.

School legislation, chiefly in regard to high schools and matters of detail, took place at intervals during the intervening years, but it was is 1871 and 1874 that the final legislation under Dr. Ryerson's auspices took place. That of 1871 was strikingly progressive and took a wide range. That of 1874 was largely supplemental and remedial.

The Act of 1871 introduced into our school law for the first time some important principles, which, as yet, had not received legislative sanction. They were chiefly those which related, among others, to the following matters:

1. Governmental, combined with improved local, inspection of schools.

2. A high and fixed standard of qualifications for inspectors of public schools.

3. The abolition of non-certificated township superintendents of schools, and the substitution therefor of duly licensed county inspectors.

4. The institution of simultaneous and uniform examinations in the several counties for teachers desiring certificates of qualification. This principle was soon extended to other examinations, including competitive examinations in counties, etc.

REVIEW OF THE SCHOOL LEGISLATION OF 1871.

At Dr. Ryerson's request I prepared for him and wrote the text of his education report for 1870. In that report I reviewed in detail the various provisions and improvements introduced into our school system by the School Act of 1871. I reproduce here the more salient points of that report, touching upon the reasons for the passing of that progressive measure, and indicating some of its main features. I said:—

So many and important have been the changes recently made in the law affecting our System of Public Instruction, that it may be well, as a preliminary to a discussion of those changes, briefly to refer to a few facts relating to the history and progress of our School System.

In 1844, our municipal system (on which our then elementary School Law was engrafted), was in its infancy. The principle of local self-government was new, and much opposition was experienced in giving effect to the School Law then in operation. The theory of local taxation for the support of schools was in some places vigorously opposed, and in others regarded as a doubtful experiment. Even as late as 1850, some municipalities refused to accept the improved law enacted that year, or act under its provisions, and thus deprived their constituents of the great boon of popular education. It is only six years since the last disability, caused by such refusal, was removed,—thus uniting the entire Province in a cordial acceptance of the School Law.

The following brief statistical references will illustrate the growth and advance of our School System:—

In 1844, there were but 2,610 Public Schools, in 1870, there were 4,566. In that year, (1844), the school population was 183,539—of which 96,756 children attended the Public Schools, while 86,783 (or nearly as many more) were reported as not in attendance at any school whatever.

In 1870, the school population was 483,966—of which 420,488 children were in attendance in our schools, and 63,478 reported as not in attendance— not one-seventh, instead of nearly one-half of the children of school age, as in 1844. In 1844, the whole sum available for the support of the Public Schools was about $280,000—of which, approximately $190,000 were raised by local taxation.[55] In 1870, the whole sum available for Public Schools was $1,712,060—of which $1,336,383 were raised by local taxation and fees—an increase of more than seven hundred per cent over 1844!

There are few Canadians who do not now refer with an mixed pride and satisfaction to the vastly improved condition of our Public Schools under the operation of the present law, revised in 1850, and now revised and extended. [56] On no one point have we greater cause for thankfulness and congratulation, than in the fact of the unanimity and cordiality with which our School System is supported by all classes of the community, by men of all shades of political feeling, and, with a single exception (and that in part only), of all religious persuasions in the Province.

OBJECTIONS TO IMPROVE OUR SCHOOL SYSTEM ANSWERED.

It is a singular and gratifying (yet in some respect it has proved an embarrassing) fact that the chief difficulty experienced in promoting the improvement of our School System has arisen from the somewhat over-sensitiveness of the friends of our Schools, lest the proposed changes should disturb the foundations of a system which they had learned to regard with so much favor and affection. This solicitude arose partly from a mistaken view of the condition and necessities of our system, and partly from a misapprehension of the scope and objects of the proposed ameliorations in our School Law. It will be my aim, however, in the following remarks to justify and illustrate the principles and policy involved in the recent important changes which have been made in our School Law.

I would, in the first place, remark that were we, in making improvements in our School System, to confine our observation and experience to our own Province alone, we might be disposed to look with complacency upon that system, and to rest satisfied with the progress which we have already made. The effect of such a state of feeling would be that we would seek to profit little by the educational experience and advancement of other countries. But such a short-sighted and unpatriotic course, though approved by some on the principle of "let well-alone," yet would not commend itself to the maturer judgment of those who are accustomed to look at the "stern logic of facts," and to take a comprehensive and practical view of the underlying causes of the social progress in other countries.

5. The fixing and rendering uniform of a higher standard of qualification for public and high school teachers.

6. Giving the profession of teaching a fixed legal status, and providing more fully and equitably for the retirement and united support, by the profession and the legislature, of worn out or disabled teachers.

7. The establishment by law of a national system of free schools.

8. Declaring the right by law, as well as the necessity, of every child to attend some school, thus recognizing the principle of, and providing for, "compulsory education."

9. Requiring, by law, that adequate school accommodation, in regard to school house, playground and site, be provided by the trustees, for all of the resident children of school age in their localities.

10. Prescribing a more systematic and practical course of study for each of the classes in the public schools.

11. Discriminating, by a clearly defined line, the course of study in public and high schools respectively.

12. Providing for the establishment and support of collegiate institutes, or local colleges.

13. Requiring municipalities to maintain high schools and collegiate institutes, equally with the public schools, and as part of the general school system.

14. Providing, at the option of the ratepayers, for the substitution of township boards of education, in place of local trustee boards.

15. Authorizing the establishment of industrial schools.

Such were the main features of the comprehensive and progressive School Act passed in 1871. In many respects it revolutionized the existing state of things. It gave a wonderful impetus to the schools, and to every department of school system—the effects of which we feel to this day.

We are a young country, placed in close proximity to a large and wonderfully progressive people. In the good providence of God, we are permitted to construct on the broad and deep foundations of British liberty, the corner-stone of a new nationality, leaving to those who come after us to raise the stately edifice itself. Apart from the vital Christianity of our people, what more lasting bond and cement of society in that new nationality, than a free and comprehensive system of Christian education for the youth of the land, such as we have sought to establish? Our aim should, therefore, be to make that system commensurate with the wants of our people, in harmony with the progressive spirit of the times, and comprehensive enough to embrace the various branches of human knowledge which are now continually being called into requisition in the daily life of the farmer, the artizan, and the man of business. In no department of social and national progress have our neighbors made greater advances, or prided themselves more justly, than, in that of free popular education. On the other hand, in no feature of progress under British institutions up to a late period has there been less satisfaction, as a whole, or less positive advancement than in that of public education. By many of our neighbors on the other side of the lines, such inertness and non-appreciation of a vital part of national life has been regarded as inherent in monarchical institutions. The fact, however, has been overlooked that the lingering effects of the long prevalence in Britain of the feudal theory, on which her social and political institutions were originally founded, has, in spite of various ameliorations in the condition of her people, exercised a sure but silent influence against the earlier adoption of the principle of the free and universal education of the people. But so surely and certainly has this latent feeling of opposition to popular education given way before the prevalence of more enlightened views, that, even in the most monarchical countries of Europe, the desire felt and the efforts put forth for the diffusion of public education in all its comprehensiveness and fulness have been remarkable. Nevertheless, even among ourselves, that principle of latent opposition to popular education did exist in the earlier stages of our educational history. Its gradual removal, therefore, under the beneficent operation of our School Laws, and the prevalence of juster and more patriotic views in matter of education are subjects of sincere congratulation to our people.

NECESSITY FOR THE CHANGES IN THE SCHOOL LAW OF ONTARIO IN 1871.

We will now proceed, in the light of the educational facts and illustrations which we have given from other countries, to discuss the recent improvements which have been effected in our own law.

The population of this Province, according to the recent census, is 1,620,842. The number of children of school age is 483,966, or a little over one-fourth of the whole. The number of Elementary Schools is not much below 5,000, and are maintained at an annual cost of nearly $1,800,000, or one dollar per head of the population. Such being the magnitude to which our Educational System has grown, every man will feel how imperative it is upon us to see that that system is as thorough and complete in all of its details as possible; and that in no respect should it be allowed to fall below the standard now reached by the other educating countries to which we have referred.

So long as our system of schools was in its infancy, and might be fairly regarded as yet an experiment, so long as we confine our efforts to mere elementary organization and be content with very moderate results. Experience has shown, however, that without great care and constant effort the tendency of all systems of education, and ours among the rest, is to a state of equilibrium, or to a uniform dead level of passable respectability. This is the stage in its history, as elsewhere, at which our system has arrived, and at which, as we have explained, many of its friends are disposed to leave it. But those who have carefully studied the subject in all its bearings, and have looked more closely into the educational history, the progress and failures of other countries, know full well that our school system would fall behind that of other countries and become stationary, unless it embodies within itself from time to time the true elements of progress, and provides fully and on a sufficient scale for the educational wants of the youth of the country.

Since 1850 it was left to the ratepayers in each school division to decide annually whether the schools should be free or partly supported by rate-bill on pupils attending the school. The principle, that a Public School education is the right of every child in the land, and that every man should contribute, according to his property, to the education of every child in the community, by whose influence and labors such property is protected and rendered valuable, had greatly obtained, so that Free Schools had increased from one hundred to five hundred per annum, until upwards of four thousand of the four thousand four hundred Public Schools were made free by actual experiments, and by the annual discussions and votes in these primary meetings of the people. The demand was very general for several years, that all the Public Schools should now be made free by law, and all local disputes on the subject be thus terminated. This has now been happily accomplished by the new law.

It is not necessary to go farther into detail in this retrospect, as the foregoing extracts indicate the scope and spirit of the improved Act of 1871.

HON. ADAM CROOKS ON THE SCHOOL INSPECTION LEGISLATION OF 1871.

In his speech before the Legislative Assembly on the 18th of February, 1877, the first Minister of Education for Ontario, in referring to the improved system of school inspection introduced by the Act of 1871, and the more certain tenure of office secured to County Inspectors under that Act, said:

> "I have also been ready to say that most valuable results were secured by the change in the law in 1871, under which the present mode of school inspection took the place of the old plan of local superintendence. Inspectors now must possess high qualifications, both as teachers and in scholarship, while the emoluments of the office make it an object of ambition to every school teacher; and we have many teachers in the Province who posses qualifications of the high standard prescribed for Public School Inspectors. The tenure of the office of County Inspector is such as should secure their impartiality. So long as an Inspector discharges his duties efficiently, he can be removed only by a two-thirds majority of the County Council. It is unlikely that such two-thirds majority would be found unless the Inspector had given reasonable cause for his dismissal. It would not be wise therefore to alter the tenure by which County Inspectors hold office."

EFFECT OF THE SCHOOL ACT OF 1871 IN THE COUNTY OF HALDIMAND.

The following valuable testimony as to the great improvement in our schools which was wrought through the agency of the School Act of 1871, is highly suggestive and practical in its character. What is true of Haldimand, as here expressed, is also true of other parts of the Province.

In an address to the teachers of Haldimand in 1873, Mr. Inspector Harcourt, M.P.P., said:—

"No one, whose attention has been called to the matter, could imagine the miserable condition of the majority of the school-houses of 1871. At that time there were not ten properly furnished buildings in Haldimand. Many of them with low ceilings, broken floors and damaged windows, had for seats nothing better than the antiquated bench facing the wall. Too cold or too hot by turns in winter, and suffocating in summer. With nothing to attract and everything to discourage scholars, we wonder that an intelligent public has so long tolerated their existence.... In the main, however, I am especially gratified at the improvements effected. In two years sixteen brick buildings have been erected; all of them substantial and well furnished—some of them models of neatness and finish. In a dozen sections preparations are being made for replacing the old houses, so that we have good reason to hope that in a year or two, at furthest, our country will no longer be noticeable for the miserable style of its school-houses."

"Connected with the question of progress in certain branches of study, in relation of which I might say of cause and effect, are the two items of Examination of Teachers and School Accommodation. The provisions now in force for the examination of teachers are such that, if wisely carried out, the standard of the profession must be raised, and along with it the status of our schools.... The fact that somehow or another teachers received first and second class certificates, three or four years ago, who could not now obtain a third; that while it was exceptional for an applicant to fail then, those who succeed now are but thirty per cent. of the whole is known to all of us....

"To summarize the foregoing statements we HAVE progressed since 1871, swiftly in one particular, slowly and steadily in several others."—*Address, pages 5-7.*

EFFECT OF THE SCHOOL LAW OF 1871 IN THE COUNTY OF SIMCOE (SOUTH.)

At the inauguration of the new school-house in Barrie in 1872, the Rev. Wm. McKee, B.A., Inspector of Schools in South Simcoe, stated what had been the salutary effect of the School Law of 1871 in his county. He said:—

During my visits to the schools I found many of the school-houses of a very inferior description—being rude log buildings, old and dilapidated, with seats and desks of a corresponding character, often situated on the edge of the road, and without wells, offices, playgrounds or fencing of any kind; so that it is quite certain and plain the requirements of the new School Law have not come into force at all too soon, so far as the interests and advancement of education in this part of Ontario are concerned. Indeed truth obliges me to state that in the Riding which forms my field of labour—and I believe the remark will hold true with still greater force in regard to North Simcoe—the school-houses which are sufficiently large, well ventilated, fully furnished, and provided with an adequate supply of requisites are very few—perhaps less than half-a-dozen all told. It is true, however, that since the New School Law and Regulations came into operation there are indications of a change for the better in regard to the matters to which I have alluded. I could mention not less than twelve or fourteen school sections in which steps have *already* been, or are being taken for the erection of new school-houses which are designed to replace the old buildings, and which, in regard to adequate school accommodation, are also intended to meet the requirements of the New School Law, and to be in every way suitable for school purposes. And it is to be distinctly noticed that in all the cases to which I have referred, the *initiative* has been taken by the people or the trustees themselves; and I, for my part, feel that I cannot but regard this as a very significant fact—a very hopeful and encouraging symptom. I look upon it as an omen for good, and as an important and gratifying evidence of the favourable and successful working of the New School Law and Regulations. For being intimately acquainted with the southern part of the county for the last fifteen years, I have no hesitation in maintaining that the effects spoken of, or the action taken by school trustees or the people, can be fairly traced to no other cause than to the working and influence of the New School Law and Regulations. I can testify that latterly—I mean particularly since the passing of the New School Act—I have marked among the people of these townships a deepening sense of the importance of a sound education, and likewise an increasing desire to encourage and promote it. I have noticed, also, I think, both among trustees and parents, a growing conviction that not only the efficiency of the teacher, but, also the discipline and spirit of a school, the progress of children in their studies, their proper training, and their successful education, are far more intimately connected than it was one time imagined, with the style and character of the schoolroom in which the work of instruction is carried on, and with the kind of school accommodations provided for and enjoyed by pupils.[57]

CHAPTER V.

A SPECIAL CHAPTER ON THE STATE EDUCATION IN THE "OLDEN TIME" IN UPPER CANADA.

In this special chapter, I insert a series of interesting papers, illustrative of what may be called the interior or domestic character of school life in its various phases, in Upper Canada, from the time of the passing of Dr. Ryerson's first School Act, in 1846, to the passing of his last School Act, in 1871. These papers give a graphic, bird's-eye view of the state of the school, school houses and school teachers in the years gone by. They are by representative men—inspectors, public men and school teachers, and they are, therefore, interesting and valuable, as giving the result of the personal observation of these gentlemen.

The personal experience of the Hon. J. Sandfield Macdonald is of an earlier date than those which follow, and refers to one of the most noted of the old District Grammar Schools. It is highly interesting as a reminiscence of the early training of one of our most noted public men, and one, under whose auspices, the important School Act of 1871 was passed.

Hon. J. Sandfield Macdonald's school days—His Reminiscences of them.

At a public dinner given to the Hon. J. Sandfield Macdonald in 1870, he thus referred to his early school days:—

"My friend, Judge Jarvis, has referred to my early life, and has very properly remarked that this is the country that offers the widest field to the industrious, or to a man of energy if he only possesses a modicum of brains…. It is true what the Judge states that I arrived in Cornwall forty years ago next autumn…. I was engaged in a dry goods store. But the Judge has told you that I was not satisfied with that state of things. I went to the school here, which has had a reputation it may be proud of ever since the time of the late Bishop Strachan. It was the school that educated the Boultons, the McGills, and the Jarvises. In the school I entered, and there I had to strive with those who were able to be maintained by their parents. I worked against them at a great disadvantage, and would have succumbed but that I was cheered on by my venerable preceptor. Many others have struggled in that school of whom Canada should be proud. One of them particularly. He was one of the brightest and most talented of the men our eastern district can boast of. But providence has thought proper to take him away from his sphere of usefulness. Need I say that I refer to that ornament of the Bench, the late Chancellor Vankoughnet.—Were Dr. Urquhart able to boast of no other pupil but that honourable gentleman, he might have retired on his laurels. If that old gentleman had not sent me a letter of encouragement I would not have been here, as I was about to break down for want of means. This letter was written in 1835, and … I cannot help shewing what was thought of me by one who had the most perceptive idea of the ability of his pupils. This letter had the effect of making me bear up in my struggle with my superiors in position and was as follows:

"'These certify that the bearer, Mr. John S. McDonald, was a pupil in the Eastern District School, from the 19th Nov., 1832, to the 23rd Dec. last; that during that period his industry and application were close and assiduous, and that his progress in the several branches of study, to which he directed his attention, was highly respectable, and very considerably exceeded what is usually made in the same space of time; that the perseverance manifested in overcoming the difficulties to be encountered at the outset of a classical and mathematical education, called forth the particular remark and approval of his teacher, as indicating considerable energy of character, and as an earnest of future success in the prosecution of his studies. Moreover, that his general deportment during the same period, was most exemplary, and becoming, evincing at all times a kindly disposition towards his fellow students and a most respectful deference to the discipline of the school; and that, if the good opinion and good wishes of his teacher can on any occasion profit him, he is justly entitled to both.'"

"I owe all the spirit of independence which I have maintained throughout my career, to my learning in that school. After I left school I went into the study of the law, in the office of the late Mr. McLean."

EDUCATION IN THE COUNTY OF WELLINGTON UNDER DR. RYERSON'S ADMINISTRATION.

The following admirable resumé of the former state of education and of educational progress in the county of Wellington, and indeed throughout Ontario generally, was given in an address on "Then and Now," delivered before a public meeting in Guelph, in May, 1880, by Hon. Charles Clarke, ex-Speaker of the House of Assembly. After some preliminary remarks, Mr. Clarke said:—

Little more than thirty years ago, much of the country, now known as the county of Wellington, was a wilderness. The territory north of Guelph was almost unsettled, beyond the townships of Nichol, and the settled portion possessed but few residents. In Wellington, the upper tier of townships had scarcely been entered upon, and names of places now "familiar as household words" were unknown. Such roads as there were had been simply cut through the bush, and had experienced little other improvement than that which the axe, the handspike, the logging chain and fire had afforded. Peel was in the early stage of settlement; Maryboro was almost unknown; Minto was really a *terra incognito*; Luther was, in popular estimation, a vast and irreclaimable swamp; Arthur had a mere handful of settlers; Mount Forest was a nameless and unbroken government reserve for a town plot, covered with virgin forest; Elora possessed some half-dozen houses; such places as Harriston, Palmerston and Drayton were not even a dream of the future; and the gravel roads, thrifty villages, and smiling farms which now make pleasant travel from the northern bank of the Grand River to the utmost bounds of Wellington, were covered with thick and luxuriant growth of maple, hemlock, elm and cedar. Everything was in primitive shape, and yet the mark of future progress was made, here and there, and coming events cast their shadow. Oxen were far more numerous than teams of horses, and neither could be regarded as plentiful. The axe was more busy than the plough, and regularly prepared more acres for the annual sowing. Money was scarce, produce was low in price, barter was the rule and not the exception, postal communication was defective, wages were poor, and "hard times" were as commonly talked about and as earnestly believed in as to-day, when, measured by the past, the term is comparatively meaningless. There was a feeling of despondency throughout the community, and people were divided as to the cause of the general depression. Some blamed the Rebellion of a few years before; others said that the effects of Family Compactism had not yet died away; and still others attributed all evils to the newly effected Union between Upper and Lower Canada. There is little wonder that, at such a time, schools and schoolmasters were under the weather, and reckoned as but of "small account" by many of our people.

EARLY SCHOOL LEGISLATION IN 1841, 1843 AND 1846.

Thanks to the energy, however, of a noble few, prominent amongst whom stood Egerton Ryerson, the Government of that day took steps to obtain information as to the system of public education in force in some of the states of the American Union and in Europe, and, taking Massachussetts and Prussia as a guide, enacted a sweeping amendment to School Act for Upper Canada, in the ninth year of Her Majesty's reign, and put it into operation in 1847. In 1841, the first Common School Law had been passed, and in 1843 it was amended, but the system was defective and unproductive of expected results.

Under it, townships were divided into school sections, by township superintendents, who were practically uncontrolled, and therefore, in many instances, arbitrary, and these divisions were unequal in size, often unnecessarily small, and frequently unfairly made. The consequence of this state of things was unpopularity of the law, and a pretty general conviction that common schools were too often common nuisances. The report of the Superintendent of Education, for 1847, tells us that the system produced "miserable school-houses, poor and cheap teachers, interrupted and temporary instruction and heavy rate-bills." In some districts, before the passage of the amending School Act, 9 Vic. Chap. 20, the District Council had never imposed a school assessment, depending for school maintenance entirely upon the small legislative grant apportioned to each district, and an equivalent raised solely by rate-bills or voluntary contributions. No uniformity existed in the use of class books, the township superintendent or the teacher, or even the parent dictating what should be employed in each particular section. In 1846, no fewer than 13 different spelling books, 107 readers, 35 arithmetics, 20 geographies, 21 histories, and 16 grammars, were used in our Common Schools, besides varying class books on other subjects.

INFERIOR QUALIFICATIONS OF TEACHERS AND VARIED METHODS OF TEACHING.

The methods of teaching were almost as numerous as the teachers, and followed no specified rule. Sometimes it was by classes, often by individuals, and in other cases by an extensive use of monitors, being generally a mixture of the three styles, and nearly always a higgledy-piggledy, go-as-you-please arrangement, as easy as possible to the teacher, and as unproductive of good results to the pupil as such indefinite work might be fully expected to be. And the character of the teachers, speaking in general terms, and not forgetting many bright exceptions, was not above suspicion. Certificates were granted by township superintendents, who too often relieved the charitable, and the district council, by thrusting into the school-house the ne'er-do-wells, the infirm, the crippled, the sickly and the unfortunate, who, under ordinary circumstances, would have become dependent upon the good nature and benevolence of their fellow-citizens. In one district a superintendent, after the passage of the new School Law, was compelled to give notice that he would not grant certificates to any candidates unless they were strictly sober, and that he would cancel the certificates of all teachers who suffered themselves at any time to become intoxicated. And, we are gravely informed, the result was that a majority, not all, of the hitherto intemperate teachers became thoroughly temperate men, and that the incorrigible were dismissed. The quality of the teachers may be guessed at very fairly, it is safe to say, from the salaries paid to them. In 1845, the average was £26 2s, or $104.40; in 1846, £26 4s, or $104.80; and in 1847, £28 10s, or $114, and this, too, for the most part, exclusive of board. Had the schools been kept open during the whole of the teaching months of these years, the salaries would have averaged $134 in 1845, $147 in 1846, and $148 in 1847. It must be borne in mind that, in those days, male were much more numerous than female teachers, so that the smaller amounts generally paid to those of the gentler sex had comparatively little influence in lessening the general average. The parsimony and poverty of the people had much to do, of course, with the quality of the teacher, for men who could obtain higher wages at almost any other occupation, through physical or intellectual superiority, would not waste time and opportunity to earn more than the paltry pittance paid to the pedagogue, simply through philanthropic desire to advance the interests of the rising generation.

Dr. Ryerson's Test of the Intelligence of a School Section.

Says Dr. Ryerson, in the report to which I am indebted for these facts: "This small compensation of teachers is the great source of inefficiency in the common schools. Persons of good abilities and attainments will not teach for little or nothing so long as they can obtain a more ample remuneration in other pursuits." He adds, in language as truthful, and as worthy of notice to-day, as when it was written: "People cannot obtain good teachers any more than good lawyers or physicians without paying for their services." And, as he says in the next sentence, so say we all, and so I am happy to observe are many of our school corporations saying all over the province: "The intelligence of any school section or corporation of trustees may be tested by the amount of salary they are disposed to give a good teacher." If Egerton Ryerson had said and done nothing more than this, he would have deserved the gratitude of every teacher in Ontario, simply because he had the courage to put upon record a sentiment which, at the time when he used the words, was eminently unpopular, and a direct and stinging rebuke to nearly every school-board then existent. In those days, cheap teachers were wanted, and the supply equalled the demand, while the pockets of the charitable were saved, a semblance of education was kept up, and the county poorhouses were not required so long as every other school section provided for one, at least, of those who would, in these days, be generally regarded as eligible candidates for admission thereto. The amount of interest taken in educational matters was not evidenced in small salaries alone.

The Character of the School-house also a Test.

The school-house, in its quality, too often matched the teacher. Of 2,572 school-houses in Upper Canada in 1847, 49 only were of brick, and 84 of stone, the others being frame and log. Of the 2,500, 800, or about one-third, were in good repair; 98 had more than one room; 1,125, or less than half, were properly furnished with desks and seats; only 367 were provided with a suitable play-ground; and not more than 163, out of 2,572, had necessary outbuildings. Coming nearer home, we find that the municipalities now comprised in the county of Wellington contained, in 1847, 43 school-houses, of which one was built of stone, 9 were frame, and 33 were log, and the report states that only 13 were good, 25 were middling, and the balance were inferior. When we remember the standard of "goodness" in those days, when school authorities at Toronto were thankful for small favors in rural districts, we can have some faint idea of the character of the buildings pronounced inferior. It is probable that they came up to the style of accommodation of the Mapleton school, in Manitoba, which I find described in the last report of the Superintendent of Protestant Schools for that Province, as follows: "Found that since my last visit the school-house has been floored; it still required plastering and ceiling and weather-boarding." What sort of a building it was before these improvements were effected, it doesn't require a very active brain to imagine, and when you have the picture in your mind's eye you will have some conception of the pleasures of teaching in the "good old times," of less than half a century ago, in Upper Canada.

School Condition of the County of Wellington in 1847.

Returning to 1847, we are told that in the whole of Wellington District, composed of the territory now forming the three counties of Wellington, Waterloo and Grey, there were 102 schools, of which only 22 possessed good buildings. Let us glance for a moment at the then state of finances of the school corporations in which we feel most interested. Guelph township, including the village of Guelph, raised $507.38 by the municipal assessment, for school purposes, realized $556.75 from rate-bills, and received $416.69 from the legislative grant, or a total of $1,480.82, wherewith to pay seven teachers, maintain, more or less efficiently, ten schools, and afford instruction, good, bad or indifferent, as the case might be, to 517 scholars. The township of Puslinch was nearly abreast of Guelph, and kept up 10 schools, paid 13 teachers, and had 558 scholars on the roll, at an outlay of $1,381.86, but it must be remembered that if two or three teachers were employed, at different portions of the year, in one school, they increased the grand total of teachers for the year. It may have been that, while thirteen appear to have been engaged, there were not more, and probably less than ten employed for the full teaching year. In 1847, Erin had the highest number of scholars of any municipality in the county, having returned a total of 585, in six schools, and with eleven teachers, at an outlay of $1,039.06. Amaranth was at the foot of the list, with one school, one teacher, thirty-eight scholars, and an outlay, made up from rate-bill, assessment and legislative grant, of $68.04. Peel and Wellesley, combined, had one school, three teachers,—employed at some portion or other of the year,—and spent $80.52. Nichol (including Fergus and Elora), Eramosa and Garafraxa made returns,—the name Garafraxa being spelt with a double r, as I have found it to be in all old official documents,— but Pilkington, Arthur, Maryboro, Luther and Minto do not appear to have had school organization, not even municipal existence, while, of the whole county of Grey, Derby and Sydenham were alone mentioned in the return. It may be interesting to know—although I am aware, from painful experience, that listening to strings of figures is not the most enlivening occupation in the world,—that the whole amount paid for school purposes, in the county of Wellington, for that year, was $5,862, of which $5,763 was given to teachers, and that the average cost for each pupil taught was $2.10. One other fact may be adduced which will enable you to form a still clearer estimate of the educational status of Upper Canada at the date referred to. The Chief Superintendent had, in forms and regulations issued by him, specified the lowest general standard of qualification for teachers, but was forced to believe that a much lower standard had been acted upon by school visitors. These visitors were clergymen, magistrates and district councillors,—equivalent to our reeves,—and any two of them could examine a teacher, test his or her qualification, pretty much as they deemed best, and grant a certificate, available only for one school and one year, it is true, but nevertheless renewable, and answering every purpose of the certificate of to-day. It is not difficult to imagine a much more easy and varying examination, under such circumstances, than that which an improved system soon rendered necessary, and the quality of teachers so produced need not be further particularized.

We have thus obtained some glimpse of the THEN of our educational facilities of a generation ago. The picture might be elaborated. It would be easy to fill in details from memory; to tell how the blind oft times led the blind; how the ignorant teacher insured the ignorant pupil; and how "schooling" was frequently a farce, and mere waste of time....

GREAT EDUCATIONAL ADVANCE MADE BY THE PROVINCE OF ONTARIO SINCE 1847.

That the Province has made enormous strides in population, wealth, intelligence and importance, during the last thirty years, admits of no doubt. Our forests have disappeared, an improved system of agriculture has followed, manufactories have sprung up, railways have connected every county, a daily press has become an established and indispensable institution, the telegraph has economized time by practically annihilating distance, while numerous inventions and discoveries have created new wants, and supplied as rapidly as they have made them. Without losing our characteristic love of hard work—I here speak of everybody in general, and nobody in particular, and purposely avoid all personal allusions—and that industrial enterprise which springs from it, we have become a reading and much more cultured people. The scholar, endowed with physical capacity equal to that possessed by an illiterate competitor, is worth more than he in the factory, the workshop, the store, the mill, the mine, or on the sea or farm. Cultivated brain has a market value, and book learning is no longer despised, or regarded with half contempt, as the mark distinguishing the mere dreamer from the worker. To possess the "Reason Why" is no proof now-a-days of physical and practical inferiority; to know a little of everything, and everything of something, is not now the peculiar privilege of the English Gentleman. Little wonder is there, therefore, that what the school has helped to bring about, should tend to make the school more valued. That such has been its effect we have but to look around to see. Where in 1847, we, in Upper Canada, had 2,863 school houses, our last returns show that we possess more than 5,000, and while the number has so largely increased the advance in value has been in much greater proportion. In 1847 we had, in all Upper Canada, but 49 school-houses built of brick; now we boast of 1,569 built of that material, or over thirty times as many. In 1847 we had eighty-four constructed of stone; now we claim more than 500. In 1847 half of our school buildings were of logs; now not more than a seventh are of that primitive character. There are no returns of money cost of buildings or of amount expended in their erection in 1847, but we find that the expenditure for all school purposes in that year, inclusive of teachers' salaries, was $350,000, while for 1877, for erection and repairs of school-houses, fuel, etc., alone we paid $1,035,390, and a total for school purposes of $3,073,489, or, in round numbers, nine times as much as in 1847. The improved financial value of the teacher is another strong testimony, willingly borne by the people, to their increased interest in education, for, as a rule, a free people will not pay for that which they fail to appreciate. In 1847 there was paid for teachers' salaries a total sum of $310,398. In 1877 the amount was $2,038,099. In 1847 there were 3,028 teachers employed, while in 1877 there were 6,468. In 1847, board was often given in addition to the nominal salary, and was, in fact, part of the teacher's remuneration. Grant that the teachers here enumerated as serving in 1847 were employed eight months in that year—which is more than the average—and put board at $2 per week, which was higher than was the average rate in those days—the average payment to each teacher would not exceed $170, and this was fully equal to, if not greater than was actually allowed. In 1877 the average amount paid to each teacher was $315. The larger amount willingly paid in 1877 for the support of Free Schools, than was unwillingly given in 1847, for the maintenance of rate-supported schools—for payment was then made under protest, and the school law was exceedingly unpopular, while rate-bills and contributions were nearly everywhere necessary, in addition to municipal assessments, to make up the teachers' salaries—is yet another proof of the hold which the educational movement has taken upon the judgment and sympathy of the people of Ontario. In 1847, too, pupils were grudgingly taught, at a cost of $2.80 per head, while in 1877 the average was $6.20. And when we add to all these things the fact that, in 1847, only 124,829 pupils attended our common schools, out of a school population of 230,975, or scarcely one in two, while in 1877, out of a school population of 494,804, not less than 490,860 names were entered on the roll, it is needless to say anything further in illustration of the marked contrast between the two periods, of the immense superiority of the present over the past condition of our schools, and of the public opinion which is necessary to their effective maintenance.

GREAT ADVANCE ALSO IN THE STANDARD OF TEACHING ABILITY.

And the standard of teaching ability, in so far as literary acquirements go, has kept pace with the progress which has otherwise characterized the history of a scholastic generation. We have long got past the period when any two magistrates, any two reeves, or even any two clergymen, could grant permission to teach, and annually invest the teacher with legal status. We subject our examiners themselves to examinations, have uniformity in the character of our examination papers, and propound questions to candidates which fully and fairly test their educational attainments. We have gone beyond *that*, and instituted county Normal Schools—for such our Model Schools may be fairly termed—at which we require applicants for a certificate to still further establish their fitness for the work upon which they seek to enter. We have not reached perfection, but we have travelled a long distance in the direction in which it lies. We have made every school practically free, built up a High School system which opens up to all seekers after higher education ample opportunity to prepare for the University course, at a minimum of cost, and placed our University upon such a footing that its advantages are not the exclusive privilege of the well-to-do, but are proffered to even the poorest student who cares to submit to a period of self-denial, and lose a little extra time in early life, for the purpose of securing them. As a people we have done no more than, probably not so much as, we ought to do, with the view of placing educational facilities within the reach of every child born or brought into the Province, but we have, nevertheless, ventured and effected more than has been attempted in many older and more wealthy lands. We have the consciousness of having done our duty, according to our lights. In our long-settled sections of country the school-house bell is within the hearing, or the school-house itself is within sight of nearly every family. In newer portions of the Province, wherever half-a-dozen or so of clearances are commenced, in the wilds of Muskoka or Algoma, provision is made for the instruction of the little ones who bless those backwoods' homes. The school-master is abroad throughout the land, and is doing much to ensure a glowing future for our country, and when his work is done, and he is compelled to retire from his labors, we willingly open the public purse and give to him that which keeps him above absolute penury, and assures him that, while Ontario cares only to help those who possess the disposition to help themselves, she is neither ungrateful nor forgetful. And, seeing all these things, we cannot help feeling that our youthful Province may modestly and yet proudly lift her head amongst the nations of the earth, assured that there are none who can reproach her with neglect of the first and best interests of those little children whom God has entrusted to her keeping.

STATE OF EDUCATION IN UPPER CANADA IN 1847-1849.

From an elaborate report prepared by the Rev. W. H. Landon, School Superintendent, to the Municipal Council of the district of Brock (county of Oxford) in 1849, I make the following extracts. The first refers to the educational supineness of the people:—

"Up to a recent period (say the last two years), the people, generally, seems to have entered upon no enquiries, and to have formed no just conclusion on the subject of education, or the proper means of imparting it. They seemed to think, if they thought at all, that all schools were equal, and that all teachers who could read, write, etc., in a better manner than their pupils were equally good.... As to books, it was supposed that any one, or any ten of the fifty different varieties of spelling books in use, with the English Reader, was all that was requisite for the reading classes, while a few treatises on arithmetic taken at random from the almost endless variety with which the country was flooded, would supply the means of imparting a knowledge of the science of numbers, and two or three grammars by as many different authors, would supply material for the grammar class and complete the stock of text books for the schools."...

Mr. Landon draws the following graphic picture of the school-house "shanties" of those days. He also gives a vivid view of the interior:

"The school-houses in many instances (though not in all) are miserable shanties made of logs loosely and roughly put together; the interstices filled with clay, portions of which are from time to time crumbling down filling the place with filth and dust. Under your feet are loose boards, without nails, across which, when one walks, a clatter is produced equal to that heard in a lumber yard. Over your head are the naked rafters, stained with smoke and hung with cobwebs and dust. Two or three little windows, generally half way up the walls, admit the light; and a rough door which does not fit the opening, creaks upon its wooden hinges.... The writing desks are generally long sloping shelves pinned up against the walls as high as the breasts of the pupils who sit before them. The seats are without backs and from eighteen inches to two feet high. Sometimes we have a master's desk, but awkwardly constructed, for the most part too high for the sitting posture and too low for the standing one.... We have no blackboards, no maps and no illustrative apparatus of any kind.

"When we enter one of these schools, we behold a picture of discomfort and misery. The children are perched upon the benches before described: but as they have no support for their backs, and as only the taller of them can reach the floor with their feet, marks of weariness and pain are visible in their features and postures. Some to procure rest and ease to their aching frames have drawn up both feet upon the bench and are sitting cross-legged like a tailor on the shop board. Others stooping forward, rest their elbows upon their knees, with one hand supporting their chins and with the other holding up their books before their weary eyes; while all avail themselves of every possible excuse to change their position and so obtain relief. Some asking permission to go out, others to get a drink, and many constantly flocking to the teacher's desk with words to be pronounced, sums to be examined and corrected, pens to be mended, or difficulties to be explained, in connection with grammar, or other lesson, etc. So that the place is filled with noise and disorder, rendering study impossible and anything like the cultivation of cheerful and benevolent affections entirely out of the question."...

Then follows an example of the character of the teaching "in a school in the centre of one of the largest and wealthiest townships" in the district of Brock:

—

"This school was taught by a person who in his youth had enjoyed what we term superior advantages, being connected with a family of highest respectability. Notice of my intended visit had several days before been sent to the teacher. The female pupils had ... decorated the place with evergreens and bouquets of flowers. The room, though humble and coarse, was neat and tidy. When I entered, the class in the fourth book of lessons was reading. A book was put into my hands and I desired them to proceed.... When they were done reading I proceeded to examine them on the lesson. Great Britain was mentioned in the lesson and allusion made to her people and institutions. My first question, therefore was—Where is Great Britain? From the vacant and surprised stare with which this question was received I was satisfied that they had no clear conception of what Great Britain was.... I finally asked what is the form of Government in Great Britain? As no answer was given, I ... asked whether a King, Queen or President governed in Great Britain? To this question a pupil, aided by the teacher, who whispered in her ear, replied a Queen. I than asked her name.... After a good deal of hesitation, a young woman of eighteen or twenty years of age, replied "Queen Elizabeth!"

THE OLD LOG SCHOOL HOUSE AND ITS BELONGINGS.

In connection with the realistic picture of education in the County of Oxford, in 1847-49, sketched by the Rev. W. H. Landon, District Superintendent, the following dual pictures of "The Old Log School" and "The Pioneer Teachers," taken from the Toronto *Globe* of 1887, will be found to be highly interesting. The pictures are graphically drawn by a teacher, and from a teacher's standpoint. Speaking of the representative teacher of a former generation recalling the past, he said:—

The old days come up vividly before him, when he first engaged in the work in some country district, engaging to devote to it the best energies of body and mind, for, it may be, some such munificent salary as eight or ten dollars a month, said salary to be supplemented by the saving in expense effected through the process formerly so much in vogue of boarding around. How well he remembers the old log school house, with its low ceiling on which a tall man could easily lay his hand; the narrow apertures, fitted with a few panes of 7×9 glass which served for windows; the floor of unplaned boards, whose crevices were either compactly filled with accumulations of dust and litter characteristic of the school room, or worse still, yawning to swallow up pen-knife and slate pencil as they would ever and anon drop from the fingers of some luckless wight, started from the half slumber into which the drowsy monotony of the ill-ventilated school room had beguiled him, by the stentorian tones, or possibly the vigorous cuffs, of the master of ceremonies. Very distinctly the vision of such a school room of the old type, though at a date much less than fifty years ago, rises before the writer as memory carries him back to the little Canadian hamlet in which his boyhood was passed. The desks, so as far any were provided, consisted of a wide shelf fixed at a pretty sharp angle against the wall, and extending all around the room, with an intermission only at the narrow space occupied by the door.

This primitive arrangement was sometimes supplemented with a long, flat table composed of three or four loose planks in the rough, supported by wooden benches or horses placed transversely beneath. The seats were of planks or slabs, likewise unsmoothed, constructed by driving rudely hewn legs into holes bored with a large augur, at a suitable angle, in the lower surface of the plank or slab. These legs often projected an inch or so above the surface of the seat. It could not be said of these rude structures as in Cowper's "Evolution of the sofa," that "the slippery seat betrayed the sliding part that pressed it," for between the projecting legs and the innumerable "splinters" the unhappy occupant was in much greater danger of being impaled and pinned fast than of slipping off. Perhaps it was better so, for in view of the great height usually given them, the fall, for a small child, while it would most surely have been a "laughing matter," might yet have proved a serious one.... It was certainly a strange and cruel infatuation which constrained our grandfathers to think that the proper position for a boy or girl at school was upon a narrow perch, without back or arm support of any kind, and with the feet dangling some six or eight inches above the floor.

The picture of the old school bench would not be accurate without reference to the warping of the plank which was pretty sure soon to take place, with the result of raising one or other of the diagonal legs an inch or two from the floor, thus converting the seat, when filled with its living, aching load, into a tilting board, provocation of many a trick from the omnipresent mischievous boy of the school, and resulting in many a blow from the palm or cane of the irate master, which would, of course, generally descend upon innocent ears or shoulders.

What a picture did the wooden desks and walls of those old-time school houses present, worn smooth with the elbows, smeared with the jackets, variegated with the ink, carved with the jack-knives and stained with the tears of boisterous and blubbering boys and rosy-cheeked, hoydenish or timid girls. What burlesque, too, upon every intelligent idea of education were the processes carried on in them. From nine o'clock to twelve, and from one till four, six long hours, as marked by the sun's shadow on the rude dial marked out on the windowsill, did the work go on.

Murray's Reader, and in the most ambitious districts his Grammar, Walker's Dictionary, Walkingame's Arithmetic, Goldsmith's Geography and somebody's spelling-book, with slate and pencil, a scanty supply of paper and ink, and pen shaped with a keen pen-knife from a quill picked up from the wayside or plucked ruthlessly from the wing of some reluctant "squawking" goose, would complete the scholar's outfit. It is the hour for preparation of the reading lesson. The school room resounds with the loud hum of a score or two of boys and girls all "studying aloud" with a most distracting din, and all the heads and bodies swaying constantly and simultaneously back and forth as an accompaniment to the voice. This voice in the case of perhaps a majority would be modulated without the slightest relation to the contents of the printed page, while the thoughts of the ostentatiously industrious student would be busy with some projected game or trick for the coming recess. And yet how often would the Scotch school master's eye gleam with pride and pleasure when he had, by dint of persuasion or threat, succeeded in getting every boy and girl engaged in the horrible, monotonous chant.

Then the recitation—what a scene of confusion and stripes, tears and bellowings. Perhaps it was the column of spellings. A few, fitted by nature with memories adapted for that kind of work, would make their way in triumph to the head of the long semicircular class. But woe, woe to the dullards and the dunces, under a regime whose penalty for missing a word a foot and a half long would be, very likely, two or three strokes on the tingling fingers or aching palm with the pitiless hardwood ferule, this process being occasionally varied as some noisy or idling youngster was called up from a back seat to be visited with a still sterner chastisement for some trifling misdemeanor…. The writer can recall instances and experiences innumerable, the infliction being sometimes accompanied with a caution to tell no tales at home under pain of a worse infliction. In his own case he well remembers the wrath of his father, who would have thought it wrong and encouraging insubordination to listen to any complaints against the master, when, on occasion of the victim of a tendency to juvenile pranks being dangerously ill with scarlet fever, and that father being called on by the doctor to annoint his back with some soothing lotion, he found said back striped and checked with a network of "black and blue." It is needless to add that at this point ended both the writer's experience under that schoolmaster and the schoolmaster's term of engagement in that district.

As a significant comment upon the moral effects of the regime of the schoolmasters of the old school the writer may add that one of his most vivid memories of the mental status produced by the school training referred to is that of an intense longing for the day when he should be large enough to repay that old schoolmaster in his own coin. That day came. The flagellated boy, transformed into a tolerably lusty youth, found himself face to face with his quondam tormenter. But his long cherished wrath speedily gave place to pity for the decrepit, friendless and lonely old bachelor, whose days were drawing to a close, with no loving hand of wife or daughter to minister to their feebleness.

THE PIONEER TEACHERS, AND THE TRIALS OF "BOARDING ROUND."

The writer of the foregoing paper pictured roughly the rural Canadian school of forty or fifty years ago. It may not be without interest to have that picture supplemented with a glimpse of rural Canadian life as seen by the schoolmaster of the period. The "boarding 'round" system afforded him excellent facilities for observation. The venerable custom of boarding round died, no doubt, a good many years ago, so far as Canada is concerned.... But thirty or forty years ago it was, in some parts of Canada at least, almost a matter of course that the teacher should "board 'round." When a school became vacant or a new and ambitious settlement had reached the pitch of development at which a school was deemed a necessary sequent to the carpenter's shop, the smithy and the shoemaker's shanty, one of the first steps was, of course, to pitch upon a suitable candidate for the scanty honors and still more scanty emoluments of the village pedagogue. Probably some influential member of the community had a son or a daughter in the teens, who was thought pretty well up in "the three R's." If so, it would usually be deemed quite unnecessary to look farther. In fact it would, in such a case, be useless for an outsider to contest the constituency. It never entered the unsophisticated heads of the trustees to invite competition by advertising for candidates "to state salary expected." This method of putting up professional talent in a kind of Dutch auction is an evolution of our present "best educational system on earth." Our grandfathers went about the business in a different way. The coming teacher being fixed upon, the next step was for the candidate himself, or some interested relative or friend on his behalf, to circulate a subscription sheet. A form of heading would be prepared somewhat in the following style:—"We, the undersigned residents of Smithton District, being desirous of securing the services of Henry Schoolman as teacher of the district school, hereby agree to engage the services of said H. S. for the period of six months, and to pay him at the rate of £1 2s 6d for each and every pupil we hereunto subscribe or send to said school. We further agree to supply the teacher with board in proportion to our several subscriptions; also to furnish our proportions of wood for the use of said school. Signed, etc."

The average juvenile Canadian made, no doubt, a much more merciful, and often much more efficient, teacher than the ex-soldier, or broken-down tradesman from the Old Country. One of the first duties of the newly-fledged teacher would be to go carefully over his treasured list of subscribers and ascertain, by a careful arithmetical calculation, the exact number of weeks and days for which he was entitled to board and lodging at the house of each of his respective patrons. The next step would be to find out, by personal or written enquiries, at what time it would be most convenient for each family to open its doors to him. This process, and the subsequent installation in each home would, it may well be imagined, be trying ordeals to the young and bashful pedagogue.... The receptions accorded the poor itinerant would be, of course, as various as the feelings, dispositions and circumstances of the householders, or, more strictly speaking, of the presiding divinities of the parlor and the kitchen, especially the kitchen. In many cases he would quickly feel at home. The welcome would be cordial, the hospitality ungrudging, the companionship agreeable. In such cases the bashful beginner would soon be able to shake off the intolerably humiliating dread of being regarded as an intruder, an interloper, or half-mendicant. But in numerous instances, as may readily be conceived, the situation would be most galling to a sensitive nature. The over-worked, perpetually tired and fretful mistress of the house would receive him with an ill-concealed frown or an involuntary sigh. To her he represented just so much addition, for so long a time, to her hourly toils and cares, already too heavy to be borne.

Unwashed specimens of "the heritage of the poor" would swarm in every corner. The fear and awe which secured him immunity for a time would soon wear away, and as they were replaced with the familiarity that breeds contempt, he would be exposed to all manner of well-meant advances and indignities. The scorn at the roughly-spread supper table would be a scramble, and the twilight hour, which, if he happened to have a spice of romance in his composition, he would fain have consecrated to quiet thought or fancy, would be made hideous by a juvenile pandemonium, as amidst stripes and cuffs and yells and tears the unruly flock would finally be got to bed. These, of course, were the ill-regulated householders, but they exist.

Well does the writer remember some personal experiences in this delightful phase of the professional life of an earlier day—not much more than half a semi-centennial distant. The old, dingy farmhouse, the bare floors, the hard seats, the utter absence of everything in the shape of books or other literature, the teeming olive branches at every age and stage of development, the little "spare" bedroom, whose sole furnishings consisted of the bed and bedding, on whose hard floor he reclined for lack of chair and table evening after evening for hours after he was supposed to be in bed, reading by the feeble rays of a tallow candle the ponderous volumes of Dr. Dick's philosophies, which had been kindly loaned him by a friend, and which were devoured with an eagerness begotten of a genuine hunger, though out of all proportion to the literary merits of the works.

THE OLD SCHOOL HOUSE.

Rude and unfinished and uncomfortable as it was, "The Old School House" would be sure to bring up to many an "old boy" tender memories, which would be recalled in after years in words somewhat like those in poetic form as follows:

It stood on a bleak country corner,
    The houses were distant and few;
A meadow lay back in the distance,
    Beyond rose the hills to our view.
The road, crossing there at right angles,
    Untraversed by pomp and array;
Were cropped by the cows in the summer,
    I've watched them there many a day.

In memory's hall hangs the picture,
    And years of sad care are between;
It hangs with a beautiful gilding,
    And well do I love it, I ween.
It stood on a bleak country corner,
    But boyhood's young heart made it warm;
It glowed in the sunshine of summer,
    'Twas cheerful in winter and storm.

The teacher, O well I remember,
    My heart has long kept him in place;
Perhaps by the world he's forgotten,
    His memory no touch can efface.
He met us with smiles on the threshold,
    And in that rude temple of art,
He left, with the skill of a workman,
    His touch on the mind and the heart.

Oh! gay were the sports of the noontide,
    When winter winds frolicked with snow;
We laughed at the freaks of the storm-king,
    And shouted him on all aglow.
We flashed at his beautiful sculpture,
    Regardless of all its array;
We plunged in the feathery snow-drifts,
    And sported the winter away.

We sat on the old-fashioned benches,
    Beguiled with our pencil and slate;
We thought of the opening future,
    And dreamed of our manhood's estate.
I cast a fond glance o'er the meadow,
    The hills just behind it I see;

Away in the charm of the distance,
Old school house! a blessing on thee!

Mr. Canniff Haight, in Canada of "Fifty Years Ago," gives the following account of the common school education of his day:—"The schoolhouse was close at hand, and its aspect is deeply graven in my memory. It was a small, square structure, with low ceiling. In the centre of the room was a box stove, around which the long wooden benches, without backs, were ranged. Next the wall were the desks, raised a little from the floor. In the summer time the pupils were all of tender years, the elder ones being kept at home to help with the work. I was one of a lot of little urchins ranged daily on hard wooden seats, with our feet dangling in the air for seven or eight hours a day. In such a plight we were expected to be very good children, to make no noise, and to learn our lessons. It is a marvel that so many years had to elapse before parents and teachers could be brought to see that keeping children in such a position for so many hours was an act of great cruelty. The terror of the rod was the only thing that could keep us still, and at that often failed. Sometimes, tired and weary, we fell asleep and tumbled off the bench, to be awakened by the fall of the rod. In the winter time, the small school was filled to overflowing with the larger boys and girls. This did not improve our condition, for we were more closely packed together, and were either shivering with the cold or being roasted with a red-hot stove.... I next sat under the rod of an Irish pedagogue—an old man who evidently believed that the only way to get anything into a boy's head was to pound it in with a stick through his back. There was no discipline, and the noise we made seemed to rival a bedlam.—*pp. 17, 18.*

"As far as my recollection goes, the teachers were generally of a very inferior order, and rarely possessed more than a smattering of the rudiments of grammar and arithmetic. They were poorly paid, and "boarded round" the neighbourhood. But it is not improbable that they generally received all that their services were worth.... The school-houses where the youth were taught were in keeping with the extent of instruction received within them. They were invariably small, with low ceilings, badly lighted, and without ventilation."—*pp. 157, 158.*

A School Teacher's Personal Experience in 1865.

From the Toronto *Mail* of November 28th, 1888, I select the following graphic account of the personal experience of a school teacher in 1865:—

"'Yes," said an old teacher to a representative of the *Mail* yesterday, "education has been wonderfully revolutionized in Ontario during the last twenty-five years. It was in January, 1865, that I first took up the birch, swaying it until I cautiously made up my mind to quit when the new Act requiring higher qualifications came into force in 1871. At that time the school houses in my county were all constructed of logs, and more uninviting buildings than these were not to be found in the country. It did appear that the ratepayers were more led to educate their children out of a feeling of latent and legal compulsion, than out of duty and parental regard. The life of a teacher in those days was not the high-toned one of to-day. Let me give my own experience, and when I have related it you will see how much there is in the complaints and grumblings of the existing generation of school teachers.

"'A school became vacant in the neighboring township, and I made up my mind, armed as I was with a first-class certificate awarded me by the County Board of Examaminers, that I would apply for the position.

"'I went to two influential men in the neighborhood and succeeded in coaxing them to go with me to the trustees of the school. We arrived at the section in due time, and after making due enquiries proceeded to the house of one of the trustees, who had the reputation of knowing everything worth discovering in the school law of the period. I felt an awful dread and confusion come over me when in the presence of that trustee. I was introduced, and I immediately told my errand. The horny-handed son of toil gave me one of those inscrutable looks that nearly sunk me to the earth. He coughed slightly, jerked his head back, put his two hands in the pockets of his trousers, and immediately proceeded to business.'

"'So yous wants the school, does you?'

"'I do, sir.'

"'Well, I might as well tell ye at once that the teacher we intend hiring must be better than the present one. He is a curse to the children of this section, with his grammar and his jography, and all his other fal da rals. Why, sir; my son Bill comes home the other night and says he,

"'Father, what is grammar?'

"I says, Bill, I never studied grammar, and you see how I am able to get along without it. Grammar is no good for ploughing or cutting up that slash fornent the house."

"Well," says the boy, "would you tell me what our teacher meant by saying that Berlin is on the Spree?" I then got mad, and says I, "Bill, never let me hear ye say anything more about these things. Sure they were never taught to us from the New Testament when I was in school."

But that is not all, the boy began to say to himself, orthography, etymology, syntax, and prosody, going over them again and again, until I says to Moriah, "is the child getting mad, wife!"

No sooner had he heard that than he began to say, "Noun, adjective, pronoun, adverb, preposition, noun, adjective, pronoun, preposition," as before. I then got afeard the child was clean crazy, and when I was in the act of rising to catch hold of him, says he, "Father, the earth is not flat, it is a round ball and goes round."

"Och, och," says I, "that spalpeen of a school master has driven my son mad."...

So I calls a meeting, and my two colleagues, Thomas Ginty and Edward Crawford, and myself, met at the school house and dismissed the rascal.

When the leader of education of school section No. 5 —— stopped, I turned to my companions, not knowing what qualifications were expected of me.

The trustee continued:—"Can you read?" "Yes." "Can you cipher?" "Yes." "Do you know how to count by long division?" "I do." "You don't know grammar?"

Here was the crucial test. I resolved, however, to get out of it the best way possible, and replied:—"I don't like grammar, and don't know much about it," which was true. "Good."

The trustee smiled sweetly and said:—"The school is yours; but, remember, no grammar or jography, or out you go."

I was taken to the other trustees, and in their presence I was put through the same examination as above recorded.

The bargain was struck there and then. I was promised fifteen dollars a month board from house to house, with the condition that I should put on the fires in winter, and keep the school house clean—a herculean task in those days.

On the morning that I was to assume my pedagogic duties, I arrived at the school house about 8 a.m., and at once proceeded to build a fire. I never can forget the feeling of utter loneliness which came over me, as I stood opposite a fireplace wide enough to accommodate an ox. On the walls of the building were three maps, of what countries I do not now remember, because geography was proscribed during my *regime*. Daylight was seen through the walls. The seats were of the most primitive character, while my own desk resembled more the top of a toboggan slide than the rostrum of one who was teaching the young idea how to shoot. There was no fence round the building, the play ground being illimitable in its dimensions and capacities. In short the whole of the surroundings of this rural academy congealed all literary aspirations, and it was little wonder that the boys and girls meeting there, and pretending to be drinking at the fountain of knowledge, grew up utterly destitute of the first principles of a rational and suitable education.

The children arrived, and I immediately began to assert my authority as the head of the institution. I made a short speech, telling the children that nothing would be taught in my school but reading, writing and 'rithmetic, adding that the ten commandments would be included in the curriculum. I got along famously that day with the pupils, and as I was told afterwards, when my charges went home and told their parents the new order of things, I was universally pronounced the greatest teacher of the age. I lodged that night with Trustee Fallis, my examiner. He was delighted with the reports given by Bill of my mode of teaching, and in a moment of confidence told me that the school was mine as long as I liked to keep it. I humbly thanked him, and retired to my room, where I found Bill, the heir of the house, in innocent slumber. Bill did not by any means prove a pleasant bed-fellow. Occasionally his feet were found where his head should be, and he repeatedly called out, "No grammar! Hurrah!" Next morning I rose, and after breakfast majestically strode through two feet of snow to the log school house, and then put in another day's grinding.

At four o'clock the trustees met and handed me a badly written and worse spelled manuscript, which on perusal I found to be the list of houses I was to board at during the coming three months.... Now, sir, continued the dominie, I put in a whole year of that kind of work; listened to all the gossip of the neighborhood, slept occasionally on the floor, nursed all the babies of the section, and just as I thought that my position was secure, disaster overcame me. One of the trustees had a daughter of prepossessing appearance, and I could not resist the temptation of falling in love with her. When the news got abroad that I was paying attentions to her, the section began to talk adversely of myself. Complaints were soon heard as to my teaching. Some said that I was teaching grammar on the sly, and that I was partial to some of the children. The result of it all was that a meeting of the board took place, and, despite the protests of Thomas Ginty, I was, in the language of modern times, "fired."

"Now," continued the old teacher, "the moral of what I told you is this:— Compare the log school house, its internal arrangements and play grounds, with those of to-day throughout the whole country, and you have the greatest exemplification possible of the progress made by Ontario during the last quarter of a century. There is scarcely a section now but has its brick school house, with surroundings attractive and neat. The teacher is given ample opportunity to cultivate the minds of his pupils to the highest pitch possible, at least as far as requisite for the general affairs of life. The old prejudices against teaching anything else but the three R's are gone. You have the walls of the buildings ornamented with maps, charts and other appliances. Text-books are provided of the most modern character, while a rigid system of examinations acts as an incentive to the teacher and makes him an instructor in fact and reality. Lastly, we have an intelligent and cultured class of teachers, and taking all things into consideration, they are well paid, and still better, their services are year by year becoming more appreciated. A better class of people now act in the capacity of trustees, and as years roll by a still more intelligent class will be found in these positions.

REMINISCENCES OF EDUCATION IN THE CITY OF HAMILTON IN 1852.

In conversation with a Reporter of the *Hamilton Times* in 1888, Mr. James Cummings, who, after thirty-seven years service on the City Board of Education, thus related his early educational experience:—

"At the time I first became connected with the board in 1852," said Mr. Cummings, "education was at rather a low ebb, not only in Hamilton, but throughout the country. Dr. Ryerson had just commenced his excellent common school scheme and in 1847, had established a training school for teachers in Toronto. Hamilton had decided to adopt the common school system and the reorganization of the schools was just being effected. Previous to that time the education of the children of the better class was almost wholly in the hands of private school teachers. There were a few small school rooms in the different wards, but they were wretched places, where usually fifty children were crowded into a small room reeking with fetid atmosphere. On the site of the present Cannon street school was a small frame grammar school, at which many of the present leading citizens received the ground-work of their education. A great reform was inaugurated here in the year 1852. Under the new Ryerson Act of 1850 trustees were clothed with new powers, and we immediately proceeded to reorganize the schools here on the new plan. Tenders were let for the erection of the present Central school and for ward schools in different parts of the city. Mr. (now Dr. J. H.) Sangster was appointed head master, and to him was entrusted the appointment of teachers, and he was made responsible for the efficiency of the schools. He had been a teacher in the Ryerson model school in Toronto, and he appointed as his assistants thoroughly trained graduates of that excellent institution. This was the founding of Hamilton's excellent common school system. It kept improving from year to year and soon closed out the private schools. Larger ward schools were erected, and since that day Hamilton has taken a high position educationally in the Province."

EDUCATION IN THE COUNTY OF SIMCOE, 1852-1872.

Dr. Ryerson was invited to open the new Public School in the town of Barrie in 1872. Before the ceremony was proceeded with a letter was read from Judge (now the Hon. Senator) Gowan, who was unable to be present, referring to his long services in the cause of education in the County of Simcoe. He said:—

"Ever since I came to this country, nearly thirty years ago, I have been connected with the school system, having held the office of Trustee of the Grammar School, and the position of Chairman of the Board of Public Instruction from its first institution till superseded by recent enactment, and, with the exception of my friend, Mr. Dallas, I am the only member of the original Board now living.

"I have seen the gradual improvement in the school system, and the improvement in the schools in this country from very small beginnings to the present advanced and most prosperous condition, so you will understand my disappointment in not being able to be present on the interesting occasion of laying the corner-stone of the Public School house of Barrie, by the Chief Superintendent of Education.

"My position as Secretary and Treasurer of the Grammar School, and Chairman of the Board of Public Instruction, in this, the largest county in Ontario, brought me in constant communication with the Education Office in Toronto; and I can say that the able, zealous, and wise administration of the school law by Dr. Ryerson and his assistant, Dr. Hodgins, has, here at least, had a happy effect—fostering the increase of schools, securing their better management, giving them efficient teachers, and providing the means, within easy access to all, of securing a good common education to the youth of this country, and a very superior education in the Grammar Schools."

Mr. (now Judge) Boys, gave a sketch of the educational history of Barrie as follows:

"Twenty years ago there was no Public or Common School, not, however, without school accommodation, as we were then included in what was known as School Section No. 1 of the adjoining Township of Vespra. We had no building specially set apart as a school house, but a rented room then sufficed to carry on the daily teaching embraced within the section.... Twenty years ago one teacher took charge of all our scholars—both male and female—and if there is any doubt as to his labor having been great, there can be none as to his salary having been small, for he subsisted on a sum of £60 per annum.

"In January, 1854, Barrie became possessed of a school of its own, and built a school house of frame 24 × 36, just about large enough to fill up one room in the building we are now erecting. It was, no doubt, at the time it was built, amply large, yet I find, from the record of the school, that such was the growth of the town by September, 1854, non-residents were refused admittance to the Barrie school on the ground of its over-crowded state, the average attendance of males being seventy—the females were then taught in another building by a female teacher. This state of things continued for nearly a year, when a separate school was established for Barrie, which brought some relief to the over-crowded building. But it was evident that more school accommodation would have to be supplied, and I see by the minute book of the school, that a new school house was talked of so far back as January, 1855. The new school house, however, never came. The difficulty at last was settled by an enlargement of the old building, which then assumed the appearance it now presents. With the enlarged school house, supplemented by some rented rooms, the schools of Barrie have ever since continued to the present time. It took time to convince our people of the imperative necessity there was for a large outlay in providing a new school house. But the ratepayers became convinced at last, and gave their hearty approval to an expenditure which will enable us, during the next year, to erect a school building suitable to the place, and one worthy of the trouble you, sir, have taken to be present at its official commencement. During the time I refer to, a Grammar School building of brick was erected and enlarged, and a Separate School building put up.

"To-day, with your kind assistance, we have inaugurated a system of Public School accommodation which, with our school known as the Barrie School, Separate and High Schools, will ultimately provide for the educational wants of the neighborhood. I use the expression 'inaugurated a system,' because I hope and trust that our efforts in this direction will not be slackened on the completion of this building.... We believe this building will be worthy of the honor you have done us in coming here to-day, we also believe at some future day, we shall have a system of Public School accommodation worthy of the life-long and successful efforts you have made to give to Ontario an almost perfect system of education. It is seldom that public men are asked to assist in building a monument to themselves, but I have asked you to do so on this occasion, for I look upon buildings of this nature as memorials of your well-directed public work during the last thirty years, and when you have gone to your long home, and the envy—aye—and the malice of your enemies are forgotten, your name associated with the noble work you have accomplished, will be handed down from generation to generation, and each school section throughout the country will contain a monument to your memory, as enduring as the foundations of this continent."

CHAPTER VI.

PERSONAL CHAPTER RELATING TO THE REV. DR. RYERSON.

In Dr. Ryerson's personal sketch of his early history he gives the following particulars as to his student and teacher life:

I was born on the 24th of March, 1803, in the Township of Charlotteville, near the Village of Vittoria, in the then London District, now the County of Norfolk.... The district grammar-school was then kept within half-a-mile of my father's residence, by Mr. James Mitchell (afterwards Judge Mitchell), an excellent classical scholar; he came from Scotland with the late Rt. Rev. Dr. Strachan, first Bishop of Toronto. He treated me with much kindness. When I recited to him my lessons in English grammar he often said that he had never studied the English grammar himself, that he wrote and spoke English by the Latin grammar. At the age of fourteen I had the opportunity of attending a course of instruction in the English language given by two professors, the one an Englishman, and the other an American, who taught nothing but English grammar. They professed in one course of instruction, by lectures, to enable a diligent pupil to parse any sentence in the English language. I was sent to attend these lectures, the only boarding abroad for school instruction I ever enjoyed. My previous knowledge of the *letter* of the grammar was of great service to me, and gave me an advantage over other pupils, so that before the end of the course I was generally called up to give visitors an illustration of the success of the system, which was certainly the most effective I have ever since witnessed, having charts, etc., to illustrate the agreement and government of words.

This whole course of instruction by two able men, who did nothing but teach grammar from one week's end to another had to me all the attraction of a charm and a new discovery. It gratified both curiosity and ambition, and I pursued it with absorbing interest, until I had gone through Murray's two volumes of "Expositions and Exercises," Lord Kames' "Elements of Criticism," and Blair's "Lectures on Rhetoric," of which I still have the notes which I then made. The same professors obtained sufficient encouragement to give a second course of instruction and lectures at Vittoria, and one of them becoming ill, the other solicited my father to allow me to assist him, as it would be useful to me, while it would enable him to fulfil his engagements. Thus, before I was sixteen, I was inducted as a teacher, by lecturing on my native language. This course of instruction, and exercises in English, have proved of the greatest advantage to me, not less in enabling me to study foreign languages than in using my own.

While working on the farm I did more than ordinary day's work, that I might show how industrious, instead of lazy, as some said, religion made a person. I studied between three and six o'clock in the morning, carried a book in my pocket during the day to improve odd moments by reading or learning, and then reviewed my studies of the day aloud while walking out in the evening…. A kind friend offered to give me any book that I would commit to memory, and submit to his examination of the same. In this way I obtained my first Latin grammar, "Watts on the Mind," and "Watts' Logic."

My eldest brother, George, after the war, went to Union College, U. S., where he finished his collegiate studies. He was a fellow-student with the late Dr. Wayland, and afterwards succeeded my brother-in-law as Master of the London District Grammar School. His counsels, examinations, and ever kind assistance were a great encouragement and of immense service to me.

I felt a strong desire to pursue further my classical studies, and determined, with the kind counsel and aid of my eldest brother, to proceed to Hamilton, and place myself for a year under the tuition of a man of high reputation both as a scholar and a teacher, the late John Law, Esq., then head master of the Gore District Grammar School. I applied myself with such ardour, and prepared such an amount of work in both Latin and Greek, that Mr. Law said it was impossible for him to give the time and hear me read all that I had prepared, and that he would, therefore, examine me on the translation and construction of the more difficult passages, remarking more than once that it was impossible for any human mind to sustain long the strain that I was imposing upon mine.[58] In the course of some six months his apprehensions were realized, as I was seized with a brain fever, and on partially recovering took cold, which resulted in inflammation of the lungs by which I was so reduced that my physician, the late Dr. James Graham, of Norfolk, pronounced my case hopeless, and my death was hourly expected.

After a severe illness Dr. Ryerson happily recovered.

His narrative states that, "the next day after my recovery, I left home and became usher in the London District Grammar School, applying myself to my new work with much diligence and earnestness, so that I soon succeeded in gaining the good-will of parents and pupils, and they were quite satisfied with my services,—leaving the head master to his favorite pursuits of gardening and building!

In 1872, Dr. Ryerson wrote to Mr. Simpson McCall, of Vittoria and asked: "Will you have the kindness to let me know what is your own recollection as to the attendance at the school, especially in the winter months, and the impression of the neighborhood generally as to its efficiency during the two years that I taught it?" Mr. McCall replied as follows: I can assure you that I have a vivid recollection of the London District School during the winters of 1821 and 1822, being an attendant myself. I also remember several of the scholars with whom I associated, viz: H. V. A. Rapelje, Esq., late Sheriff of the County of Norfolk; Capt. Joseph Bostwick, of Port Stanley; James and Hannah Moore.

The number generally attending during the winters of those two years, if I remember correctly, were from forty to fifty.

The school while under your charge was well and efficiently conducted, and was so considered and appreciated throughout the neighborhood at the time; and after you left the charge of the London District School it was generally regretted in the neighborhood.

I remember hearing this frequently remarked not only by pupils who attended the school under your tuition but also by their parents.

"During two years I was thus teacher and student, advancing considerably in classical studies, I took great delight in "Locke on the Human Understanding," Paley's "Moral and Political Philosophy," and "Blackstone's Commentaries," especially the sections of the latter on the Prerogatives of the Crown, the Rights of the subject, and the Province of Parliament."

In an address before the Ontario Teachers' Association in 1872, Dr. Ryerson said: "As it has of late been stated, so confidently and largely, that he had yet to learn the elements of his native tongue. Such had been the representations on the subject, that he had begun to suspect his own identity, and to ask himself whether it was not a delusion that he had in boyhood not only studied, but, as he supposed, had mastered Murray's two octavo volumes of English Grammar and Kame's Elements of Criticism and Blair's Rhetoric, of which he still had the notes that he made in early life; and had been called to assist teaching a special class of young persons in English Grammar when he was only fifteen years of age; and whether it was not a fancy that he had taught, as he supposed, with some degree of acceptance and success, what was then known as the London District Grammar School for two years, and had subsequently placed himself for a year under an accomplished scholar in order to read Latin and Greek. Somewhat disturbed by these doubts, he thought he would satisfy himself by writing to the only two gentlemen with whom he was now acquainted, who knew him in these early relations. In reference to these statements he would read the correspondence on the subject." (See the foot notes appended.)

THE REV. DR. RYERSON AS A TEACHER.

As to Dr. Ryerson's influence as a teacher, Rev. Dr. Ormiston thus referred to it at the Ontario Teacher's Convention in 1872. He said: "The teacher has a reward peculiar to his work—a living, lasting memorial of his worth. The feelings of loving reverence which we entertain for those who have awakened our intellectual life, and guided us in our earliest attempts at the acquisition of knowledge, are as enduring as they are grateful. I shall never forget, as I can never repay, the obligations under which I lie to the venerable and honorable Chief Superintendent, Dr. Ryerson, not only for the kindly paternal greeting with which, as principal, he welcomed me, a raw, timid, untutored lad, on my first entrance into Victoria College, when words of encouragement fell like dew-drops on my heart, and for the many acts of thoughtful generosity which aided me in my early career, and for the faithful friendship and Christian sympathy which has extended over nearly thirty years, unbroken and unclouded, a friendship which, strengthened and intensified by prolonged and endearing intimacy, I now cherish as one of the highest honors and dearest delights of my life; but especially for the quickening, energizing influence of his instructions as professor, when he taught me how to think, to reason and to learn. How I enjoyed the hours spent in his lecture-room—hours of mental and moral growth never to be forgotten! I owe him much, and but for his presence here to-day, I would say more of what I think and feel of his character and worth. He has won for himself a place in the heart of many a young Canadian, and his name will be ever associated with the educational advantages and history of Ontario. May he be spared for many years to see the result of his labors, in the growing prospects and success of the common schools and educational institutions of this noble and prosperous province, whose best interests he has patriotically done so much to promote."

In 1882, after Dr. Ryerson's death, Dr. Ormiston thus referred to his experience at Victoria College, then under Dr. Ryerson's presidency. He said:

—

"In the autumn of 1843, I went to Victoria College, doubting much whether I was prepared to matriculate as a freshman. Though my attainments in some of the subjects prescribed for examination were far in advance of the requirements, in other subjects I knew I was sadly deficient. On the evening of my arrival, while my mind was burdened with the importance of the step I had taken, and by no means free from anxiety about the issue, Dr. Ryerson, at that time Principal of the College, visited me in my room. I shall never forget that interview. He took me by the hand; and few men could express as much by a mere hand-shake as he. It was a welcome, an encouragement, an inspiration, and an earnest of future fellowship and friendship. It lessened the timid awe I naturally felt towards one in such an elevated position—I had never before seen a Principal of a College—it dissipated all boyish awkwardness and awakened filial confidence. He spoke of Scotland, my native land, and of her noble sons, distinguished in every branch of philosophy and literature; specially of the number, the diligence, the frugality, self-denial and success of her college students. In this way he soon led me to tell him of my parentage, past life and efforts, present hopes and aspirations. His manner was so gracious and paternal—his sympathy so quick and genuine—his counsel so ready and cheering—his assurances so grateful and inspiriting, that not only was my heart *his* from that hour, but my future career seemed brighter and more certain than it had ever appeared before.

"Many times in after years have I been instructed, and guided, and delighted with his conversation, always replete with interest and information; but that first interview I can never forget, it is as fresh and clear to me to-day as it was on the morning after it took place. It has exerted a profound, enduring, moulding influence on my whole life. For what, under God, I am, and have been enabled to achieve, I owe more to that noble, unselfish, kind-hearted man than to any one else.

"As a teacher he was earnest and efficient, eloquent and inspiring, but he expected and exacted rather too much work from the average student. His own ready and affluent mind sympathized keenly with the apt, bright scholar, to whom his praise was warmly given, but he scarcely made sufficient allowance for the dullness or lack of previous preparation which failed to keep pace with him in his long and rapid strides; hence his censures were occasionally severe. His methods of examination furnished the very best kind of mental discipline, fitted alike to cultivate the memory and to strengthen the judgment. All the students revered him, but the best of the class appreciated him most. His counsels were faithful and judicious; his admonitions paternal and discriminating; his rebukes seldom administered, but scathingly severe. No student ever left his presence, without resolving to do better, to aim higher, and to win his approval."

THE REV. DR. RYERSON AND HIS NATIVE COUNTY OF NORFOLK.

Mr. P. K. Olyne, in the *New Dominion Monthly* for July, 1869, in an article on "Norfolk, or the Long-Point County," thus referrs to its settlement and to the boyhood there of Dr. Ryerson:—

"After undergoing many hardships which were only a foretaste of what they had to endure in the future, a company arrived in the Long Point region about the year 1780. This was then a solitary wilderness. These pioneer

Loyalists went to work with zeal unsurpassed in clearing away the forest, in building roads and erecting houses as commodious as it was possible to erect out of rude materials. Among those who first came to the Long Point country, worthy of particular notice, were Colonel Ryerson, Colonel Backhouse, Walsh and Tisdale. In the pioneer home of Joseph Ryerson might have been seen a remarkably bright lad. Being extremely fond of books, he spent his spare moments in studying. So regular was his habits in this respect, that when a neighbour would drop in and ask for Egerton, the answer was sure to be: "You will find him in such a place, with a book." Notwithstanding he was placed in a position where opportunities for gaining an education were very meagre indeed, yet he overcame all obstacles—obstacles that he could not forget in after life, and which, like a true patriot, he set himself to remove. How much Dr. Egerton Ryerson, Chief Superintendent of Education, has done for the educational interests of Canada the reader is left to judge for himself. Of late the Doctor has made a practice of visiting the home of his childhood annually. Not always by rail and stage has he accomplished the journey from Toronto, but still clinging to the sport of his youthful days he would set forward in an open boat, and paddling it himself along the shores of the lakes would finally reach the place so dear to him, and which, no doubt, brought afresh to his memory many recollections both joyous and sad.

"A rude log schoolhouse was constructed by the early settlers as soon as they could do so conveniently. A fire-place extended along nearly a whole side of the building. Logs of considerable length were rolled into this in cold weather for fuel, before which rude benches or hewed logs were placed as seats for the instructor and pupils. The close of the teacher's term was denominated "the last day." It was customary on this occasion for the children to turn the pedagogue out of doors by force, and for this purpose some whiskey was generally provided as a stimulant. Such was the state of educational institutions in the days of young Ryerson. What advancement has education made since? We trace it step by step as onward it has advanced, until to-day Norfolk can proudly boast of institutions and teachers second to none of the kind in the world."

In 1851, Dr. Ryerson sent to each County Council specimens of maps, charts, natural history, prints, etc., to the value of $30, the Council of the County of Norfolk, acknowledged the gift in a very hearty manner. In reply to the County Council, Dr. Ryerson said:—

From the Municipal Council of my native county, I have never experienced unkind opposition, but have been encouraged by its patriotic co-operation: and it affords me no small satisfaction, that that same Council is the first in Upper Canada to acknowledge the receipt of the documents and maps referred to—that the resolution of the Council was seconded by an old school-fellow, [59] and couched in terms to me the most gratifying and encouraging; and that my first official letter of a new year, relates to topics which call up the earliest associations of my youth, and are calculated to prompt and impel me to renewed exertions for the intellectual and social advancement of my native land.

To the County Board of Public Instruction he said:

"I hope the poorest boy in my native County may have access to a better common school than existed there when I was a lad. What I witnessed and felt in my boyhood, gave birth to the strongest impulses of my own mind, to do what I could to place the means and facilities of mental development and culture within the reach of every youth in the land."

"I am more than gratified, I am profoundly impressed, that such efforts are made for the interests of the young, and of future generations in the County of Norfolk. That county is dear to me by a thousand tender recollections; and I still seem to hear in the midst of it, a voice issuing from a mother's grave, as was wont formerly from the living tongue, telling me that the only life worthy the name, is that which makes man one with his fellow-men, and with his country."

In September, 1864, Dr. Ryerson thus referred to the trip in his frail skiff to his native county of Norfolk in the preceding month:

"In my lonely voyage from Toronto to Port Ryerse the scene was often enchanting and the solitude sweet beyond expression. I have witnessed the setting sun amidst the Swiss and Tyrolese Alps from lofty elevations, on the plains of Lombardy, from the highest eminence of the Appenines, between Bologna and Florence, and from the crater summit of Vesuvius, but I was never more delighted and impressed (owing, perhaps, in part to the susceptible state of my feelings) with the beauty, effulgence, and even sublimity of atmospheric phenomena, and the softened magnificence of surrounding objects, than in witnessing the setting sun on the 23rd of June, from the unruffled bosom of Lake Erie, a few miles east of Port Dover, and about a mile from the thickly wooded shore, with its deepening and variously reflected shadows. And when the silent darkness enveloped all this beauty, and grandeur, and magnificence in undistinguishable gloom, my mind experienced that wonderful sense of freedom and relief which come from all that suggests the idea of boundlessness—the deep sky, the dark night, the endless circle, the illimitable waters. The world with its tumult of cares seemed to have retired, and God and His works appeared all in all, suggesting the enquiry which faith and experience promptly answered in the affirmative

With glorious clouds encompassed round
  Whom angels dimly see;
Will the unsearchable be found;
  Will God appear to me?

"My last remark is the vivifying influence and unspeakable pleasure of visiting scenes endeared to me by many tender, and comparatively few painful recollections. Amid the fields, woods, out-door exercises, and associations of the first twenty years of my life, I have seemed to forget the sorrows, labors and burdens of more than two score years, and be transported back to what was youthful, simple, healthy, active, and happy. I can heartily sympathise with the feelings of Sir Walter Scott when, in reply to Washington Irving, who had expressed disapprobation in the scenery of the Tweed, immortalized by the genius of the border minstrel, he said:

"'It may be partiality, but to my eyes these gray hills and all this wild border country have beauties peculiar to themselves. I like the very nakedness of the land. It has something bold, and stern, and solitary about it. When I have been for some time in the rich scenery of Edinburgh, which is ornamented garden land, I begin to wish myself back again among my honest gray hills, and if I did not see the heather at least once a year I think I should die.'

"Last autumn I lodged two weeks on the farm on which I was born, with the family of Mr. Joseph Duncan, where the meals were taken daily in a room the wood-work of which I, as an amateur carpenter, had finished more than forty years ago, while recovering from a long and serious illness."[60]

CLOSING OFFICIAL ACTS AND UTTERANCES OF DR. RYERSON.

An entire revision and consolidation of the laws relating to public and high schools took place in 1874, in which Dr. Ryerson took a leading part. But the revision related chiefly to details and to the supply of former omissions in the law.

The last important official act of Dr. Ryerson was to arrange for the educational exhibit of the department at the Centennial Exhibition in 1876. That was most successfully carried out; and, at the close of that exhibition, the following highly gratifying "award" was communicated to the then venerable ex-chief, after he had retired from office. The award was made by the American Centennial Commission, and was to the following effect:

> For a quite complete and admirably arranged exhibition, illustrating the Ontario system of education and its excellent results; also for the efficiency of an administration which has gained for the Ontario Department a most honorable distinction among government

educational agencies.

This award was quite a gratification to the now retired chief of the Department, then in his seventy-third year, and amply repaid him, as he said, for many years of anxious toil and solicitude, while it was a gratifying and unlooked-for compensation for all of the undeserved opposition which he had encountered while laying the foundations of our educational system.

In a letter to a friend toward the close of his official career, Dr. Ryerson thus explained the principles upon which he had conducted the educational affairs of the Province during his long administration of them. He said:—

During these many years I have organized and administered the Education Department upon the broad and impartial principles which I have always advocated. During the long period of my administration of the Department I knew neither religious sect nor political party; I knew no party other than that of the country at large; I never exercised any patronage for personal or party purposes; I never made or recommended one of the numerous appointments of teachers in the Normal or Model Schools, or clerk in the education office, except upon the ground of testimonials as to personal characters and qualifications, and on a probationary trial of six months.

———————

I believe this is the true method of managing all the public departments, and every branch of the public service. I believe it would contribute immensely to both the efficiency and economy of the public service. * * * It would greatly elevate the standard of action and attainments and stimulate the ambition of the young men of the country, when they know that their selection and advancement in their country's service depended upon their individual merits, irrespective of sect or party, and not as the reward of zeal as political partisans in elections or otherwise, on their own part, or on that of their fathers or relatives.

The power of a government in a country is immense for good or ill. It is designed by the Supreme Being to be a "minister of God for good" to a whole people, without partiality, as well as without hypocrisy, like the rays of the sun; and the administration of infinite wisdom and justice and truth and purity.

———————

I know it has been contended that party patronage * * * is an essential element in the existence of a government. * * * The Education Department has existed—and it is the highest public department in Upper Canada—for more than thirty years without such an element, with increasing efficiency and increasing strength, in the public estimation, during the whole of that period. Justice, and virtue, and patriotism, and intelligence are stronger elements of power and usefulness than those of rewarding partisans; and if the rivalship and competition of public men should consist in devising and promoting measures for the advancement of the country and in exercising the executive power most impartially and intelligently for the best interests of all classes, then the moral standard of government and of public men would be greatly exalted, and the highest civilization of the whole country be advanced.

In a series of letters published in defence of his administration of the Education Department in 1872, he thus pointed out the character of his difficult and delicate task. He also gave a brief glance at what had been accomplished by the Department since he took office in 1844. He said:—

The Department of which I have had charge since 1844, and during several administrations of government, is confessedly the most difficult and complicated, if not the most important, of any department of the public service. Since 1844, it has devolved on me to frame laws, and to devise, develop, and administer a system of public instruction for the people of this Province. That system has been more eulogized by both English and American educationists, and more largely adopted in other British colonies, on both sides of the globe, than any other system of public instruction in America.

The system of popular education in Ontario has opened a free school to every child in the land, and proclaimed his right to its advantages; it has planted a school house in nearly every neighborhood, and in hundreds of instances, made the school house the best building in the neighborhood; it has superseded the topers and broken-down characters, so common as teachers of a former age, by a class of teachers not excelled in morals by the teachers of any other country, and who, as a whole, compare favorably in qualifications with those of any State in America; it has achieved a uniformity of excellent text-books, earnestly prayed for by educators in the neighboring States, and has spread throughout the land books of useful and entertaining knowledge to the number of nearly a million of volumes; it is the nearest approach to a voluntary system of any public school system in the world; and it has developed larger resources than that of any other State in America, in proportion to the wealth and number of inhabitants.

This unparalleled success is due to the Christian feeling, the energy, patriotism and liberality of the people of this Province; but it has been imposed on me to construct the machinery, devise the facilities and agencies by which so great a work has been accomplished, and to do what I could to encourage my fellow-countrymen in its promotion.

The administration of laws generally is by learned judges, by the pleadings of learned counsel, and the deliberations of selected juries; but the administration of the school law and system is through the agency of several hundred elected councils, and nearly twenty thousand elected trustees,—thus embodying, not the learned professions, but the intelligence, common sense, feelings and interests of the people at large in the work of school administration and local self-government.

REASONS FOR DR. RYERSON'S RETIREMENT AS CHIEF SUPERINTENDENT OF EDUCATION.

In "The Story of My Life," I gave the following reasons, amongst others, which induced Dr. Ryerson to propose a change in the headship of the Education Department. I said: "For many years after confederation Dr. Ryerson felt that the new political condition of the Province, which localized, as well as circumscribed, its civil administration of affairs, required a change in the management of the Education Department. He, therefore, (as early as in 1868, and again in 1872) urged upon the Government the desirability of relieving him from the anomalous position in which he found himself placed under the new system. The reasons which he urged for his retirement are given in a pamphlet devoted to a 'defence' of the system of education, which he published in 1872, and are as follows:—

"When political men have made attacks upon the school law, or the school system and myself, and I have answered them, then the cry has been raised by my assailants and their abettors, that I was interfering with politics. They would assail me without stint, in hopes of crushing me, and then gag me against all defence or reply.

"So deeply did I feel the disadvantage and growing evil of this state of things to the department and school system itself, that I proposed, four years ago last December, to retire from the department, and recommended the creation and appointment of a Minister of Public Instruction. My resignation was not accepted, nor my recommendation adopted; when, two months later, I proposed that, at the commencement of each session of the legislature, a committee of seven or nine (including the Provincial Secretary for the time being) should be elected by ballot, or by mutual agreement of the leading men of both parties, on the Education Department; which committee should examine into all the operations of the department for the year then ending, consider the school estimates, and any bill or recommendations which might be submitted for the advancement of the school system, and report to the house accordingly. By many thoughtful men, this system has been considered more safe, more likely to secure a competent and working head of the department, and less liable to make the school system a tool of party politics, than for the head of it to have a seat in Parliament, and thus leave the educational interests of the country dependent upon the votes of a majority of electors in one riding. This recommendation, submitted on the 30th of January, 1869, has not yet been adopted; and I am left isolated, responsible in the estimation of legislators and everybody else for the department—the target of every attack, whether in the newspapers or in the Legislative Assembly, yet without any access to it or to its members, except through the press, and no other support than the character of my work and the general confidence of the public."

Dr. Ryerson's Letter of Resignation in 1868 and Reply To it.

The salient points of Dr. Ryerson's letter of resignation, dated 7th December, 1868, and addressed to Hon. M. C. Cameron, Provincial Secretary, are as follows:—

"I have the honor to submit to the favourable consideration of the Lieutenant-Governor in Council what, some three weeks since, I submitted to the individual members of the Government, namely, that

"The Department of Public Instruction shall be under the management of a member of the Executive Council, to be designated 'Minister of Public Instruction,' who shall be an *ex officio* member of the Toronto University and of the Council of Public Instruction, and who, in addition to the powers and functions vested in the Chief Superintendent of Education, shall have the oversight of all educational institutions which are or may be, aided by public endowment or legislative grant, to inspect and examine, from time to time, personally or any person appointed by him, into the character and working of such institution; and by him shall all public moneys be paid in support or aid of such institutions, and to him they will report at such times and in such manner as he shall direct....

"Our system of public instruction has acquired such gigantic dimensions, and the network of its operations so pervades every municipality of the land, and is so interwoven with our municipal and judicial systems of government, that I think its administration should now be vested in a responsible Minister of the Crown, with a seat in Parliament; and that I should not stand in the way of the application to our varied educational interests of that ministerial responsibility, which is sound in principle and wise in policy. During the past year I have presented a report on school systems in other countries, with a view of improving my own; and the Legislative Assembly has appointed a Select Committee for the same purpose. I have, therefore, thought this was the proper time to suggest the modification and extension of the Department of Public Instruction....

"While, in addition to the duties imposed upon me by law as Chief Superintendent of Education, I have voluntarily established a system of providing the municipal and school authorities with libraries, text-books and every description of school furniture and school apparatus—devising and developing their domestic manufacture. I have thus saved the country very many thousands of dollars in the prices as well as the quality of the books, maps, etc., etc. I can truly say that I have not derived one farthing's advantage from any of these arrangements, beyond the consciousness of conferring material, intellectual and social benefits upon the country."...

To this letter the Government of the Hon. J. Sandfield Macdonald replied, through Provincial Secretary Cameron, on the 30th of January, 1869, as follows:—

"In acknowledging your letter of the 7th December last, placing your resignation of the office of Chief Superintendent of Education in the hands of His Excellency the Lieutenant-Governor, and suggesting that the Department of Public Instruction should be placed under the more direct management of the Government, through a Minister, to be designated 'the Minister of Public Instruction,' holding a place in the Executive Council and a seat in the Legislative Assembly, thus bringing this department, in common with all other branches of the Government, within the control of the people through the responsible advisers of the Crown. I am directed by His Excellency the Lieutenant-Governor, to thank you for the valuable suggestions contained in your letter, and to request that you will continue to discharge those important duties, which you have performed for a quarter of a century with so much credit to yourself and benefit to the people of this Province, until His Excellency's advisers shall have more fully considered your suggestions, and matured a measure for placing your department under the direct supervision of a member of the Executive Council.

"The services that you have rendered your country, and your now advanced age, fully warrant your asking to be relieved from the further discharge of your arduous duties; but knowing your vigor of mind and energy of character, His Excellency ventures to hope that compliance with the request now made will not prove too great a tax upon your energies, or interfere seriously with any other plans you may have formed for the employment of the remaining years of a life devoted to the moral and intellectual improvement of your fellowmen."

To this letter Dr. Ryerson replied on the 30th January, 1869, as follows:—

"I have the honour to acknowledge the receipt of your letter of this date conveying the most kind expression of his Excellency the Lieutenant-Governor in regard to myself and my past humble services, and the request that I would continue in my present office until His Excellency's advisers should be able to mature a measure to give effect to the recommendations of my letter of 7th of December last respecting the direct responsibility of the Education Department to Parliament, and the creation of the office of Minister of Public Instruction to be filled by a responsible Minister of the Crown, having a seat in Parliament. The more than kind reference to myself on the part of His Excellency has deeply affected me, and for which I desire to express my most heartfelt thanks.

"I beg to assure you for the satisfaction of His Excellency that I will subordinate every inclination and contemplated engagement, to the great work of the Education Department and the system of Public Instruction, as long as I have strength and may be desired by the constituted authorities to do so.

"I have found that the apprehensions first expressed by the Hon. M. C. Cameron, as Chairman of the Education Committee of the Legislative Assembly during the late session, that connecting the Department of Public Instruction with the political Ministry of the day might draw the system of Public Instruction into the arena of party politics and thus impede its progress, is largely shared in by thoughtful men, and that my recommendation has been coldly received generally, and strongly objected to in many quarters.

"Under these circumstances I have been led to review the whole question; and aided by the experience which the recent session of the Legislature has afforded, I would respectfully suggest that, until a better system can be devised, a committee of say seven or nine members of the Legislative Assembly (to be presided over by the Provincial Secretary) be elected by ballot, (or if not by ballot, by the mutual agreement of the leaders of both parties in the House,) at the commencement of each session, to examine into the working, and report upon all matters relating to the Education Department and its administration, as well as upon any measures which might be suggested for the promotion of Public Instruction. The Provincial Secretary, being *ex officio* Chairman of such Committee, would be able to bring before it any thing that had required the interposition of, or had been brought before the Government during the year and meriting the attention of the Committee. The Committee being chosen by ballot, or by mutual agreement on both sides of the House, would preclude the character of party in its mode of appointment, and give weight and influence to its recommendations. In this way the Education Department, necessarily so identified with matters affecting popular progress and enlightenment would, it its whole administration be more directly responsible to Parliament and through it to the people than any other Public Department is now, and that without being identified or connected with any political party, and on the occasion of a vacancy in the Administration of the Department, a selection and appointment could be made free from the exigencies of party or of party elections, upon the simple and sole ground of qualifications for the office and with a view of promoting the interests of public education irrespective of sect or party."

DR. RYERSON'S LETTER OF RESIGNATION IN 1872 AND REPLY TO IT.

On the 10th of February, 1872, Dr. Ryerson addressed a letter to the Hon. Edward Blake, then Premier of Ontario, in which he said:

"After much deliberation, I have thought it advisable to address you in respect to my long desired retirement from the Education Department, of which I have had charge longer than any Judge has ever occupied the Bench in Canada, and to a greater age....

"The infirmities of age must compel me to retire before long; and I have thought my immediate or early retirement would enable the Government to exercise its discretion more freely in regard to the Department, and system of Public Instruction....

"In case you concur in what I have above intimated, I would suggest the creation of the office of Minister of Public Instruction, and the appointment of yourself to it, as is the Premier in Lower Canada, bringing the University, U. C. College, Institutions of Deaf and Blind, as well as the Normal, High and Public Schools, under direct governmental supervision.

"In the practical administration of the Education Department an abler, more judicious and reliable man cannot be found than Dr. Hodgins, who has been in the Department twenty-seven years—who was first educated to business in a retail store in Galt, and afterwards in a wholesale establishment in Hamilton with the Stinsons—clerk in the same establishment with Mr. Charles McGill, M.P., and was offered to be set up in business by the Stinsons or admitted as a partner within a year or so if he would remain, but he chose literature and went to Victoria College in 1840, where I found him; and on account of his punctuality, thoroughness, neatness, method, and excellent conduct, I appointed him on trial first clerk in my office in 1844; and having proved his ability, I wrote to him when I was in Europe, to come home to his widowed mother in Dublin, and spend a year in the great education office there, to learn the whole system and management—I having arranged with the late Archbishop Whately and other members of the National Board, to admit Mr. H. into their office to study the principles and details of its management and of the Normal and Model Schools connected with it. Mr. Hodgins did so at his own expense, and losing the salary for the year; at the end of which he returned to my office with the testimonials of the Irish National Board, as to his diligence and the thorough manner in which he had mastered the modes of proceeding in the several branches of that great Education Department. He also brought drawings, of his own make, of the Dublin Education Offices, Normal and Model Schools. Then since you know that Mr. Hodgins having taken his degree of M. A., has proceeded regularly to his degree of law in the Toronto University, and has been admitted to the Bar as Barrister at Law. He is, therefore, the most thoroughly trained man in all Canada for the Education Department; and is the ablest, most thorough administrator of a public department of any man with whom I have met. I think he has not been appreciated according to his merits; but should you create and fill the office of Minister of Public Instruction, you may safely confide the ordinary administration of the Education Department to Dr. Hodgins, with the title of my office.

"In the meantime you can make yourself familiar with the principles and branches, and modes of its arrangement. Whatever you may find to approve of in my policy and course of procedure, I have no doubt you will have the fairness to avow and the patriotism to maintain, whatever may be your views and feelings in regard to myself, personally; and if you find defects in, and can improve upon, my plans or proceedings, no one will rejoice at your success more than myself. I enclose a printed paper, which will afford information of the details of the Department....

"I may add that should I retire from my present office, I would have no objections, if desired, to be appointed Member of the Council of Public Instruction and give any assistance I could in its proceedings as the result of my experience."

In his reply, dated 12th of February, 1872, Mr. Blake said:—

"I have your note of the 10th instant, marked private, proposing your retirement and the reconstruction of the Education Office, and enclosing copies of a former official correspondence on the same subject. At this late stage of the session, and under the present pressure of public business, there is no probability of our giving this matter the consideration which it deserves, and it must therefore be postponed till the recess, when, if you will have the goodness to put yourself in communication with the Provincial Secretary, as on the former occasion, the subject will receive the early and earnest attention of the Government."…

Nothing further was done in this matter until 1876, when Dr. Ryerson finally retired from office on full salary, after having filled his responsible post for nearly thirty-two years.

A FEW WORDS, PERSONAL TO THE WRITER OF THIS RETROSPECT.

Having been intimately concerned in all of the events and educational matters to which I have referred in the foregoing Retrospect, it may not be out of place for me to add a few words of a personal character in conclusion.

At the end of this year I shall have completed my more than 45 years' service, as chief of the staff of the Education Department of Ontario.

For over 40 years I enjoyed the personal friendship of the distinguished man whose memory we honor here to-day—32 years of which were passed in active and pleasant service under him.

The day on which he took official leave of the Department was indeed a memorable one. As he bade farewell to each of his assistants in the office, he and they were deeply moved. He could not, however, bring himself to utter a word to me at our official parting, but as soon as he reached home he wrote to me the following tender and loving note:—

171 Victoria street, Toronto,
Monday evening, February 21st, 1876.

My Dear Hodgins,—I felt too deeply to-day when parting with you in the Office to be able to say a word. I was quite overcome with the thought of severing our official connection, which has existed between us for thirty-two years, during the whole of which time, without interruption, we have labored as one mind and heart in two bodies, and I believe with a single eye to promote the best interests of our country, irrespective of religious sect or political party—to devise, develop, and mature a system of instruction which embraces and provides for every child in the land a good education; good teachers to teach; good inspectors to oversee the Schools; good maps, globes, and text-books; good books to read; and every provision whereby Municipal Councils and Trustees can provide suitable accommodation, teachers, and facilities for imparting education and knowledge to the rising generation of the land.

While I devoted the year 1845 to visiting educating countries and investigating their system of instruction, in order to devise one for our country, you devoted the same time in Dublin in mastering, under the special auspices of the Board of education there, the several different branches of their Education Office, in administering the system of National Education in Ireland, so that in the details of our Education Office here, as well as in our general school system, we have been enabled to build up the most extensive establishment in the country, leaving nothing, as far as I know, to be devised in the completeness of its arrangements, and in the good character and efficiency of its officers. Whatever credit or satisfaction may attach to the accomplishment of this work, I feel that you are entitled to share equally with myself. Although I know that you have been opposed to the change, yet could I have believed that I might have been of any service to you, or to others with whom I have labored so cordially, or that I could have advanced the school system, I would not have voluntarily retired from office.[61] But all circumstances considered, and entering within a few days upon my 74th year, I have felt that this was the time for me to commit to other hands the reins of the government of the public school system, and labor during the last hours of my day and life, in a more retired sphere.

But my heart is, and ever will be, with you in its sympathies and prayers, and neither you nor yours will more truly rejoice in you success and happiness, than

Your old life-long Friend and Fellow-laborer,
E. RYERSON.

J. GEORGE HODGINS, Esq., LL.D.

While in England, in reply to a retrospective letter from me at the close of that eventful year, Dr. Ryerson wrote as follows:—

"LONDON, December 12th, 1876.

"DEAR HODGINS,—

.   .   .   .   .

"Had we been enabled to work together, as in former years, we would have done great things for our country, and I could have died in the harness with you. But it was not to be so.... I have no doubt it will be seen that the hand of

God is in this, as it has been in all our work together for more than thirty years.

> "Your ever Affectionate Friend,
> "E. RYERSON.

"J. George Hodgins, Esq., LL.D."

Under these circumstances how can I, therefore, regard without emotion the events of to-day? They bring vividly to my recollection many memorable incidents and interesting events of our educational past known only to myself. They also deeply impress me with the fleeting and transitory nature of all things human. The Chief and sixteen counsellors, appointed and elected to assist him, (besides more than twenty persons connected with various branches of the Department) have all passed away since my first connection with the Department in 1844.[62] His great work remains, however, and his invaluable services to the country we all gratefully recall to-day, while his native land lovingly acknowledges these services in erecting this noble monument to his memory. Truly indeed and faithfully did Egerton Ryerson make good his promise to the people of this Province, when he solemnly pledged himself, on accepting office in 1844—

"To provide for my native country a system of education, and facilities for intellectual improvement not second to those of any country in the world."

God grant that the seed sown and the foundations thus laid with such anxious toil and care—and yet in faith—may prove to be one of our richest heritages, so that in the future, wisdom and knowledge, in the highest and truest sense, may be the stability of our times!

J. G. H.

Toronto, 24th May, 1889.